OLIVER CROMWELL

PETER GAUNT

BLACKWELL *Publishers*

with the Historical Association

General Editors: *Muriel Chamberlain, H. T. Dickinson and Joe Smith*

Titles in Print

Forthcoming titles

Germany under the Nazis
Richard Bessel

British Politics 1832–1885
John Bourne

The Italian Renaissance
Peter Denley

The Whig Supremacy
H. T. Dickinson

The German Reformation
C. Scott Dixon

The Enlightenment
Martin Fitzpatrick

The American Revolution
Keith Mason

Gladstone
Neville Masterman

The Cold War (2nd ed)
Joe Smith

John F. Kennedy
Geoff Stoakes

The Historical Association, founded in 1906, brings together people who share an interest in, and love for, the past. It aims to further the study and teaching of history at all levels: teacher and student, amateur and professional. This is one of over 100 publications available at preferential rates to members. Membership also includes journals at generous discounts and gives access to courses, conferences, tours and regional and local activities. Full details are available from The Secretary, The Historical Association, 59a Kennington Park Road, London SE11 4JH, telephone: 0171-735 3901.

For my Parents

Copyright © Peter Gaunt 1996

The right of Peter Gaunt to be identified as author of this work has been asserted in accordance with the Copyright, Designs and Patents Act 1988.

First published 1996
First published in paperback 1997

Blackwell Publishers Ltd
108 Cowley Road
Oxford OX4 1JF, UK

Blackwell Publishers Inc
350 Main Street
Malden, Massachusetts 02148, USA

British Library Cataloguing in Publication Data
A CIP catalogue record for this book is available from the British Library

Library of Congress Cataloging in Publication Data
Gaunt, Peter
Oliver Cromwell / Peter Gaunt
p. cm. — (Historical Association studies)
Includes bibliographical references and index.
ISBN 0-631-18356-6 — ISBN 0-631-20480-6 (pbk)
1. Cromwell, Oliver, 1599-1658. 2. Great Britain—History—
Puritan Revolution, 1642-1660—Bibliography. 3. Head of state—Great
Britain—Biography. 4. Generals—Great Britain—Biography.
I. Title. II. Series.
DA426.G38   1996
941.06'4'092—dc20   95-20324
[B]   CIP

Printed and bound in Great Britain by T. J. Press Ltd, Padstow, Cornwall

This book is printed on acid-free paper

CONTENTS

PREFACE

This is a biographical study of Oliver Cromwell (1599–1658). It focuses quite tightly on his life and career and does not attempt to give a broader history of the mid-seventeenth century. Part I briefly introduces some of the key issues, including the mythology surrounding Cromwell, the differing interpretations which have been advanced and the reasons for those differences, and the nature and reliability of the surviving source material. Part III, which can be read as an extended conclusion, summarizes the major themes of Cromwell's life, including appearance, character, health and wealth, military abilities, political outlook and religion. Part II, by far the longest part and the core of this book, gives an analytical account of Cromwell's life, broadly chronological in structure, and subdivided on that basis into five chapters.

Given the nature and objectives of the series in which this book appears, it would have been inappropriate to have advanced largely untested and potentially controversial new theories here; in part, this book is intended as an up-to-date synthesis of the best existing work on Cromwell. However, over the past fifteen years or so I have conducted extensive research on Protectoral central government; accordingly, the final chapter of Part II, on the Protectorate, rests quite heavily upon original research and, reflecting my specialist research interests, explores in unusual depth both the constitutional powers of Cromwell in theory and in practice and his relationship with the Council.

Throughout the book, great stress has been laid upon Cromwell's surviving letters and the extant texts of his major public speeches, and, wherever possible, they have been drawn upon as the principal sources. Quotations from Cromwell's speeches have generally been drawn from I. Roots (ed.), *Speeches of Olvier Cromwell* (Everyman's Library, London, 1989), reprinted by permission of J. M. Dent. Quotations from Cromwell's letters have generally been drawn from W. C. Abbott (ed.), *The Writings and Speeches of Oliver Cromwell* (copyright © 1937 by the President and Fellows of Harvard College) (4 vols, 1937–1947; reissued 1988), reprinted by permission of Oxford University Press and Harvard University Press. Endnotes have been used very sparingly, in general only to indicate the source of a direct quotation. Thus readers should turn to the select bibliography for reference to the many works of other historians which I have used and upon which this book in large part rests. However, it would be wrong not to acknowledge here my debts to two outstanding studies – Barry Coward's *Oliver Cromwell* and the collection edited by John Morrill, *Oliver Cromwell and the English Revolution* – which appeared while this book was at an early stage and whose findings, where appropriate, have been incorporated in this study. The final chapter of Part II draws upon material which I originally published as '"The Single Person's Confidants and Dependants"? Oliver Cromwell and his Protectoral Councillors', in *The Historical Journal* 32 (1989); I am grateful to the editor of that journal for permission to reuse the material here. The same section also draws upon my still largely unpublished Ph.D. dissertation, 'The Councils of the Protectorate, from December 1653 to September 1658' (University of Exeter, 1983), supervised by Professor Ivan Roots; I remain deeply in Professor Roots's debt for the judicious guidance which he offered and for the informed enthusiasm which he inspired. I am grateful to Margaret Jackson and Emma Whinton, two colleagues at Chester College, for reading and commenting upon the text in draft form. For all errors of fact, interpretation and style which remain, I am wholly and solely responsible.

Throughout this book, all dates are old style, but the year has been taken to begin on 1 January.

Peter Gaunt
Chester

PART I

INTRODUCTION

subsequently became a rather undignified collector's item and passed from hand to hand until, in 1960, that believed to be his was bequeathed to Sidney Sussex, his old Cambridge college, and buried or immured near the college chapel. His body, buried in an anonymous pit at the place of execution, probably lies somewhere under the teeming traffic and urban sprawl of the Marble Arch area, which has long engulfed the site of old Tyburn tree.

Within a few years of Cromwell's death in 1658 and his exhumation and execution in 1661, however, doubts began to circulate about the identity of the body mutilated at Tyburn and about the true resting place of his mortal remains. Occasional rumours were reported by Pepys and other near-contemporaries, but not until the eighteenth century did the uncertainties and alternative stories begin to find their way into print and so to a wider audience; speculation reached new heights during the nineteenth century, stoked by the Victorian fascination with all things funereal. A variety of theories have been advanced, resting upon old and suitably vague traditions, accounts passed down from generation to generation from gnarled servants and friends of the Cromwells, and plain wishful thinking. Based upon the assumption that at some point between his death in September 1658 and the exhumation of January 1661 Cromwell's corpse was buried or reburied somewhere other than the designated vault in the Abbey in order to protect it from vengeful royalists, the stories would have his mortal remains resting undisturbed in the soil of London, Cambridgeshire, Northamptonshire or Yorkshire. And where no claim can be made to the physical remains, there is always Oliver the ghost to stand in. His spectre has allegedly been seen stalking the Holborn and Tyburn areas of London and around the tithe barn at Old Basing, ensconced in Hampton Court and Long Marston Hall, wandering again the fields of his triumphs at Naseby and Worcester, and visiting room thirteen of the Gold Lion in St Ives with a mistress in attendance. At least these sites have genuine Cromwellian connections and were visited by him in life or by his exhumed remains in 1661. But what of Apsley House, the London home of the Duke of Wellington, built nearly a century and a half after Cromwell's death, in which he supposedly appeared at the height of the Reform Bill crisis? or Brampton Bryan park, near a castle which saw action in the civil war but one never visited by Cromwell, through which the devil dances with Oliver's spectre every 3 September? In short, Cromwell has become almost an ever-present figure, a many-headed, many-bodied monster, linked in death and after with more parts of the country than any ruler since King Arthur.

Improbable or absurd as they are, there is a more serious side to all these rather questionable tales, for the stories of Cromwell's travels in and beyond the grave are but posthumous echoes of Cromwell in life. Once more, Cromwell seems to have been everywhere, to have stayed in more mansions than Queen Elizabeth I at her most expansive and to have destroyed more castles than Henry VII, gunpowder and death duties put together, to have desecrated more churches than is surely possible for a mere human and to have left more clothes, armour and assorted trinkets around the country than the most absent-minded or open-handed tourist. As one eighteenth-century traveller and writer put it, 'whenever I enquire about ruins, I always get the same answer, that it was some Popish place destroyed by Oliver Cromwell'.[2] The diary of Francis Kilvert records a rich crop of stories about Cromwell and his times circulating in rural Wiltshire and Radnorshire during the 1870s. For example, in August 1871 Kilvert was told by a 'patriarch' of ninety-one why the local 'Rattlebones' inn was so named:

> Rattlebones was one of Oliver Cromwell's chiefs. In a battle Rattlebones was wounded in the stomach and all his entrails came pouring out. But Rattlebones found a tile and holding it against his stomach kept his entrails in while he went on fighting. 'Well done, Rattlebones', cried Oliver, 'fight away and I'll give you Sherston and Pinckney.'[3]

Some of these stories are patently absurd or are well known to be false – Cromwell's reputed presence in a whole litany of towns and villages during the civil war years which in reality were never visited by him, strongholds supposedly wrecked by Cromwell which in truth had fallen ruinous during the sixteenth century, the original tower of Ely Cathedral brought

down, not by the local boy made bad, but by medieval storms
and subsidence, the artillery pieces nearby supposedly used by
Cromwell to bombard the Cathedral which in fact date from
the nineteenth century, and the countless churches stripped
of ornament under the influence of a Cromwell assuredly,
but of Thomas and his followers during the sixteenth-century
Reformation, not of Oliver and the mid-seventeenth-century
parliamentarians. Others are harder to prove or disprove.

Even where physical destruction did take place during or
in the wake of the civil war, the association with Cromwell
in person is often erroneous. We know that in the 1650s
Cromwell was commander-in-chief of the army and became
head of state, and it is all too easy to approach the 1640s with
this in mind, to pre-date Cromwell's dominance, to assume
that he was the leading figure in the parliamentary cause
from some point early in the 1640s and thus to ascribe all
subsequent actions and policies to his influence or personal
involvement. Yet despite the all-embracing manner in which
some writers and popular historians identify every battlefield
and parliamentary regiment, every desecrated church and
ruined castle with Oliver Cromwell in person, his travels,
though extensive, did not take him to all parts of the country
and to all the theatres of war and, in the early stages of
the civil war at least, his political and military influence was
very limited. The slighting of castles after the civil war was
parliamentary policy, not the initiative of Cromwell; he was
personally involved in the deliberate destruction of only a
handful of fortresses. Again, such cleansing of churches by
stripping out images and ornate decoration as did occur in the
mid-seventeenth century was the policy of Parliament and Parliament's local agents; very little iconoclasm was undertaken
by Cromwell in person or by troops under his direct and
immediate command. The colourful stories and the sweeping
if lazy association of every event and location with a single man
have their place and tell us much about the richness of folk
memory and the limitations of popular history. However, if we
are to come close to discerning the real man, then the myth
of the omni-present, all-powerful Cromwell, who completely
dominated the parliamentary cause from the outbreak of the
civil war in 1642, if not earlier, should be laid aside.

Historical Assessments

> He had once conceived the design of writing the Life of Oliver Cromwell, saying that he thought it might be highly curious to trace his extraordinary rise to the supreme power, from so obscure a beginning. He at length laid aside his scheme, on discovering that all that can be told of him is already in print; and that it is impracticable to procure any authentick information in addition to what the world is already possessed of.[4]

Alas, the world was thereby denied Samuel Johnson's view of Cromwell, a biography which would doubtless have contained full measure of pungent views and striking epithets. But the good doctor's judgement that, by the early 1780s, everything that could be said about Cromwell had already appeared in print and that no new information or interpretations remained to be expounded, proved spectacularly wide of the mark. The literature on Cromwell, already extensive by the late eighteenth century, has continued to pour from the presses, some of it scholarly and judicious, some of it dreadful or irredeemably biased. England's only non-royal head of state is also by some way our most closely and frequently studied ruler, and biographies of Cromwell far outnumber those of any English or British monarch. As well as straightforward accounts of the life and times, there have appeared specialist studies of Cromwell the soldier and Cromwell the politician, of Cromwell's religious beliefs and of his foreign policy, psychological studies, verses of all sorts, stage plays and screenplays, and a stirring though historically inaccurate feature film. There is also an annual journal of Cromwellian studies and an academic and historical society whose principal aim is to promote the understanding of Cromwell's life and times. Bound up inseparably if sometimes unhelpfully with the history of the civil wars and interregnum, the man and his times remain popular topics in schools, colleges and universities. Such is the bulk of material produced on Oliver Cromwell, with more known to be forthcoming, that one could almost speak of a Cromwell 'industry'. Over two centuries since Dr Johnson felt that nothing more could be said, Cromwellian studies are still booming.

From his own lifetime to the present day, Cromwell's standing and reputation have always aroused great passions and provoked heated debate. Even people whose interest in history is minimal seem to have strong opinions about Cromwell and believe that they know something about him. He is a figure whom few approach with neutral feelings and a genuinely open mind. In the late nineteenth century many MPs and peers reacted with horror to the proposal of the Prime Minister, Lord Rosebery, to erect a statue of Cromwell within the Palace of Westminster. Rosebery's refusal to push the issue to a vote, for fear of defeat, contributed to a collapse in his authority and the fall of his government shortly after. The statue was subsequently erected, but outside the Palace; Rosebery paid for the work largely out of his own pocket, though he attempted to do so anonymously. In 1902 Huntingdon's MP led similar and successful opposition to plans to erect a statue of Cromwell in the town of his birth. In more recent years, the tercentenary of Cromwell's death in 1958 was certainly not ignored, but it passed off in rather subdued fashion, and during the 1960s the reigning monarch reportedly vetoed proposals by a Labour government to include Cromwell's image on a postage stamp. From time to time, lively correspondence for and against Cromwell flares up in the letters pages of local and national newspapers, often tied to the suggestion that Britain needs another Cromwell to ride forth Arthur-like from Avalon to rescue the country from political, social, economic or moral decline. Cromwell remains a controversial figure.

It has always been so. Cromwell often puzzled his contemporaries, friends and enemies alike, and they were much divided in their assessments of him. To some, he was during the Protectorate 'a Matchless Prince', a successful soldier and a courageous politician who, as a second Moses, was leading the nation into the Promised Land of true reformation. To others, he was 'the Devil of later times, who Butcher-like made cruelty his profession and was never better than when he had his sword sheathed in his Countrymen's bowels' and who had 'enchained' the whole nation. Contemporary detractors frequently alleged that, when reminded of the rights and liberties enshrined in Magna Carta, Cromwell would show his contempt for the document by snapping back 'Magna Farta'.[5] A slightly later history claimed that he similarly referred to the Petition of Right as 'the Petition of Shite'.[6] Many of his early biographers, writing both before and after the Restoration, produced some gloriously ambivalent judgements, reflecting their own indecision and their admiration for the man as well as condemnation of him. Although it appeared after the potentially distorting sea-change of the Restoration of the Stuart monarchy in 1660 and was written by a figure who was never personally close to him, Clarendon's assessment of Cromwell is a masterpiece. Its final judgement, that Cromwell 'will be looked upon by posterity as a brave bad man', is oft-quoted, but the preceding review of his character, policies and achievements deserves to be better known. Following immediately upon an account of his death, Clarendon opens his assessment by commenting, 'he could never have done half that mischief without great parts of courage, industry and judgment'. Cromwell's rise from humble beginnings to great power had been achieved through a mixture of unsurpassed wickedness bolstered by 'a great spirit, an admirable circumspection and sagacity, and a most magnanimous resolution'. He was adept at winning over opponents through persuasion and strength of character and displayed 'a wonderful civility, generosity and bounty' towards those who obeyed him. Those who still stood out he crushed ruthlessly and illegally, though in the main 'he seemed to have great reverence for the law, rarely interposing between party and party'. He achieved 'entire obedience' at home and respect and glory abroad. Wherever possible, he held back from violent retribution and 'was not a man of blood'. 'In a word,' Clarendon concluded, 'as he had all the wickedness against which damnation is denounced, and for which hell-fire is prepared, so he had some virtues which have caused the memory of some men in all ages to be celebrated.' Clarendon's assessment is remarkably ambivalent; if anything, it explores the virtues at greater length than the damnable wickedness.[7]

At no time has there been anything approaching complete agreement in the historical assessment of Cromwell's character, career and achievements. In the light of the sheer quantity

and very variable quality of material written by each generation since his death, such lack of unanimity is hardly surprising. There have always been discordant voices, reappraising
Cromwell, standing above or swimming against the tide. But
undeniably there have been distinct trends in Cromwellian
studies. Despite some grudging regard for his achievements,
particularly the active and partly successful foreign policy
which contrasted so sharply with the largely inactive or unsuccessful policy of Charles II, works published in the post-
Restoration era were predominantly and predictably negative
and condemnatory. Whatever may have been private opinions, in histories, pamphlets, sermons and plays published
during the reigns of Charles II and James II, Cromwell was
overwhelmingly portrayed as an ambitious and hypocritical
king-killer, a cruel yet cowardly tyrant, not above personal
greed, villainy and immorality, who had been in league with
the devil. In the wake of the Glorious Revolution and Revolution Settlement of 1688–9, not only was there heightened
interest in Cromwell but also some more favourable interpretations, particularly by historians who were themselves
nonconformists or who at least supported the new statutory
toleration of Protestant dissenters and who therefore praised
what they took to be the same air of toleration practised
under Cromwell. In the late seventeenth century and on
into the eighteenth, writers of all persuasions made allusions
to Cromwell, comparing contemporary political issues and
figures with the former Protector, sometimes to praise them,
but more often still to damn them. Indeed, in the eighteenth
century as a whole, despite some kinder views and attempts at
favourable reassessment – again, the active foreign policy was
often favourably compared to the often supine or unsuccessful
Hanoverian foreign policy – portrayals of Cromwell remained
largely negative. To Tories, Cromwell was a wicked and god-
less usurper who unforgivably had killed God's anointed, while
to Whigs he was a hypocrite, a man who had betrayed the
cause of liberty in favour of his own ambitions.

It was the Victorians who 'rediscovered' Cromwell and saved
him from a generally condemnatory press. In a turnabout
caused or at least strengthened by the appearance of Thomas
Carlyle's *The Letters and Speeches of Oliver Cromwell* in the 1840s,

many Victorian writers presented an image of Cromwell which they believed to be truer to the original and which, regardless of the veracity of that belief, was noticeably more favourable than those of the preceding generations. The Victorian Cromwell was often portrayed as a liberal – or even a Liberal – hero, a man ahead of his times who had worked for political and religious liberties, a constitutional monarchy and a proper balance between the rights of the governed and the governors, but who had held back the political chaos and social turmoil – the dangerous, destructive revolution – which the radicalism of the 1640s, like the radicalism of the Chartists at home and the events of 1848 on the Continent, seemed to threaten. For many Victorian and early twentieth-century historians, most notably S. R. Gardiner and C. H. Firth, Cromwell was the acceptable face of reform, a man possessed of a character which was highly complex but through which decency and liberal toleration came shining through.

Despite both the undeniable service performed by Carlyle in making available Cromwell's own words and the profound insights contained in the works of Gardiner and Firth, in many ways still Cromwell's greatest biographers, subsequent generations have criticized aspects of their assessments as at best muddled and incomplete, and at worst wholly misconceived. The historiography of Cromwell provides the supreme example of the old adage that each generation needs to rewrite its own history, and twentieth-century biographers have moved on, modifying or abandoning Victorian portrayals and giving us new images of the man. During the 1930s and early 1940s there was a short-lived fashion for portraying Cromwell as a military dictator in the mould of the dictators of contemporary Europe; initially, many such comparisons were intended to be complimentary. The current trend is to fight shy of sweeping praise or condemnation and instead to attempt to place Cromwell more firmly within his own mid-seventeenth-century context and to tailor any judgement accordingly. Interpretations aimed at portraying Cromwell's policies as precursors of modern liberalism and religious toleration are now deemed anachronistic and are very much out of fashion. Instead, strenuous attempts are made to understand Cromwell's own religious beliefs and motivations and to employ that understanding as the key which may unlock other aspects of his character, aims and actions. Yet the unhelpful and often forced attempts to liken Cromwell to other historical figures continue. As well as the enduring comparisons with Caesar, Nero, Machiavelli or the Borgias, each generation has likened Cromwell, for good or ill, to contemporary figures – to Lord Wharton during William III's reign and to the Duke of Marlborough during Queen Anne's, to Charles James Fox at home and to Robespierre and Napoleon abroad during the reign of George III, to both Joseph Chamberlain and Paul Kruger during the Boer Wars, and to Hitler, Mussolini, Franco and Stalin during the 1930s and 1940s. The present generation has merely added to this gallery of ghosts, with attempts to liken Cromwell to President Zia of Pakistan and to Margaret Thatcher. Modern historians believe that they are coming nearer to the real Cromwell, that by paying close attention to contemporary sources and to Cromwell's contemporary context they are uncovering more about the man and his times, that they are stripping away past generations of overpainting and tarnish to reveal the original colours, and that by demythologizing Cromwell they will recover a truer, purer picture. Future generations may not wholly agree.

The Sources

> Ours is a very small enterprise, but seemingly a useful one; preparatory perhaps to greater and more useful, on this same matter: The collecting of the *Letters and Speeches of Oliver Cromwell*, and presenting them in natural sequence, with the still possible elucidation, to ingenuous readers. This is a thing that can be done; and after some reflection, it has appeared worth doing. No great thing: one other dull Book added to the thousand, dull every one of them, which have been issued on this subject! But situated as we are, new Dulness is unhappily inevitable; readers do not reascend out of deep confusions without some trouble as they climb.[8]

The great Victorian historian and man of letters Thomas Carlyle had long toyed with the idea of writing a biography of Oliver Cromwell and certainly compiled notes on the man and his times. But the biography never appeared. Instead, in the process of trying to get to grips with Cromwell, Carlyle became aware of the limitations of existing biographies – he dismissed them all as 'worthy of oblivion, – of charitable Christian *burial*' – and of the need to uncover the true Cromwell by a re-examination of the surviving contemporary documents by and about him. Intermittently and uncertainly at first, Carlyle's thoughts and actions turned away from traditional biography and to the compilation of an edition of Cromwell's own letters and speeches, letting the man speak for himself – though with plenty of interpretation or 'elucidation' by Carlyle – and thus, he felt, both avoiding and correcting generations of prejudice, misunderstanding and myth. 'It is from his own words . . . well read, that the world may first obtain some dim glimpse of the actual Cromwell, and see him darkly face to face', he asserted.[9] The result, *The Letters and Speeches of Oliver Cromwell*, was first published in 1845. It quickly went through several editions, was subsequently revised and enlarged, and remained in print in one form or another for almost exactly a century.

In the introduction to his work, Carlyle claimed to have gathered the 'authentic utterances of the man Oliver himself . . . from far and near; fished them up from the foul Lethean quagmires where they lay buried'.[10] In reality, the fishing cannot have been too taxing or the quagmires too dark and foul. Versions of many of Cromwell's letters and speeches were published during his lifetime, in something approaching a word-for-word form, and other utterances and conversations were summarized in the weekly newspapers and in other memoirs and diaries, some of which were published during the civil war and interregnum, some – for example, those of Bulstrode Whitelocke and Edmund Ludlow – not until several decades after Cromwell's death. In addition, many of Cromwell's letters, though never published at the time, were carefully preserved, either as original holographs or in more or less contemporary transcripts, and by the mid-nineteenth century were in the well-known and well-catalogued collections of the British Museum and the Bodleian Library. The existence of such material was no secret and Carlyle was far from being the first historian to reproduce versions of Cromwell's letters and speeches from printed and unprinted sources. But he was the first to gather this material together and to publish as much of it as possible, uncut, in a single collection. After the appearance of the first edition, a steady 'leakage of new Cromwell matter . . . oozed in' upon Carlyle 'from the whole world',[11] and subsequent editions, revised first by Carlyle himself and then, after his death, by S. C. Lomas and others, grew steadily as this new material was added. More still had been uncovered by the 1930s and 1940s when an American academic, W. C. Abbott, produced a much larger assemblage of Cromwellian material, *The Writings and Speeches of Oliver Cromwell*. Where Carlyle had contented himself with brief linking passages and tart elucidations, this huge and weighty four-volume set, running in total to well over 3,500 pages, is dominated by Abbott's leaden and generally rather uninformative prose. Inevitably, a trickle of Cromwellian material, very little of it of much weight or significance, has come to light since the publication of Abbott's fourth and final volume in 1947.

Through the work of Carlyle, Abbott and others, we know of several hundred letters written by Cromwell and several score speeches and utterances made by him. Some of the letters, most notably the standard, impersonal administrative and diplomatic correspondence of the Protectorate, were doubtless drafted and prepared by others, with Cromwell personally contributing little more than his signature. This sort of correspondence, common to all reigns, tells us much about the formal workings of government and little about the character, aims and aspirations of the individual ruler. But throughout the period of the civil wars, from the early 1640s to the early 1650s, Cromwell wrote a large number of letters to family, friends and political colleagues in London and the provinces, to the Speaker of the House of Commons, the Committee of Both Kingdoms, the Committee of Both Houses and the Rump's Councils of State, letters generally dominated by news of the latest military developments but also revealing much about the state of his body and mind, his views on church and state, politics and religion, his hopes and his fears. Even during the Protectorate, when Cromwell was head of state, the flow of these more personal letters massively diminished but never quite dried up. There can be no doubt that they were written by Cromwell himself and reflect his own thinking, however hesitant or muddled that thinking may, on occasion, have been. Through his letters, Cromwell comes alive as few other early modern monarchs come alive, and we can discern something of the essence of the man.

The speeches and other recorded conversations present more difficulties. The speeches themselves, particularly those delivered to Parliament or parliamentary committees during the Protectorate, appear to have been Cromwell's own and there are few signs that he employed a speechwriter. On occasion, he may have discussed the general line and elements of the contents with his advisers and confidants, particularly his Protectoral Council and his secretary of state, but the form, tone and words seem to have been Cromwell's alone. The real difficulty is in the records of the speeches as they have come down to us. There survive no manuscripts of the speeches, whether in full or in note form, written by Cromwell himself. Indeed, when in January 1658 the Commons approached him for a written copy of the speech he had delivered the day before, he claimed not only that he possessed no such copy but also that he could not recall even four lines of the speech itself. Doubtless the main thrust of a speech and perhaps a few choice phrases and images were decided upon in his mind if not in note form beforehand, but the speeches do seem to have been largely and genuinely extempore. Thus for texts of these long set-piece speeches, some of them reportedly lasting two hours or more, we rely upon versions produced from the hastily taken notes and inevitably incomplete memories of members of the audience. The results, many of them printed at the time, convey the ideas, arguments of the originals – probably many of the very words and phrases – but they cannot be treated as entirely complete, accurate and faithful transcripts. Where two separate versions of the same speech survive, a significant number of variations often show up.

Cromwell's other recorded utterances, accounts of speeches which he made as an MP in the Long Parliament during the 1640s and of his contributions to political debates at Putney and elsewhere, versions of discussions with Whitelocke, Ludlow, Sir Thomas Fairfax, John Rogers and various foreign ambassadors, need to be used with even more care, for they have often come down to us only through the flawed and distorting mirror of assorted parliamentary and private diaries, memoirs, autobiographies and diplomatic dispatches, many of them written with self-justification in mind or with an axe to grind. For the same reason, their comments about Cromwell, as well as their versions of utterances by him, must be treated with caution.

The approach adopted here is to rely most heavily upon accounts written and known to have been disseminated – though not necessarily published – during Cromwell's own lifetime, contemporary with the events and developments they relate. The best sources, principally Cromwell's own writings and speeches and, to a lesser extent, strictly con-temporary newsletters, newspapers and the dispatches written by London-based diplomats, as well as the official records of Cromwell's Protectorate government, have therefore provided the backbone of this study. Other accounts, those known to have been written, revised and published many years later, after Cromwell's death and the Restoration of the Stuart mon-archy, and those which appeared during Cromwell's lifetime but written by political or religious opponents of Cromwell and published with clear political or propaganda ends in mind, have been used in a much more cautious and limited way. However, there are dangers in this approach. Why should a diplomatic dispatch or a newsletter written immediately after the event it describes – which may, after all, have been tailored to meet the perceived expectations of the reader – necessarily be more reliable than the memoirs of one of the protagonists, even though those memoirs may not have been written until years after the event? For example, Edmund Ludlow became an embittered enemy of Cromwell, he probably wrote his memoirs many years after Cromwell's death and they have come down to us in a published form which we now know was edited and heavily amended for political ends by another hand. And yet we also know that, for a time, Ludlow was close to Cromwell and probably had unique insights into some of his thoughts, hopes and fears. Ludlow's published *Memoirs* have been used here only very selectively and hedged around with warnings, but other historians might well view this approach as over-cautious and likely thereby to exclude much valuable information available from no other source. Moreover, although on occasion the range and reliability of the surviving sources for a particularly crucial event or development are discussed in Parts II and III, in a work of this length it is impossible to assess the nature and likely veracity of the source material at every stage in Cromwell's life and career. Reasons of space generally preclude both discussion of the often conflicting source material and explanation of which have been judged reliable and so given greater credence.

Wherever possible, Cromwell's life and career are related through his own words. There are periods when Cromwell falls uncharacteristically and unhelpfully silent, forcing a more heavy reliance upon other sources, and it is also clear that the surviving accounts of his speeches and conversations are to a greater or lesser extent compressed, paraphrased or, by accident or design, distorted. Nevertheless, the letters – very much stronger for the 1640s and early 1650s than for the years of the Protectorate – and the speeches and other utterances – which really come into their own during the period 1653–8 – together provide a biographer with a wealth of invaluable material by and about Cromwell, their quality and quantity surpassing those of any other pre-nineteenth-century English ruler. Through his own words, however imperfectly they have come down to us, we may, as Carlyle puts it, 'here best of all . . . expect to read' the story of 'Oliver's Character, and that of Oliver's Performance in this world'.[12] Indeed, even if we read them as masterpieces of deception, self-deception or hypocrisy, Cromwell's own words are surely the best approach to the man.

Divided Opinions

It becomes more and more apparent to one, That this man Oliver Cromwell was, as popular fancy represents him, the soul of the Puritan Revolt, without whom it had never been a revolt transcendently memorable, and an Epoch in the World's History . . . And then farther, altogether contrary to the popular fancy, it becomes apparent that this Oliver was not a man of falsehoods, but a man of truths . . . An earnest man, I apprehend, may gather from these of Oliver's, were there even no other evidence, that the character of Oliver . . . is much the reverse of that mad jumble of 'hypocrisies,' etc. etc., which at present passes current as his.[13]

Having worked carefully through his surviving letters and speeches, Carlyle agreed that Cromwell was the dominant character of what he termed the 'Puritan Revolt' but, running against trends then current, he felt that he was a man of truth and acquitted him of the then widely accepted accusations of falsehood and hypocrisy. Although Carlyle's work caused or coincided with a general move towards more kindly interpretations of Cromwell, by no means all historians were and are convinced of his essential truthfulness. Even on his own terms and in his own words, his actions and aspirations between the mid-1640s, when he began to play a significant political and military role on the national stage, and his death in 1658, contain so many apparent inconsistencies that a prima facie case can be made out for hypocrisy and falsehood. Even when the myths have been stripped away, Cromwell still comes across as a hugely complex figure, whose career was marked by a number of twists and turns, most of them to his own benefit. Current historical writing, popular or academic, is by no means all in Cromwell's favour.

By employing the evidence of Cromwell's career, it is quite possible to make a strong and plausible case for him being an ambitious dissembler, a man who used people, institutions and events ruthlessly though in an underhand manner to further his own breathtaking ambitions, an arch hypocrite. Firstly, it can be argued that Cromwell was a power-hungry megalomaniac, from the outset aiming at the highest office. During the 1640s he had fought against the King and, rather tardily perhaps but then very enthusiastically, pushed for the trial and execution of Charles I. Yet in the 1650s he became head of state, assumed semi-monarchical powers and was certainly attracted to suggestions that he take the crown and become king in name. Thus his stance up to January 1649 was all a pretence, for he wanted Charles I dead and the

Stuart monarchy abolished not on lofty political or constitutional grounds but merely to clear the way for King Oliver, a long-standing ambition he realized in practice and almost in name during the Protectorate. Secondly, it can be argued that his changing attitude towards Parliament betrays his wafer-thin commitment to justice and liberty. During the 1640s he rose to power in the service of the Long Parliament, but then turned against Parliament, violently and illegally ejecting the Rump in April 1653, setting up a non-elected body to replace it and thereafter extensively purging both his Protectorate Parliaments. Where Charles I had contented himself with abrupt though perfectly legal dissolutions and a botched attempt to arrest five MPs, Cromwell resorted to military-backed coups, mass purges and the subversion of established parliamentary rights and liberties. Thirdly, it can be argued that Cromwell's changing political outlook betrays unpleasant duplicity and dangerous ambition. During the 1640s Cromwell appeared to support radical demands for sweeping reforms, in order better to secure and promote the rights and liberties of the people. But in the 1650s, firstly as head of the army and then as the political head of state, he can be portrayed as an increasingly conservative and reactionary politician, dropping and turning against a long list of more radical figures who were formerly political colleagues or personal friends, using military backing to impose his increasingly extensive and repressive powers, and illegally subverting rights and liberties. Once again, the charge is that Cromwell had cynically and insincerely hitched a lift on the bandwagon of the parliamentary cause, only to betray that cause once it had served his purpose, namely the acquisition of power, and then to exercise that power to very different and repressive ends, ends much blacker and grimmer than anything which Charles I had attempted. All of these accusations were made during Cromwell's own lifetime, all have been repeated by subsequent historians and biographers and all can be supported by evidence drawn from Cromwell's career. Many other historians believe that this is a gross misreading of the man, but it is very difficult conclusively and unambiguously to prove that this interpretation is incorrect.

In truth, there are so many uncertainties and inconsistencies in Cromwell's career that almost any event and action can be read in a good or bad light. For example, the ruthless way in which Cromwell's capture of Drogheda and Wexford in Ireland and – less well known – of Basing House in England were followed by much bloodletting has provoked furious debate among later generations of historians over the rights and wrongs of these 'massacres'. Again, two very different interpretations can be placed on the way in which, during the Protectorate, Cromwell had a handful of the most vocal and troublesome opponents of his regime exiled to the Channel Islands, Isles of Scilly or Isle of Wight for a time. On the one hand, this can be seen as Cromwell acting mercifully, preferring that they should live in exile rather than be brought to the block or the gallows as the inevitable consequence of a formal trial. On the other hand, this could be seen as Cromwell acting brutally and illegally, exiling people without due process of law when he feared that a trial would prove politically embarrassing or end in an acquittal, so choosing a location outside the orbit of English law to deny them the opportunity of legitimately gaining their freedom.

There are also many curious incidents and events, which in the long or short term proved very much to Cromwell's benefit, and in which his own role and involvement appear suspicious. For example, in winter 1644–5 he took the lead in promoting the Self-Denying Ordinance under which all members of the Lords and Commons who held military command would have to surrender that command. The Ordinance was passed, but Cromwell was then excepted from its provisions by Parliament and retained his command. The end result was an increase in his own power through the removal of many other military commanders who disliked or opposed him. Did Cromwell hope and expect from the outset to be excepted from the Ordinance, in which case his promotion of it would be a prime example of duplicitous self-advancement, or was it just a lucky and unforeseen windfall? Again, in June 1647 a junior officer, Cornet Joyce, seized the captive King, making Charles directly a prisoner of the parliamentary army rather than of Parliament. Cromwell played the innocent, but the move may have suited his own plans and he had met Joyce just a few days before. In autumn 1648 Cromwell spent many weeks in northern England, besieging an isolated castle still held by the then broken royalist rebels, by accident or design not returning to London until a few hours after the army, in the shape of Colonel Pride, had ruthlessly purged the Long Parliament on the morning of 6 December. Once more, he was able to keep his hands clean and to deny direct involvement, though once more the event fitted in very neatly with his own plans and he moved swiftly to gain the maximum advantage from the new situation. Similarly, Cromwell claimed that he had neither hand in, nor prior knowledge of, the carefully laid plans to push through the resignation of the Nominated Assembly in December 1653, but he benefited from that resignation, the plans had been laid and executed by several of his closest military and civilian colleagues and many of them went on to be rewarded with high office in the new Protectorate regime. It is easy to see why some historians believe that Cromwell's hands were by no means as clean as he made out and that duplicity, subterfuge or personal ambition were key and sometimes poorly concealed components of Cromwell's *modus operandi*.

The way in which Cromwell chose to explain some of his actions and decisions, the very language which he employed in letters and speeches, also lend themselves to dark interpretations. Cromwell repeatedly claimed that God was controlling events, that his own actions were moulded or directed by a very interventionist, providential God, that he sought God's will on how he should proceed and that divine instruction shaped subsequent events. To many modern ears this sounds strange or unbelievable. In a modern world far more secular than Cromwell's there is a strong temptation to dismiss all this as cant, to argue that Cromwell was quite consciously pursuing his own very secular policies and his own all-too-mortal ambitions, and that he was merely cloaking these policies and ambitions in a covering of religious mumbo-jumbo in order better to conceal them or to win support and respect for them. Recently, many historians have rejected this approach as far too cynical and have argued not only that Cromwell had a deep and sincere religious faith but also that, if we are to come close to understanding the man and his times, we must try to immerse ourselves in the same sort of deeply religious and providential atmosphere which moulded Cromwell and many of his contemporaries alike. However, some current historians still see a large element of deception and self-deception in Cromwell's habit of explaining his actions in terms of God's will and God's intervention. Many contemporaries, too, suggested that much of this was insincere cant, a thin veneer beneath which dangerous ambitions seethed.

Here, as in so many aspects of Cromwell's character and career, the evidence can be interpreted in several very different ways and employed to reach starkly differing conclusions. It is not even clear whether Cromwell had any consistent, long-term goals and, if so, what they were. From the point at which he began to acquire a clear national influence during the first civil war until his death in 1658, was his quest the pursuit of personal power and glory, the promotion of political and social reform, the extirpation of all trace of royalist tyranny or the spiritual reformation of the people to bring them closer to God? Or did Cromwell's goals shift to a greater or lesser degree from year to year? Given the great and repeated changes which occurred in England and in Britain as a whole between 1640 and 1658, it would be surprising if Cromwell's perception of what was achievable and what was right did not alter. In particular, his outlook as a senior army officer during the 1640s when Charles was still on the throne may well have been sharply different from his views as head of the interregnum state from December 1653. Flexibility in means, if not in ends, in changing circumstances is understandable and no sign of deceit or duplicity. Perhaps Cromwell had no consistent goals but instead changed his perceptions and objectives repeatedly as he was unexpectedly tossed higher and higher by the storms which shook the nation time and again between 1640 and 1658. Cromwell's own words, 'no one rises so high as he who knows not whither he is going', may hint at this.[14]

Even once we have stripped away much of the mythology about Cromwell which has grown up in the three and a half centuries since his death and have got closer to him by examining his own words and the words of contemporaries and by attempting to place him in his mid-seventeenth-century context, Cromwell remains a baffling and many-faceted figure. Historians approaching Cromwell with preconceived views will almost certainly be able to find elements which fit and substantiate those views. Historians approaching Cromwell with genuinely open minds will see different things and will paint different pictures of the man. No biographical study, and certainly not one of this length, can hope to produce a definitive portrait. However, the effort is – almost – always worthwhile. Whether they find Cromwell to be hero or villain, whether they praise or condemn him, surely no historians can deny his greatness or his enormous impact upon his times. An obscure and minor country gentleman in 1640, Cromwell rose rapidly as a brilliant and naturally gifted soldier and more steadily as a politician of influence and real skill. He made important, perhaps decisive, personal contributions to the military victory of Parliament over the royalist forces, within eight years of first picking up a sword in earnest he became commander-in-chief of the parliamentary armies, he led campaigns which crushed Scotland and helped subdue Ireland, so uniting Britain into a more workable whole, and he retained command of an overwhelmingly loyal and disciplined army until his death. In the wake of the first civil war, he played an increasingly prominent political role in decisions concerning the future government and constitution of the nation, he was perhaps the key driving force in all the revolutionary acts of 1647–9, by 1653 he had become the leading power-broker in making or breaking regimes, and from December 1653 until his death in September 1658 he was head of state, presiding over a reasonably stable regime which maintained order at home, won Britain respect and territory abroad and appeared always to have a firm grasp on power. Cromwell divides historians still as he divided his contemporaries, but he always fascinates and can never be ignored.

PART II

THE LIFE AND CAREER

INTRODUCTION TO PART II

Oliver Cromwell's life and career unfolded through a number of fairly distinct phases. Of course, his growing experience of the world probably influenced subsequent actions and decisions, just as he may have had consistent, long-term goals and objectives to which he held firm throughout his adulthood. No one's life can be neatly dissected into completely separate and self-contained compartments. But in the case of Cromwell, perhaps more than of most prominent figures, there are good grounds for making a number of broadly chronological divisions. Down to the early 1640s, Cromwell was a provincial gentleman, and he played only a very limited role in national or local politics, his obscurity confirmed or perhaps magnified by the paucity of contemporary documentation which survives from these years. During the decade or so from the outbreak of civil war down to 1651, Cromwell was an increasingly important figure in national politics through his parliamentary activities, but his principal stage and power-base was the army. It was as the successful military commander, active in many different theatres and frequently on the move, and as the increasingly influential guiding hand over army politics and the army's political ambitions, that Cromwell really acquired and exercised power down to 1651. For the remaining seven years of his life, from 1651 until his death, his power continued ultimately to rest upon army backing, but he ceased to campaign in person and increasingly became the London-based political leader, shaping mainstream national politics and, from December 1653, formally guiding the nation as an ostensibly civilian head of state. In several broadly similar maelstroms, the figure who led the uprising, coup or revolution then disappeared and a second, very different figure moulded the post-revolutionary reconstruction – Robespierre giving way to Napoleon and Lenin to Stalin are often cited as examples. But in many ways Cromwell had to play both parts. He became one of the leaders of the armed struggle, of crushing military victory, of regicide and the dismantling of the old regime, but he also led the repeated attempts at reconstruction thereafter. Here lie the roots of many of the tensions and seeming inconsistencies apparent in Cromwell's career from 1642 until his death.

2

EARLY LIFE, 1599–1642

We know little about Cromwell's life before the calling of the Long Parliament in 1640 and the outbreak of the civil war in 1642. True, the bare outline is clear enough – baptism, marriage, children, and so forth – but it amounts to a rather thin story. We do not possess the detailed information to paint a rounded picture of the man, his life and his character. In large part, this is because we lack personal evidence from Cromwell himself. Apart from his signature on a number of legal documents, there survives just a handful of letters and personal correspondence written by him before 1640. Nor, it appears, does Cromwell figure largely in any surviving caches of family, estate or business papers. From the 1640s onwards we have letters and speeches in abundance, but unfortunately Cromwell very rarely referred back to his early life. Indeed, we have little more than the vague assertion in a speech of 1654 that 'I was by birth a gentleman, living neither in any considerable height, nor yet in obscurity.'[1] Beyond that, his post-1640 correspondence contains no rosy anecdotes about his boyhood, his speeches of the 1650s no poignant tales of his early life in East Anglia. Cromwell seems neither to have written an autobiography or personal memoir nor to have worked closely with, and confided in, a biographer.

As a result, his earliest biographers and other contemporary writers, although sketching in a few details, tended to pass over the early life quite swiftly and to become detailed only from the 1640s onwards. Moreover, even strictly contemporary works cannot be treated as infallible, for many of them contain full measure of bias, invention and confusion. Later works are even less reliable and the stories which they tell about Cromwell's early life need to be treated with extreme caution. There are many such stories, most of which appear apocryphal or completely fanciful – that as a baby Cromwell was snatched away by a pet monkey and carried on to the roof of Hinchingbrooke House; that as a child he fought with, and gave a bloody nose to, the young Prince Charles who had accompanied his father, King James I, on a trip to Hinchingbrooke; that he played a king in a school play but stumbled over his robe and dropped his crown on ascending the stage; and that as a child he was saved from drowning in a pond by a young clergyman who told Cromwell to his face years later that, far from saving him, he wished that he had held him under. Several post-Restoration writers lovingly told stories of his wicked, dissolute early manhood, dominated by debauchery. Some of these stories even circulated – anonymously – during the 1650s, including one that he had been very promiscuous as a young man, had made at least seven local women pregnant and had been known as the 'town bull of Ely'.[2] None of these stories can now be substantiated and many appear inherently unlikely.

If later, probably fanciful stories are disregarded, we are left with a noticeably shallow account. From his birth in 1599 until the eve of the civil war, Cromwell appears as a poorly lit and little-known figure. The first forty or more of his fifty-nine years – two-thirds of his life – are shadowy and sparsely recorded. This is neither surprising nor, perhaps, a very grave loss to historians. Down to 1640, Cromwell's life as a provincial farmer and small businessman, as a gentleman but one who at times only just scraped into the gentry class, would have been of no great regional or national importance. There is no reason why letters and papers of these years should have been preserved or why historians should expect to find such material still extant. Like most of the minor gentlemen of his era, like most of his contemporaries at grammar school and university, his life was passing in comparative obscurity. The political and military confrontation of the 1640s changed Cromwell's life, lifting him from obscurity and enabling him to play a substantial role in the shaping of the nation. Only from the early 1640s does he become a figure of real significance. For most historians, the sparsely recorded life before 1640 is interesting primarily in the hunt for formative experiences, for the origins of those traits and skills, beliefs and ambitions which surfaced only after – often long after – the outbreak of war.

Oliver Cromwell was baptized on 25 April 1599 in St John's Church in Huntingdon. He was at birth the second son of Robert Cromwell and Elizabeth Steward. The couple produced a total of ten children, but the other two sons – one older, the other younger than Oliver – died very young. Cromwell was thus brought up as the only son and heir in a household of seven daughters. The Cromwells were a large and locally influential family, who had risen rapidly during the sixteenth century and had acquired wealth and extensive property, much of it formerly belonging to the Catholic Church but disposed of in the wake of the Henrician Reformation. For a time they dominated the Huntingdon region as the greatest gentry family in the area. But by the early seventeenth century the family was already on the wane, in part because of the extravagant lifestyle of the head of the family, Sir Oliver Cromwell of Hinchingbrooke House on the outskirts of Huntingdon, who had succeeded his father, Sir Henry Cromwell, in 1604. Worse still, Robert Cromwell was a younger son of Sir Henry and was one of ten siblings who survived into adulthood. As the younger son in a large and declining family, his own inheritance was comparatively meagre, namely a house in Huntingdon, formerly owned by a Catholic monastic order, and some land, again most of it at one time the property of the Church, close to the town and in neighbouring parishes. Although reconstructing seventeenth-century incomes is extremely difficult, it is possible that these lands would have brought Robert Cromwell around £300 in a good year, an income which was comfortable enough but close to the bottom of the range which contemporaries held to be the income of a gentleman. Thus by birth Oliver Cromwell's social status was ambiguous. He was a member of a family which, although in decline, was still rich, powerful and influential, his grandfather and his uncle – after whom he was presumably named – were both knights and belonged to the upper reaches of the gentry class and, by marriage, the Cromwells were also tied in with a whole network of distinguished and socially elevated families in the region and beyond. However, his father was a younger son and his immediate family were, if not exactly the poor relations, certainly several pegs down the social scale compared to their kin at Hinchingbrooke.

Cromwell attended the local grammar school in Huntingdon, where Dr Thomas Beard was schoolmaster. Beard, vicar of one of the Huntingdon parishes, may have helped shape his pupil's later beliefs, but there is no evidence that Cromwell saw Beard as a seminal influence upon his life, or that Beard's views on Church or state, expounded in several published works, were outside the fairly broad mainstream of Jacobean thought. In April 1616, two days before his seventeenth birthday, Cromwell went to Cambridge University, entered as a gentleman commoner of Sidney Sussex College. But he neither completed his studies nor obtained a degree, for he left university soon after the death of his father in June 1617. Although still under age – the Court of Wards queried whether part or all of the estate should fall under the care of the Crown, but decided against it – Cromwell probably assisted in the running of his late father's estate. There is no clear evidence to reveal his whereabouts and activities over the next three years. It is, however, far more plausible that, between 1617 and 1620, Cromwell helped his widowed mother oversee the family estates around Huntingdon and perhaps gained a smattering of common or civil law at one of the London Inns of Court, than that, as is sometimes suggested, he travelled abroad or crossed to the Continent to fight in the opening rounds of the Thirty Years War. Several early biographers suggested that he attended Lincoln's Inn around this time, but the surviving admissions registers of that and the other Inns carry no record of Oliver Cromwell.

On 22 August 1620, four months after his twenty-first birthday, Cromwell married at St Giles Church, Cripplegate, London, Elizabeth Bourchier, daughter of a wealthy London fur dealer who had made a fortune, received a knighthood and bought a country seat in Essex. The match might have been facilitated by the Barringtons of London and Essex, to whom both the Cromwells and a branch of the Bourchiers were allied through marriage. Now of age and a husband, Cromwell settled down to married life in Huntingdon, running the estates and associated businesses which he had inherited from his father, sharing the house with his widowed mother and those of his sisters who remained unmarried. Cromwell's marriage seems to have been happy and between 1621 and 1638 his wife bore him nine children, most of whom survived into adulthood. Although detailed evidence of Cromwell's location and activities remains scanty, the dates of his wife's known pregnancies make it unlikely that Cromwell either travelled to the Continent or entered into military service there at any time during the 1620s or 1630s.

Cromwell lived in Huntingdon until 1631. He played a small role in the town affairs and in 1628 he was returned to Parliament as one of the town's two MPs, probably through the influence of his uncle in the soon-to-be-sold Hinchingbrooke. But his years in Huntingdon ended sadly. A power struggle developed among the leading lights of the town, when disagreements in the late 1620s over the best way to spend a bequest to the town spilled over into a personal animosity which reached fruition in 1630 when, at the request of many of Huntingdon's elite, the Crown issued a new town charter. The victorious clique ensured that, under this charter, their opponents – including Cromwell – were excluded from office and power in Huntingdon. Enraged, Cromwell protested too vigorously and was hauled before the Privy Council in London, briefly held in custody and forced to make a humiliating apology. With his uncle no longer residing close by and able to exert much influence in Huntingdon and with the new charter sealing defeat in the power struggle, Cromwell's prospects in Huntingdon were bleak. He may also have been in financial difficulties. Certainly his inheritance was not great and during the 1620s his annual landed income may have fluctuated between £100 and £300, barely sufficient to maintain the status and lifestyle of a gentleman. Facing crisis and defeat, Cromwell sold almost all his property in and around Huntingdon and moved elsewhere.

He did not move far. From 1631 the Cromwells lived in St Ives, another Fenland town, where an old Cambridge friend,

Henry Downhall, had become vicar. In St Ives he leased land and became a tenant farmer, perhaps temporarily slipping down from gentry to mere yeoman status. But his fortunes revived at the beginning of 1636, when he inherited from his maternal uncle a series of long leases and administrations over property in and around Ely. From 1636, Cromwell and his family lived in the house near St Mary's Church, Ely, which still survives, the only one of Cromwell's residences to survive in something like its condition when he lived there. Most of the property inherited in 1636 was leased from Ely Cathedral; in the late 1630s Cromwell leased further land from the Cathedral. He also inherited his uncle's job as tithe collector for the parish of Ely and outlying chapelries. By working some of the land himself, subletting the rest and perhaps running some small agriculturally based businesses – later detractors alleged that he was involved in brewing – his income probably returned to a more healthy £3–400 per year. His tax return of 1641 suggests that, by then, he was one of the twenty wealthiest residents of Ely township and although in 1643 he wrote that 'my estate is little', in the same letter he estimated that during 1641–2 he had contributed a far from negligible £1,200 to help fund Parliament's war effort in Ireland and England.[3] Cromwell's family were at Ely for roughly a decade, continuing to live there until the mid-1640s. By then, Oliver Cromwell had moved a long way from his Fenland roots.

What were the formative influences upon Cromwell during these early years? Many historians have speculated on the influence of Beard and of his tutors at Cambridge, on the consequences of Cromwell being brought up in an overwhelmingly female household, on the impact of the early deaths of his brothers, his father and of his own eldest son, also called Robert, who died in 1639 while at school at Felsted in Essex, and on the influence of his mother, who was apparently very close to her only surviving son and who continued to live with him until her death at an advanced age in 1654. Of necessity, this psychological approach to history and to long-dead figures is speculative and often inconclusive.

In similar vein, some historians look to Cromwell's geo-

graphical origins, lyrically describing the low, brooding land-
scape of the Fens and a distinct, rather dour, Fenland outlook
with which the locals, including Cromwell, were imbued. Certainly, Cromwell's knowledge of England was rather limited.
Down to 1640, most of his life had been spent in and around
Huntingdon, St Ives, Ely and Cambridge, all of which could be
encompassed by a circle of barely fifteen miles radius. He had
also visited and spent time in London and perhaps Essex too
and, given our scant knowledge of his early life, trips further
afield cannot be ruled out. But there is every indication that,
right up to the eve of the civil war, Cromwell's travels had not
extended much beyond London, the northern home counties
and parts of East Anglia.

Other historians have stressed that ill-health, apparent in
early life, became a dominant trait. In 1628 Cromwell consulted one of the greatest doctors of the day, Sir Theodore
Mayerne, who noted a number of physical and mental problems, most notably 'valde melancholicus', for which he prescribed a wonderful cocktail of drugs.[4] A slightly later and
somewhat suspect source alleged that Cromwell had repeatedly pestered his doctor in Huntingdon, calling him out during the night, 'lying melancholy in his bed' during the day,
prone not only to unfounded fears that he was dying but
also to strange visions about the town cross and about how
he would become the most powerful man in the kingdom.[5]
The story sounds apocryphal.

More reliably, perhaps, historians have looked to his
insecure social status in the years before the civil war
as a formative influence on the post-1642 Cromwell. For
many years he lived insecurely on the lower fringes of
the gentleman class and, following the humiliation and
crisis of 1630–1, may have slipped below it for a time.
After 1631 he had held little freehold land, from his
birth to the outbreak of war and beyond he lived in
modest townhouses and during the 1620s and 1630s he
worked for a living, as a farmer, tithe collector and
perhaps manager of small agriculturally related businesses.
He had held just a few, very minor offices. He had served
neither as a JP for the county nor, it seems, as an officer
in the militia. Indeed, it is very unlikely that he had

had any military experience, at home or abroad, before 1642.

How far was Cromwell interested in, influenced by and active within the political life of the nation? Down to 1640, the answer seems to be very little. Cromwell was born during the closing years of Elizabeth I's reign, grew to manhood under James I and was in his mid-twenties when Charles I came to the throne in 1625. He doubtless heard about the main events and issues of the day, but in his surviving correspondence there is no mention of national politics and in his actions no sign of real opposition to royal government. He was a minor and insignificant figure in the Parliament of 1628–9, his one recorded speech comprising bland and muted criticism of Arminianism based on an event which had occurred a decade before. During the 1630s he paid various royal exactions as required, including his knighthood fine – his payment slightly delayed but with only mild and short-lived foot dragging – and his Ship Money dues. According to a contemporary but uncorroborated allegation, in 1638 he took an interest in a dispute over a local fen draining project, offering to help gain compensation for those who stood to lose under the scheme. But there is no sign that he was opposing fen draining in principle, saw himself as fighting for essential liberties or wished to use the dispute as a vehicle for challenging the established order. Instead, then as later, he merely argued that those who legitimately held property or rights in the areas being drained should be fairly compensated. Down to 1640, Cromwell does not come across as an intensely political animal. Later stories that, at some stage during the 1630s, he felt so disenchanted with the drift of national politics that he contemplated emigrating to New England, even that he boarded a ship but changed his mind before it sailed, are unsubstantiated and implausible.

In contrast, there is no doubting that Cromwell did acquire profound and active religious beliefs at some point prior to 1640. Here, most historians now agree, lies the dominant influence over Cromwell's later career. In October 1638, in by far the most interesting of his early surviving letters, he gave an account of his conversion experience to the wife of his kinsman, Oliver St John:

Yet to honour my God by declaring what He hath done for my soul, in this I am confident, and I will be so. Truly, then, this I find: That He giveth springs in a dry and barren wilderness where no water is. I live (you know where) in Mesheck, which they say signifies Prolonging; in Kedar, which signifieth Blackness: yet the Lord forsaketh me not. Though He do prolong, yet He will (I trust) bring me to His tabernacle, to His resting-place. My soul is with the congregation of the firstborn, my body rests in hope, and if here I may honour my God either by doing or by suffering, I shall be most glad.

Truly no poor creature hath more cause to put forth himself in the cause of his God than I. I have had plentiful wages beforehand, and I am sure I shall never earn the least mite. The Lord accept me in His Son, and give me to walk in the light, and give us to walk in the light, as He is the light. He it is that enlighteneth our blackness, our darkness. I dare not say, He hideth His face from me. He giveth me to see light in His light. One beam in a dark place hath exceeding much refeshment in it. Blessed be His name for shining upon so dark a heart as mine! You know what my manner of life hath been. Oh, I lived in and loved darkness, and hated the light. I was a chief, the chief of sinners. This is true; I hated godliness, yet God had a mercy on me. Oh the riches of His mercy! Praise Him for me, pray for me, that He who hath begun a good work would perfect it to the day of Christ.[6]

From a life of sin without God, the Lord had saved the unworthy Cromwell and converted him to His ways. Henceforth, Cromwell displayed the convert's enthusiasm and most of his letters and speeches are full of these sorts of phrases and expressions, praising the work of a very active, interventionist God who was guiding not only his own life but also the events and campaigns in which he was involved. Cromwell clearly had not always felt this way – he refers to how he turned away from his very sinful past – but there is nothing in this or his other letters precisely to date this conversion or to reveal whether it occurred in a traumatic, sudden flash or via a more lengthy process of gradual enlightenment. His earliest surviving letter, of October 1626, asking Downhall to be godfather to his first son, contains none of this intense, religious language; nor does a letter of April 1631, to a Mr Newdigate, but the subject matter, the care of a hawk, perhaps precluded its use. In contrast, his letter to a Mr Storey of January 1636, concerning a lectureship at Godmanchester, is full of phrases such as 'the Lord hath by him wrought much good amongst us', 'to Him lift we up our hearts', 'I beseech you therefore in the bowels of Christ Jesus' and so forth.[7] Some historians have speculated that the conversion may have occurred around the time of his more worldly crisis of 1630–1, but firm evidence is lacking.

In the wake of his conversion, Cromwell can be identified with those who believed that the Protestant Reformation of the sixteenth century had not gone far enough in sweeping away Catholic beliefs, forms and practices, and had left the country but half-reformed. Specific objects of their criticism included the retention of certain holy days, of elaborate ceremonies within many church services and of ornate decorations within many church buildings. Twinned with this was the belief that most of the population was still sinful, wallowing in the mire of immorality, worldliness and superstition, and that the established church was not doing enough to root out these sins. They saw it as their duty to promote policies of their own and to put pressure on established institutions designed to enforce spiritual reform, 'godly reformation' as it was often termed at the time, and so bring people closer to God. Many who held these hopes and aspirations – Cromwell was certainly one of them – also believed in 'providentialism', that is, a belief that the Lord was very active and at work in the world, intervening directly to guide mortal affairs. This vocal minority were often referred to by themselves and by others as 'the godly'. At the time and since they were also often labelled 'puritans'.

In recent years historians have reconsidered the condition, composition and direction of the state Church in early Stuart England. Research continues and areas of disagreement and doubt remain, but most historians working in the field now characterize the Church of England under James I as a broad, tolerant movement, essentially Calvinist in nature but able to encompass a wide spectrum of Protestant beliefs. The godly had a place in this Church and were able to work within it in an attempt to bring about the reforms which they favoured. If the results were always much slower and more limited than they would have liked, there were none the less enough signs of change to give them some hope and comfort. Most historians argue that, in contrast, the religious policies which Charles I promoted after his accession in 1625 changed the nature of the state Church, favouring the ceremonial, high church approach associated with the Dutch theologian, Arminius, and – from 1633 – the Archbishop of Canterbury, William Laud. Many Protestants who had been perfectly happy with the Church of Elizabeth I or James I were now dismayed, viewing Charles's policies as at best an unwise and dangerous tampering with established Protestant practices and at worst an attempt to reintroduce Catholicism by stealth. The godly, who were looking for further reformation, were appalled at royal policy which, in many respects, ran directly counter to their aspirations. By 1638 at the latest – and probably by 1636 – Cromwell was among their number.

These religious views helped shape Cromwell's stance in 1640. In that year he was returned to both the Short and the Long Parliaments as one of the MPs for Cambridge. He was inconspicuous in the Short Parliament, but almost from the beginning of the Long Parliament Cromwell stood out as a firm critic of royal policies not only in religious but also in secular affairs. He lent his weight to attempts to secure lasting and significant parliamentary reform of royal government, was prominent in promoting many key initiatives during the opening two years of the Parliament and was forthright during 1641–2 in urging his colleagues to be on their guard against Catholic conspiracies at home and abroad. By the early years of the civil war, and perhaps from the opening of the Long Parliament in November 1640, Cromwell saw success for Parliament as a necessary precondition for – perhaps even as synonymous with – the achievement of religious reform.

There is no doubting the prominent role which Cromwell played during the opening years of the Long Parliament. He was appointed to a long list of committees, many of them dealing with religious matters, he often acted as a teller in formal divisions and as a messenger to the Lords, he presented petitions in favour of John Lilburne and for the protection of south-east Wales from Catholic uprising, he proposed that

Parliament appoint guardians for the Prince of Wales and that
the Earl of Essex be made commander of the militia by a parliamentary ordinance, which would not require royal assent,
he allegedly helped draft the bill to abolish episcopacy root
and branch, he moved the second reading of the bill which
eventually became the Triennial Act, and he was very active
during the opening months of 1642 in proposing practical
measures to help put the kingdom 'into a posture of defence'.
On the other hand, he also made a string of blunders – many
of these proposals were dropped or defeated, his temper
got the better of him on several occasions and his tactless
outbursts earned him reprimands, some of his speeches were
naive and counter-productive and his alleged prediction that
'few would oppose' the Grand Remonstrance proved very wide
of the mark.[8] It is also noticeable that Cromwell seems to have
played little or no part in some of the major parliamentary
events of 1640–2, such as the proceedings against the Earl
of Strafford, the debate on the Grand Remonstrance and the
preparation of the Nineteen Propositions.

Historians have advanced two quite different interpretations of Cromwell's role and position during the early years
of the Long Parliament. One version has Cromwell acting
alone at this period, an inexperienced, headstrong apprentice
politician who made many mistakes and who learnt the hard
way, by himself, through trial and error. He was related by
marriage to a number of prominent members of both Houses,
but the relationships were quite distant and did not mean
that these people were close personal friends or political
associates and mentors of the MP for Cambridge. Instead,
he was working alone. An alternative version stresses that by
1640, even before Parliament met, Cromwell was already a
junior member of a group of politicians who were or would
become leading critics of royal government, most of whom
were also close or distant kin – figures like John Hampden
and Oliver St John, the Earl of Warwick and Viscount Saye
and Sele. On the fringe of this group, Cromwell worked with
them to prepare for the coming parliament, owed his return
as MP for Cambridge to them and then worked as their agent
in the Long Parliament. It was only because of their backing
that this otherwise obscure and inexperienced figure was so

prominent so early in the Long Parliament even if, because of his inexperience, he sometimes blundered. This second interpretation may be closer to the truth, for it helps to explain not only Cromwell's double return for Cambridge in 1640 but also his otherwise unexpected prominence so early in the Long Parliament. However, such conclusions rely more upon speculation than upon conclusive proof.

During the summer of 1642, as relations with the King broke down and as it became increasingly obvious that war was approaching, Cromwell's life and career moved in a new direction. The forty years of fairly obscure provincial life and eighteen months of somewhat mixed parliamentary apprenticeship were replaced by military action. In late July the King at York directed requests to Oxford and Cambridge Universities to send their college plate to his northern HQ. During the second week of August, Cromwell, one of the local MPs, and others left London and travelled to Cambridge, gathering a small force en route, in an attempt to stop the University complying. Although some plate was dispatched before their arrival, Cromwell and his colleagues did succeed in blocking the main roads and so preventing the bulk of the college plate from being sent to the King. He also seized for Parliament the arms and ammunition stored in Cambridge Castle. Cromwell was by no means the only parliamentary activist who, with or without clear authorization from the Long Parliament, had seen fit to use a measure of force during the summer of 1642, prior to the formal declaration of war by the King on 22 August, in order to secure men, money and materials and to resist royalist attempts to do likewise. But in so doing, he – like several others – was placing himself in an exposed and potentially dangerous position. It was an early indication of the courage and resolution which would become very evident in the ensuing war.

gave him an alternative power-base which was to prove vital in post-war politics.

In the late summer of 1642 Cromwell raised and commanded a troop of sixty horse, mounted volunteers drawn from his native Cambridgeshire. Although he returned briefly to London and to Parliament in early September, much of August and September was spent in and around Cambridge, organizing the defences. When, during October, it became clear that the King's army would engage the main parliamentary army under the Earl of Essex somewhere in the west Midlands, Captain Cromwell was one of a number of minor provincial officers ordered to march with their newly raised troops to rendezvous with Essex's forces. He seems to have arrived too late to take part in the set-piece battle below Edgehill in Warwickshire on 23 October, though he and his troop may have arrived later that day and skirmished with royalists in the final stages of the indecisive engagement. He probably marched back to London with Essex's main army and took part in the stand-off at Turnham Green on 13 November, which prevented Charles I from entering his capital. However, there is no clear evidence for Cromwell's whereabouts or activities during November and December.

From the beginning of 1643 to spring 1644, his military career comes across as that of an inexperienced but keen regional commander, a man acquiring military skills and struggling to overcome local apathy as well as royalist opponents. He won through to become a star performer in his own fairly small area. It was a pattern common to perhaps half a dozen parliamentary commanders. Cromwell's movements during this period show the rather modest nature of his early military career. In March 1643 he rode via Norwich to Lowestoft, where a show of force bloodlessly cowed local royalists, and in September he went north, to confer with Sir Thomas Fairfax and others in Kingston upon Hull. These trips aside, his travels were largely confined to a small region, comprising the modern counties of Cambridgeshire, southern Lincolnshire and the eastern fringes of Nottinghamshire and Leicestershire, with passage through Hertfordshire as he travelled between the east Midlands and London. He silenced and arrested the royalist sheriff of Hertfordshire at St Albans, secured or strengthened Cambridge, Huntingdon, Peterborough and Ely, watched King's Lynn being bombarded and confiscated the plate and arms of his aged royalist uncle at Ramsey. Real military experience did not come until April 1643, when, having secured Peterborough, he bombarded the royalists within Crowland Abbey into surrender, and similar action secured Burghley House in July. As for field engagements, Cromwell took part in a confused twilight skirmish near Belton in May 1643 and relieved Gainsborough in July by crushing a royalist detachment outside the town, only to fall back the following day when a larger royalist army approached. Not until October 1643 did he take part in a full-scale battle, the modest but decisive engagement at Winceby in the south of Lincolnshire.

The battle of Winceby was a crucial engagement, for it ended royalist dreams of sweeping south into the parliamentary heartlands of East Anglia and the east Midlands. During 1643 royalist forces had been pushing south from Yorkshire, successfully overrunning much of Lincolnshire. It was this threat which Cromwell, promoted in early 1643 to the rank of colonel and given command over a horse regiment of his own, had been striving to meet and overcome. He had been one of a number of officers dispatched to hold the parliamentary heartlands, employing not only his own cavalry regiment but also other units belonging to the army of the Eastern Association under the overall command of Lord Grey of Warke; in practice, Lord Grey was absent from the region for most of 1643. Although Cromwell's direct involvement in sieges, skirmishes and field engagements was limited during 1643, he did play an important role, both by himself and acting with colleagues on a Cambridge-based committee, in securing and organizing the defences of the Isle of Ely, the exposed and vulnerable north-western flank of Eastern Association territory. He proved an able and energetic military administrator, intensely aware of the royalist threat to the area, determined to do all in his power to protect the region and to stir his less active colleagues into contributing to the defences.

Much of Cromwell's work during 1643 was directed towards raising money, the life-blood of the war effort. He wrote many letters requesting money, sometimes apologetically – 'I am sorry I should so often trouble you about the business of money: it's no pleasant subject to be too frequent upon', – sometimes flatteringly – 'I speak to wise men', he told the Mayor of Colchester – and sometimes imploringly:

> Why you should not strengthen us to make us subsist! Judge you the danger of neglect, and how inconvenient this improvidence, or unthrifty, may be to you! I shall never write but according to my judgment. I tell you again, it concerns you exceedingly to be persuaded by me . . . Lay not too much upon the back of a poor gentleman, who desires, without much noise, to lay down his life, and bleed the last drop to serve the Cause and you . . . I desire to deny myself; but others will not be satisfied. I beseech you hasten supplies. Forget not your prayers.[2]

In attempting to raise money and men, Cromwell was often exasperated by the foot-dragging he encountered, by the failure of others to share his appreciation of the approaching dangers and the best way to counter them. While on campaign in the field during June, he begged his fellow commissioners at Cambridge for reinforcements, cajoling them: 'This is not a time to pick and choose for pleasure. Service must be done. Command, you, and be obeyed!' He wrote again in August, a hasty, staccato note, with an air of panic about it, reflecting Cromwell's fear of an imminent royalist breakthrough into Cambridgeshire: 'Raise all your bands; . . . get up what volunteers you can; . . . I beseech you spare not, but be expeditious and industrious . . . You must act lively; do it without distraction. Neglect no means.'[3] In the course of 1643 further parliamentary recruits were successfully raised, many of them joining Cromwell's own cavalry regiment, which numbered over a thousand men by the autumn.

Several features of Cromwell's approach to the war show up in his letters and actions of 1643. Firstly, he became aware that fellow commanders were often unreliable and unco-operative, whether because of personal shortcomings, because they did not share his enthusiasm for winning the war or because they cared more about their own localities. In May 1643 Cromwell was scathing when Lord Grey of Groby failed to rendezvous with him as arranged and instead remained in the Leicester area to protect that town, writing bitterly to the Lincolnshire committee:

> It were better, in my poor opinion, Leicester were not than that there should not be an immediate taking of the field by your forces to accomplish the common end, wherein I shall deal as freely with him when I meet him as you can desire.[4]

On several occasions during 1643 hopes of campaigning slightly further afield with a combined army foundered on the failure of the various commanders, Cromwell included, to co-operate. In January 1644, during a rare and brief return to London, he made a speech in Parliament attacking Lord Willoughby, serjeant-major-general of the parliamentary forces in Lincolnshire. Cromwell made a number of allegations about Willoughby's conduct, including his failure to hold Gainsborough when reinforcements were close at hand, his over-hasty abandonment of Lincoln and his employment of 'very loose and profane' officers.[5]

Secondly, we can trace Cromwell's growing confidence in command during 1643. At his first field engagement, at Belton in May 1643, Cromwell was hesitant, aware that many of his troops were 'poor' and 'broken', content to deploy close to the enemy line and simply exchange shot for over half an hour. When it became clear that the royalists would not advance, Cromwell conferred with others about the best way of proceeding and reached a joint decision: 'we agreed to charge them'. His troops then moved forward at 'a pretty round trot', and charged into and routed the still stationary royalists.[6] Time and again in later battles, Cromwell would rely heavily on the effectiveness of an orderly but rapid cavalry charge. At Gainsborough a similar cavalry charge broke the main royalist body, though only after a longer and closer fight. Cromwell, however, noticed that the royalist commander,

Cavendish, had held back his own regiment and he realized that the royalists would gain the upper hand if all the parliamentarians set off in pursuit of the already broken principal royalist force. 'With much ado', Cromwell managed to draw a couple of his troops back from the chase, to form them up with his own modest reserve and then to charge, break and destroy Cavendish's regiment.[7] At Gainsborough, perhaps more than at Edgehill, Cromwell witnessed at first hand the risk in allowing cavalry to gallop off the battlefield in pursuit of opposing units and saw the advantage in keeping them on the field in good order to break any surviving elements of the enemy army. The value of well-disciplined cavalry acting in tight formation was reinforced the following day, when Cromwell had to fall back on Lincoln, harried all the way by a much larger royalist army. Two blocks of four cavalry troops apiece acted in unison, alternately standing and retiring, so holding off the royalist army and shielding their colleagues as they fell back on Lincoln. If Cromwell had won his spurs as a cavalry officer during 1643, he had also come to appreciate the tactical value of horse over foot. In August he reckoned that one troop of horse was of 'far more advantage [to] the cause than two or three foot companies; especially if your men be honest godly men'.[8]

Thirdly, Cromwell showed a strong interest in the well-being of his men, both junior officers and troopers. In his letters, he expressed great concern about the shortages of pay, clothing and boots which his men were suffering and he repeatedly begged supplies from local and central government. His concern for his men, however, went much deeper than their physical well-being. Cromwell also took an interest in their moral and spiritual standing, their strength of character and moral fibre. He attempted, he recalled in 1657, to recruit 'such men as had the fear of God before them, and made some conscience of what they did'.[9] Cromwell was never a social revolutionary. He recognized that gentlemen and persons 'of quality' were more likely to make good soldiers than were the dregs of society, and he boldly advised John Hampden at some point very early in the war, perhaps after Edgehill in autumn 1642:

Your troopers . . . are most of them old decayed serving men and tapsters, and such kind of fellows, and . . . their [the royalists'] troopers are gentlemen's sons, younger sons, persons of quality: do you think that the spirits of such base and mean fellows will be ever able to encounter gentlemen that have honour, courage and resolution in them? . . . You must get men of a spirit . . . that is like to go as far as a gentleman will go, or else I am sure you will be beaten still.

Hampden felt that the advice was theoretically sound but impractical.[10]

Cromwell, too, found that in practice he could not recruit exclusively from the upper echelons of society and during 1643, as he cast his net wider, so he shifted his argument. If, regrettably, insufficient gentlemen came forward to serve as officers, Cromwell was quite prepared to recruit socially less-elevated men – 'plain' was the adjective he often used of them – but it was important that they should be honest, faithful, sober figures. He told the Suffolk county committee in September:

It had been well that men of honour and birth had entered into these employments, but why do they not appear? Who would have hindered them? But seeing it was necessary the work must go on, better plain men than none, but best to have men patient of wants, faithful and conscientious in the employment, and such, I hope, these will approve themselves to be.[11]

It is in this context that we should place Cromwell's slightly earlier advice to the Suffolk committee, far more famous, often quoted, but often misinterpreted:

I beseech you be careful what captains of horse you choose, what men be mounted; a few honest men are better than numbers . . . If you choose godly honest men to be captains of horse, honest men will follow them, and they will be careful to mount such . . . I had rather have a plain russet-coated captain that knows what he fights for, and loves what he knows, than that which you call a gentleman and is nothing else. I honour a gentleman that is so indeed.[12]

Cromwell was not arguing that officers drawn from below the social status of a gentleman were inherently better than gentlemen, or that gentlemen necessarily made poor officers and should not be commissioned. Far from it – a gentleman who was committed to the parliamentary cause was to be honoured. But honest plain men who were aware of the issues at stake and who strongly supported the parliamentary cause were likely to make better officers than gentlemen who showed no real commitment to the struggle.

Cromwell took care that his own subordinate officers and troopers were sober, godly men and he reportedly imposed strict discipline throughout his regiment. As a parliamentary newspaper put it in May 1643, in terms perhaps a little too glowing to be accepted as the unvarnished truth, though in a tone consistent with several other newspaper reports of 1643:

> As for Cromwell, he hath 2,000 brave men, well disciplined: no man swears but he pays his twelve pence; if he be drunk he is set in the stocks, or worse, if one calls the other 'Roundhead' he is cashiered; insomuch that the countries where they come leap for joy of them, and come in and join with them. How happy were it if all the forces were thus disciplined.[13]

But at the same time Cromwell's practice of recruiting and promoting strongly committed men of non-gentry status left him open to jealousies and to accusations of undermining the established social order – 'it may be it provokes some spirits to see such plain men made captains of horse', he wrote in September[14] – just as his practice of recruiting 'godly' men who held a wide variety of Protestant religious beliefs led to accusations that he was undermining the true faith and encouraging sectaries and heretics. In June 1643 a former parliamentarian accused Cromwell of employing 'an anabaptist', of supporting a captain 'who was lately but a yeoman' and of permitting the 'defacing of churches'.[15] Later in the war, the Earl of Manchester turned on Cromwell, alleging:

> Col Cromwell raysing of his regiment makes choyce of his officers not such as weare souldiers or men of estate, but such

as were common men, pore and of mean parentage, onely he would given them the title of godly, pretious men . . . If you looke upon his owne regiment of horse, see what a swarme ther is of thos that call themselves the godly; some of them profess they have sene vissions and had revellations.[16]

Cromwell defended himself from such allegations and sought to paint a very different picture of his regiment in his letters of autumn 1643. To Oliver St John he wrote, 'I have a lovely company; you would respect them, did you know them. They are no Anabaptists, they are honest, sober Christians; they expect to be used as men', and to Thomas Barrington:

> But truly mine (though some have stigmatised them with the name of Anabaptists), are honest men, such as fear God, I am confident the freest from unjust practices of any in England, seek the soldiers where you can. Such imputations are poor requitals to those who have ventured their blood for you. I hear there are such mists cast to darken their services.[17]

Fourthly, Cromwell was adamant that God was guiding the war and that such military success as he and his colleagues achieved was brought about by God. Immediately after Belton, Cromwell wrote that 'God hath given us, this evening, a glorious victory', emphasizing that God alone had granted Parliament this victory: 'it pleased God to cast the scale', and 'by God's providence they [the royalists] were immediately routed'. Similarly, his letters describing the victory at Gainsborough and his subsequent retreat to Lincoln are full of phrases such as 'it hath pleased God to favour us', 'this relation I offer you for the honour of God, to whom be all the praise', 'it's great evidence of God's favour', 'it hath pleased the Lord to give your servant and soldiers a notable victory', and so forth. In his letter to the Suffolk committee Cromwell wrote that this and other recent victories should be interpreted 'as if God should say, "Up and be doing, and I will help you and stand by you", there is nothing to be feared but our own sin and sloth'. In September it was, again, 'the goodness of God' which had enabled Fairfax to bring reinforcements from Hull.[18] A natural consequence of his profound providentialism was Cromwell's belief that God determined the outcome of battle. As the mixed fortunes of 1643 turned to the more frequent victories of 1644–6, this belief deepened. If God was determining the outcome, parliamentary successes must be a sign that they were doing God's work, fighting for a cause which God sanctioned and supported and acting as God's appointed agents.

The battle of Winceby of October 1643 was the culmination of Cromwell's career as a local commander. Unfortunately, we have no account of the battle written by Cromwell, but other accounts confirm that, once more, Cromwell led a cavalry charge, though on this occasion he did not carry all before him. Indeed, his own horse was shot dead under him and he was nearly killed by royalists.

It was a second charge, led by Sir Thomas Fairfax, which sealed the victory for Parliament. None the less, it was from around this time that Cromwell began to receive greater attention in the newspapers, both royalist and parliamentarian, and to be looked upon as more than just one of the dashing provincial officers with sound war records who were to be found in most regions. It was in November 1643 that a pro-royalist newspaper sarcastically dubbed Cromwell 'Lord of the Fenns'.[19]

Winceby marks the end of the first stage of his military career and it is noticeable that, having spent the closing weeks of the year in Ely, he rarely returned to the east Midlands; he took little part in later clashes in Cambridgeshire and south Lincolnshire. From spring 1644 Cromwell acted on a much larger stage.

By December 1643 Cromwell had been promoted to the rank of lieutenant-general and during 1644 he served under the Earl of Manchester as second-in-command of the army of the Eastern Association. As such, he was often held back by his senior's rather lacklustre and unenthusiastic approach and the year was marked by periods of inactivity – a month before York in June as part of a larger parliamentary army besieging the royalists' northern capital, and two months based around Doncaster and Lincoln from early July to early September, engaged in only the most minor of military operations. Cromwell did take part in two of the greatest battles of the year, the crushing victory at Marston Moor on 2 July and the indecisive engagement at Newbury on 27 October. He was probably wounded in the neck at Marston Moor and may have left the field for a time, but he and his men successfully broke the opposing cavalry and then, lessons learned and discipline tight, stayed on the field to tear into the now vulnerable royalist foot.

He appeared strangely inactive at Newbury, slow to follow up Waller's initial attack and so giving the royalist forces time to reorganize and counter-charge. Against these should be placed his two campaigns in the south Midlands of March and of September to November 1644, during which he began eating into the outer edges of the circuit of royalist bases which protected the King's main capital, Oxford. Although he was not strong enough to tackle the principal bases, still less Oxford itself, he did useful work, taking Hillesden House, raiding and briefly besieging other outposts, generally harrying the King's men and tying down royalist units.

The high point of the year was undoubtedly the great victory at Marston Moor in the largest battle of the entire war. Cromwell was aware just how well he and his men had performed, in stark contrast to many other parliamentary commanders and units. His account of the battle to his brother-in-law, Valentine Walton, is a masterpiece and one of the most moving letters he wrote. Cromwell had a difficult task, to give Walton the splendid news of the smashing victory but also to break to him the news of his eldest son's death in the battle. The letter opens with a sense of foreboding, an early warning of what was to follow: 'It's our duty to sympathise in all mercies; that we may praise the Lord together in chastisements or trials, that so we may sorrow together.' Cromwell then gives an almost ecstatic account of the battle itself, as usual stressing that credit was due to God alone:

Truly England and the Church of God hath had a great favour from the Lord, in this great victory given unto us, such as the like never was since this war began. It had all the evidences of an absolute victory obtained by the Lord's blessing upon the godly party principally. We never charged but we routed the enemy . . . God made them as stubble to our swords . . . Give glory, all the glory, to God.

Then came the sting in the tail, closely followed by consolation from a man who had just lost another son, Oliver junior, dead from natural causes while serving as a junior parliamentary officer:

Sir, God hath taken away your eldest son by a cannon-shot. It brake his leg. We were necessitated to have it cut off, whereof he died. Sir, you know my trials this way; but the Lord supported me with this: that the Lord took him into the happiness we all pant after and live for. There is your precious child full of glory, to know sin nor sorrow any more . . . Truly he was exceedingly beloved in the Army, of all that knew him. But few knew him, for he was a precious young man, fit for God. You have cause to bless the Lord. He is a glorious saint in Heaven, wherein you ought exceedingly to rejoice . . . You may do all things by the strength of Christ. Seek that, and you shall easily bear your trial. Let this public mercy to the Church of God make you to forget your private sorrow. The Lord be your strength.[20]

Off the battlefield, Cromwell struggled to contain differences within the parliamentary ranks. The English Parliament's alliance with the Scottish presbyterians in December 1643 brought problems, for Cromwell – like several other English officers – had little sympathy with the strict Scottish presbyterianism, a version of which, under the terms of this alliance, was to be imposed in England and Wales once the war was won. Cromwell's own tolerant and relaxed approach, welcoming the help of any who supported the parliamentary cause and who were broadly Protestant and godly, brought him into conflict with less liberal commanders, especially those who welcomed the prospect of a strict presbyterian settlement. In March 1644 he clashed with Major-General Crawford, who was seeking the dismissal of a baptist junior officer, telling Crawford sharply:

> Surely you are not well advised thus to turn off one so faithful to the Cause, and so able to serve you as this man is. Give me leave to tell you, I cannot be of your judgment; that if a man notorious for wickedness, for oaths, for drinking, hath as great a share in your affection as one that fears an oath, that fears to sin, that this doth commend your election of men to serve as fit instrument in this work. Ay, but the man is an Anabaptist. Are you sure of that? Admit he be, shall that render him incapable to serve the public. He is indiscreet. It may be so, in some things, we have all human infirmities. I tell you, if you had none but such indiscreet men about you, and would be pleased to use them kindly, you would find as good a fence to you as any you have yet chosen.

Cromwell desired Crawford to take the man back into his favour, advising Crawford to 'take heed of being sharp, or too easily sharpened by others, against those to whom you can object little but that they square not with you in every opinion concerning matters of religion'.

Cromwell drove the message home to Crawford by asserting, rather sweepingly, that 'the State, in choosing men to serve them, takes no notice of their opinions; if they be willing faithfully to serve them, that satisfies'.[21] Here, Cromwell was indulging in wishful thinking. This broadly tolerant attitude was what Cromwell hoped to see adopted and what he did apparently practise within his own regiment. But state policy was very different. Parliament had directed that officers must sign the Solemn League and Covenant, the formal document of alliance with the Scots, thereby signifying their acceptance of the future imposition of a Scottish-style presbyterian system in England and Wales. As a baptist, this junior officer felt unable to take the Covenant and Crawford was merely executing Parliament's policy in seeking to have him removed. Cromwell was in the wrong; he had no authority to advise Crawford to disregard parliamentary policy, still less to write a different policy of his own. But Cromwell's squabble with Crawford in the spring of 1644 was as nothing compared to his major confrontation with his own commander, the Earl of Manchester, fought out in Parliament during the following winter.

Cromwell had returned to London only occasionally and briefly during 1643–4, and throughout this period he appears to have been active in Parliament only once, for a fortnight or so in January and February 1644. It is a sign of his increased status that, despite this prolonged absence, he was appointed in spring 1644 to the Committee of Both Kingdoms, Parliament's powerful executive committee. Cromwell's return to Westminster and to the parliamentary arena in November 1644 was not a happy affair. In the course of the year's campaigning, a wide rift had developed between Cromwell and the Earl of Manchester. During the winter of 1644–5, both the protagonists, backed by their supporters, sought to resolve the matter by airing their grievances in Parliament. During late November Cromwell roundly denounced Manchester via both parliamentary speeches and a detailed written account. His principal accusation was that, time and again during 1644, Manchester had been slow and unwilling to prosecute the war, holding back the Eastern Association army even when there were clear opportunities to defeat the enemy. The reason, Cromwell alleged,

> was not merely from dullness or indisposedness to engagement, but (withal) from some principle of unwillingnes in his Lordship to have this war prosecuted unto a full victory, and a design or desire to have it ended by accommodation (and that) on some such terms to which it might be disadvantageous to bring the King too low.[22]

The accusation was that Manchester was a very lukewarm supporter of military action, that he held back from fighting for total military victory, because he thought it was unachievable or undesirable, and instead sought a peaceful compromise with the King at the earliest opportunity and on terms favourable to the Crown. Cromwell supported this accusation by giving lengthy and highly detailed accounts – perhaps prepared in consultation with other commanders – of the actions of the Eastern Association army from May to November 1644, emphasizing how his own desire actively to engage the enemy whenever and wherever possible had been thwarted by Manchester, who instead kept the army idle or engaged in trivial affairs.

Manchester was by no means overwhelmed by this onslaught, nor was he silent in the face of Cromwell's accusations. He produced an equally detailed and damning account of his own. In it, he not only defended his conduct of the 1644 campaign but also levelled counter-accusations, alleging that Cromwell had displayed anti-Scottish and anti-presbyterian feelings and that he had deliberately undermined the established social and religious orders by promoting poor, common and mean men and by encouraging fanatics, sectaries and heretics. Here, Manchester was building upon much wider and potentially very damaging suspicions of Cromwell and his own troops. It was rumoured that they were not prepared to fight for a victory which would lead to a presbyterian church settlement, that Cromwell and his colleagues would rather resign or emigrate than live under a presbyterian system which would not tolerate other brands of Protestantism, and that they were hatching plots against their more presbyterian-inclined superiors, including Manchester and the Earl of Essex. These rumours seem to have been circulating so widely during the autumn that pro-parliamentary newspapers several times went out of their way to deny them. Cromwell himself in a letter of early September referred to 'the many slanders heaped upon us by false tongues', hoping that in due course the Lord would make clear to all that, notwithstanding these slanders, they were in reality seeking 'the glory of God [and] the honour and liberty of the Parliament' and were not pursuing their 'own interests'.[23] But Cromwell's own actions on the battlefield in the course of the 1644 campaign, especially at and after the battle of Newbury, were not above reproach. Not only had he been curiously slow and lethargic in committing his cavalry to the unfolding battle, but also during the following days he had done little to hinder royalist manoeuvres in the area, reportedly refusing to obey an order from Manchester to prevent the King relieving Donnington Castle on the grounds that his horses and their riders were exhausted. This might add to the suspicions that, because of their own religious opinions and their dislike of an intolerant, presbyterian settlement, it was Cromwell and his colleagues rather than Manchester who were less than enthusiastic in pushing for the military victory which would open the way to this settlement. During December and January the Earl of Manchester, with the support of the majority of the House of Lords, pressed the Commons for full consideration of Cromwell's charges and his counter-charges.

There is no doubting that Cromwell favoured 'liberty of conscience' and that he and many who served under him in the army would have had little enthusiasm for the establishment of a national presbyterian church in England and Wales and even less for the persecution of other brands of Protestantism which such a church might initiate. These apprehensions are clear in Cromwell's clash with Crawford and played a part in his attacks on Willoughby and Manchester. It is also clear that, during the latter half of 1644, Manchester and Cromwell had adopted divergent attitudes towards the religious opinions of their officers and men. Where at one time both adopted quite liberal and relaxed approaches, happy to employ men of presbyterian, independent and other viewpoints, the attitudes of both men seem to have changed after Marston Moor. With the complete defeat of the King now a distinct possibility, Manchester became increasingly fearful of the breakdown in religious and social order which might follow; a compromise peace settlement with the King, restoring strong royal government, and the restoration or imposition of a disciplined, orderly national church now seemed much more attractive to him. Conversely, Cromwell, fearful of any one religious group gaining a monopoly of power, became more critical of the Scots and their church, and during the autumn he reportedly carried out a modest purge of presbyterian-inclined officers. Perhaps shaken by the intolerant presbyterianism of the Scottish officers whom he met at the siege of York, perhaps convinced by his success at Marston Moor that the Lord favoured his 'godly' approach, perhaps fearful of the approaching strict presbyterian settlement which the sweeping victory at Marston Moor seemed to bring closer, or perhaps merely reacting to the changed attitude of Manchester and his colleagues, Cromwell's own outlook seems to have undergone a subtle but crucial change during the latter half of 1644.

None of this either invalidates the substance of Cromwell's

principal accusations against Manchester – that he was a lacklustre, inactive commander who was hankering after a compromise peace settlement – or substantiates Manchester's allegations that it was Cromwell who was holding back from military victory. From what we know about Cromwell, Manchester's allegation that Cromwell was deliberately trying to overturn the established social order – at one point he claimed that Cromwell had said that he hoped 'to live to see never a nobleman in England' – and his accusation that Cromwell deliberately and without good reason stymied the parliamentary campaign at and after the battle of Newbury, seem highly implausible. However, the truth was not fully established at the time and the rival charges and counter-charges were never investigated or pursued to any sort of final verdict. Instead, on 9 December Cromwell changed tack, perhaps realizing that he had bitten off more than he could chew and fearing defeat if he pushed on with the confrontation, perhaps because he realized that victory would be messy, opening up even deeper divisions among the parliamentary cause and so giving succour to the enemy. In one or more speeches delivered on 9 December Cromwell backed down, claiming that he did not wish 'to insist upon any complaint or oversight of any Commander-in-chief upon any occasions whatsoever', acknowledging that he himself had been 'guilty of oversights, so I know they can rarely be avoided in military matters', and 'waving a strict inquiry into the causes of these things'.[24] Whether an act of statesman-like magnanimity or face-saving retreat, Cromwell successfully proposed that the two sets of charges be taken no further and inquiries dropped. Thereafter, the Commons blocked all attempts to revive the investigation.

Cromwell's change of heart on 9 December was inseparably linked to a proposal designed to improve the future command of the parliamentary army and so bring the war more speedily to a victorious conclusion. He threw his weight behind a proposal that all members of the Houses of Lords and Commons who held a command within the parliamentary army should surrender their commissions and henceforth should not hold military command. He was careful to stress that this should not be seen as a veiled attack on any current commander, but that all those who were members of either House should stand down as an act of self-denial, enabling new officers to take the helm and guide an administratively and morally reformed army to victory. Mindful of the rumours and suspicion which surrounded him, Cromwell assured the House that his own troops idolized not him but the cause for which they fought, that they would happily follow a new commander chosen by Parliament and that 'you may lay upon them what commands you please', confident that they would be obeyed.[25] Cromwell remained in London and active in Parliament throughout January and February 1645, during which time legislation to put this proposal for self-denial into binding, statutory form was debated and further preparations were made to appoint a new commander-in-chief – Sir Thomas Fairfax to replace the Earl of Essex – and to reorganize the army into a more coherent fighting unit. Cromwell played a leading role in many of these debates.

With the Self-Denying Ordinance still under consideration, Cromwell left London in early March 1645 and returned to active campaigning. After a foray into Dorset, he resumed his attacks on the circuit of royalist bases in Oxfordshire and Berkshire. In an eight-week campaign, he captured Bletchingdon House, tried unsuccessfully to frighten Faringdon into submission, threatening 'I will not spare a man of you, if you put me to a storm',[26] harried other bases in the area, and skirmished with royalist units in the field. Writing to the Committee of Both Kingdoms on 25 April, he gave an account of this campaign, seeing in both his successes and his failures the unmistakable 'mercy' of God: 'I hope you will pardon me if I say, God is not enough owned. We look too much to men and visible helps: this hath much hindered our success. But I hope God will direct all to acknowledge Him alone in all.'[27]

In Cromwell's absence a revised version of the Self-Denying Ordinance completed its passage though both Houses on 3 April, giving all existing officers who were members of either House forty days in which to surrender their commissions. Many, including Essex and Manchester, did so upon or even before the passage of the Ordinance. Cromwell did not and remained on campaign, but his command, too, should have lapsed by 12 May at the latest. However, by that time the

King's main army was on the move, and Parliament voted to extend Cromwell's commission for a further period of forty days. Part of this he spent back in Cambridge and Huntingdon, a rare return visit, organizing improvements to local defences. On 10 June, with the King's army on the loose in the Midlands, Leicester ravaged and a major confrontation looming, the Commons extended his command once more and, at Fairfax's request, agreed to his appointment to the still-vacant post of lieutenant-general of the horse, thus making him second-in-command of the revamped New Model Army; the Lords subsequently concurred. For a further year, Parliament agreed to a succession of renewals, extending his commission for periods of three, four or six months at a time. Cromwell was not the only officer thus granted exemption from the provisions of the Self-Denying Ordinance, but it was a rare and potentially divisive step. There is now no way of knowing whether the exemption was unforeseen, saving a military career which Cromwell himself believed would end in spring 1645, or whether from the outset he hoped and expected to win such exemption. If the latter, his early and active promotion of the self-denying measure and perhaps also his support for Fairfax's appointment as the new commander-in-chief – Fairfax subsequently urged very strongly that Cromwell be retained in the army – take on a very different light.

Thus thrown a life-line, Cromwell remained on campaign during the last year of the war, from June 1645 to June 1646. He was absent from Parliament throughout almost the whole of this period. He reappeared in the House for barely a week in late April 1646, reportedly the centre of attention and 'looked on as a wonder' by fellow MPs as he passed through Westminster Hall.[28] He spent the winter of 1645–6 on campaign in the West Country rather than in London. For much of the time he was operating with Fairfax and the main army, first shattering the King's army at Naseby in Northamptonshire on 14 June, and then slowly pushing the remaining royalists into the West Country, clearing Wiltshire, Dorset and Somerset during June to September, Devon from October to the following February and Cornwall in March, and finally taking part in the siege of Oxford in May and June

1646. Highlights included further victorious field engagements at Langport, Somerset, on 10 July 1645, and at Bovey Tracey and Torrington in Devon on 9 January and 16 February 1646 respectively, and the capture by siege or storm of Bridgwater in July 1645, of Sherborne Castle in August, of Bristol and Devizes in September 1645 and of Exeter in April 1646. In September and October 1645 Cromwell led seven regiments on a short, separate campaign, in which they cleared remaining royalist bases in central southern England, principally Winchester and Basing House in Hampshire.

As usual, Cromwell's letters recounting these victories are full of references to God and accord all the credit to the Lord. If anything, this belief seems to have become more intense. Writing a month or so after the event, Cromwell recalled that at Naseby:

> when I saw the enemy drawn up and march in gallant order towards us, and we a company of poor ignorant men, to seek how to order our battle ... I could not (riding alone about my business) but smile out to God in praises, in assurance of victory, because God would, by things that are not, bring to naught things that are. Of which I had great assurance; and God did it. O that men would therefore praise the Lord, and declare the wonders that He doth for the children of men![29]

Concluding a very long and detailed account of the siege and storming of Bristol, he commented 'that all this is none other than the work of God' and that 'he must be a very Atheist that doth not acknowledge it'. He went on to stress that all the officers and men who had taken part in the operation were aware that the capture of Bristol had been achieved through the 'faith and prayer' not only of the soldiers but also 'of the people of God ... all England over, who have wrestled with God for a blessing in this very thing'.[30]

During summer 1645 Cromwell used the valour and success of parliamentary troops in battle pointedly to drive home his plea that godly men of differing persuasions be given liberty of conscience and that no over-narrow religious boundaries be imposed. In his letter to the Speaker of the House of

Commons, written immediately after the battle of Naseby, Cromwell declared:

> Honest men served you faithfully in this action. Sir, they are trusty; I beseech you in the name of God, not to discourage them. I wish this action may beget thankfulness and humility in all that are concerned in it. He that ventures his life for the liberty of his country, I wish he trust God for the liberty of his conscience, and you for the liberty he fights for.[31]

The Commons censored these sentences when they had Cromwell's dispatch published; the Lords, however, published the full version. Again, his lengthy dispatch to the Speaker relating the capture of Bristol ended with an even more explicit passage, once more omitted from the version subsequently published on Parliament's orders:

> Our desires are, that God may be glorified by the same spirit of faith by which we asked all our sufficiency, and having received it, it's meet that He have all the praise. Presbyterians, Independents, all had here the same spirit of faith and prayer; the same pretence and answer; they agree here, know no names of difference: pity it is should be otherwise anywhere. All that believe, have the real unity, which is most glorious, because inward and spiritual, in the Body, and to the Head. As for being united in forms, commonly called Uniformity, every Christian will for peace-sake study and do, as far as conscience will permit; and from brethren, in things of the mind we look for no compulsion, but that of light and reason.[32]

Cromwell retained tight discipline over his troops and employed them sparingly. During the campaign of 1645-6, he was careful to give a besieged castle or town several opportunities to surrender on terms. Even when the initial offer was spurned, Cromwell almost always granted subsequent requests for a parley once the operation was in progress. For example, when the governor of Winchester Castle refused a summons to surrender on terms, Cromwell mounted batteries against the place and sent in a second summons, again refused; he then bombarded the castle walls, eventually opening a breach which he considered stormable. At that point the governor requested and was granted a parley, which led to the surrender of the fortress on honourable terms. Cromwell pledged that no inhabitants of Winchester, soldier or civilian, would suffer 'violence or injury' from his troops and he duly enforced tight discipline over his men to prevent any looting or plundering; as an added inducement, he promised each foot soldier a 'gratuity' of five shillings.[33] At the beginning of August Cromwell had been even more concerned to avoid bloodshed during an encounter with the Dorset clubmen, a body of several hundred lightly armed locals. He tried to persuade them to disperse peacefully and, when that failed, he sent his troops in but with orders to use minimal force. Only when the clubmen had fired on and killed several of his troops did he order them to counter-attack, though even then, as he stressed in his written report on the affair, his men enforced only 'small execution upon them; I believe killed not twelve of them'. Most of them he allowed to return to their homes, dismissing them as 'poor silly creatures'.[34]

Against this mild approach, Cromwell's treatment of the royalists in Basing House, Hampshire, stands out starkly. True, Cromwell allowed them one opportunity to surrender on terms to his summons, but after its rejection no subsequent offers were made. Indeed, after the outer defences had fallen, the royalists holding out within the 'Old House' requested a parley, but this was ignored. Instead, following several days' bombardment and a night which Cromwell reportedly spent largely in prayer, his men stormed the entire stronghold with considerable violence. In his account to the Speaker Cromwell himself wrote that 'many of the Enemy our men put to the sword, and some officers of quality' and that the place had been left 'exceedingly ruined', both by the initial bombardment and by a subsequent fire. Other contemporary accounts allege that over a quarter of the garrison perished in the attack, including many civilians sheltering within the walls, and that Cromwell allowed his men to kill and to plunder in a manner which contrasted sharply with his usual practice. Basing House was a very large stronghold, its garrison had a formidable reputation for raiding the surrounding area and its presence had long been a thorn in Parliament's side. However, it is difficult to avoid the conclusion that the brutality of Cromwell's attack was due, in part at least, to a hatred of Roman Catholicism. Basing House was owned by a Roman Catholic peer and was reputed to be a haven for Catholics, soldiers, civilians and priests, 'a nest of Romanists', as Cromwell reportedly termed it in his initial, spurned summons. Certainly, explanations of the high death-toll in parliamentary newspapers stressed the Catholic faith of most of those who perished – 'agents of the Devill and Pope' – as well as noting that the defenders called for a parley too late in the operation, when they were 'not heard or not trusted'.[35]

Cromwell's direct military involvement in the first civil war ended in June 1646 with the surrender of royalist Oxford. He played no part in operations during the late summer and autumn to mop up Raglan Castle and other diehard royalist bases, and instead returned to London; his wife and children moved from Ely to London around the same time. Four years of intense military campaigning had seen Cromwell rise from a mere captain with no previous military experience to second-in-command of the parliamentary army, a battle-hardened veteran with a formidable reputation for vigorous and successful action – 'that never beheld his enemies in the face but returned from them crowned alwayes with renowne and honour, nor ever brought his colours from the field but he did wind up victory within them', as one newspaper put it in spring 1646.[36] The growing military power and prestige had brought with it potentially enhanced political influence, as yet largely untried and untested. In the wake of the Self-Denying Ordinance, he was almost the only man who possessed both a strong military power-base and the opportunity directly to guide national politics by means of a seat in Parliament. In the course of his campaigns Cromwell had travelled widely over southern England, East Anglia and the Midlands. He had also gained considerable insights into the strengths and weaknesses of his royalist opponents and his parliamentary colleagues. In particular, he had become aware of the variety of religious viewpoints, many very different from his own, encompassed by the parliamentary cause. Years later Cromwell declared that the desire to secure broad religious liberty 'was not the thing first contested for, but God brought it to that issue at last'.[37] By the end of the war he had become painfully aware

4

POLITICS AND THE ARMY, 1646–1649

In mid summer 1646 Cromwell returned to Parliament and began playing a direct and sustained role in parliamentary affairs for the first time in four years. Much had changed since 1642, when Cromwell was last active in the House for more than a few weeks at a time. Several of his parliamentary colleagues of 1642 were dead, many other MPs with whom he had sat in 1640–2 had gone, either to the grave or disabled through wartime royalism, and instead the Commons was slowly and partly refilling with new MPs, returned in 'recruiter' elections. But more than the personnel had changed. If the central problem – the need to find constitutional solutions to a range of governmental problems broadly acceptable to, and sincerely accepted by, the King, his critics and a substantial part of the nation at large – remained unresolved and just as thorny in 1646 as it had been in 1640–2, the context of that problem had changed enormously and other issues had arisen. By 1646 there were clear signs of divisions opening up among the English parliamentarians, they now had to deal with their wartime Scottish allies, there existed a large and powerful parliamentary army which might influence political developments and the experience of four years of war had seen the rise and dissemination of a range of new religious and political ideas. These problems increasingly absorbed Cromwell's time and energies from summer 1646 onwards. Increasingly, too, he felt weighed down by their burdens. On occasion during the war Cromwell's letters reveal a sense of dismay, but his correspondence of the winter of 1646–7 indicates a sustained bitterness and depression. By March 1647 he was writing to Fairfax, 'Never were the spirits of men more embittered than now. Surely the Devil hath but a short time.'[1] The certainties, the clarity and, for Cromwell, the string of overwhelming, God-given victories on the battlefield had been replaced by the slough of political infighting.

It is difficult to discover exactly where Cromwell fitted into the kaleidoscope of differing political and religious views of 1646–7. His surviving letters from this period are often thin, giving no more than tantalizing hints at Cromwell's views on the major religious, political and constitutional issues of the day. Their provenance indicates that Cromwell was based in London between July 1646 and June 1647, excepting only three weeks spent at Saffron Walden in May. He was attending Parliament quite regularly during the latter half of 1646 and on into January 1647, for he was appointed to a steady stream of parliamentary committees and frequently acted as a teller in formal divisions of the House. Thereafter, serious illness, the Saffron Walden trip and perhaps also depression and disillusionment at the drift of affairs in Parliament meant that his attendance was more sporadic. But even when he was attending assiduously, we know little about the precise role he was playing in the House. Apart from his appearances as a teller, thus indicating the position he took on the specific issues being voted upon, the parliamentary sources are rather meagre. No detailed transcript or account of a parliamentary speech made by Cromwell at this time appears to survive.

It is tempting to fall back on other sources to fill out our picture of Cromwell in 1646–7. Edmund Ludlow's *Memoirs*, for example, contain various glimpses of Cromwell, including an account of a meeting between Ludlow and Cromwell in September 1646, during which the latter expressed a profound depression at the infighting of parliamentary life and contrasted it with the purity of military service. This is consistent with the feelings which Cromwell was expressing in his own letters of winter 1646–7. However, Ludlow became a political enemy of Cromwell and the version of the *Memoirs* which has come down to us was heavily edited by another hand prior to its publication in the late seventeenth century. Again, we are given some interesting insights into Cromwell's utterances and actions during 1646–7 – not least a colourful story that at the beginning of June 1647, just before he quit Parliament for the army camp, Cromwell 'foamed and stormed' in the Commons, pledging 'before God . . . that he would never leave them [the two Houses] nor foresake them whilst he lived' – in an account published by Colonel Edward Wogan in 1648. Yet by 1648 Wogan had deserted to the royalist cause and his whole account, which seeks to justify his desertion, sets out to blacken the honesty of the leading parliamentary officers, Cromwell and Henry Ireton above all. In similar vein, Robert Huntingdon, once a major in Cromwell's own regiment, published in summer 1648 an account of the reasons which had led him to resign his commission, an account shot through with animosity towards Cromwell and full of stories showing Cromwell to be a scheming hypocrite; Huntingdon's account probably tells us more about the author's frustrated ambitions and general bitterness than it does about his former commander's actions in 1647.[2] Such sources must be used with great caution, if at all.

During the closing years of the civil war, Cromwell several times indicated his support for broad liberty of conscience and opposition to overly narrow and restrictive religious policies. In that area, Cromwell was likely to ally with those politicians who favoured a broad religious settlement and to oppose, and be opposed by, those who were proposing a much narrower religious settlement based upon a single state church, perhaps organized on presbyterian lines. In late July 1646 he wrote in defence of some villagers in East Anglia persecuted for their religious beliefs, taking the opportunity roundly to condemn all who attacked their fellows in this way:

> Truly nothing moves me to desire this, more than the pity I bear them in respect of their honesties, and the trouble I hear they are like to suffer for their consciences . . . I am not ashamed to solicit for such as are anywhere under a pressure of this kind; doing herein as I would be done by. Sir, this is a quarrelsome age; and the anger seems to me to be the worse, where the ground is things of difference in opinion; which to

cure, to hurt men in their names, persons or estates, will not be found an apt remedy.[3]

Some of the Commons divisions of 1646–7 in which Cromwell acted as a teller concerned religious matters, and again Cromwell attempted, usually unsuccessful, to reject or water down proposed restrictions upon religious practice. For example, at the end of December he was teller in a vain attempt to defeat a resolution to forbid the 'expounding' of scriptures by the unordained.

Cromwell's political and constitutional views during the first year of uneasy peace are less apparent. In August 1646, Cromwell wrote that the King had given 'a very general answer' to the Newcastle Propositions,[4] but this was no more than a passing comment. Cromwell was one of many MPs involved in negotiations with Parliament's Scottish allies, but direct negotiations with Charles himself were still at an early stage and Cromwell seems to have made no clear statement of his own views on the content or direction of any constitutional settlement. In political terms, he was probably far closer to the so-called independents, who wished to impose quite extensive new controls over royal power, than the so-called presbyterians, who favoured the re-establishment of royal government on minimal terms.

After his desire to protect liberty of conscience, it was dismay at attacks upon the parliamentary army which seems to have motivated Cromwell most strongly during this period. In many ways these issues cannot be separated, for all parties came to view the position of the English army as crucial to other developments. Weakening or completely breaking the power of the parliamentary army was seen as a desirable or essential preliminary move both by politicians who wished to conclude a speedy constitutional agreement with the King on mild terms and by those who wished to reimpose a state church and narrow religious discipline. It therefore follows that many of the overt attacks upon the army launched during 1646–7 may have had political or religious factors underlying them, just as Cromwell and others may have sprung to the army's defence, at least in part, because they also wanted to impede feared political and religious development. Certainly, in his surviving letters and also in several of the parliamentary divisions in which he served as teller, military concerns and his fears for the well-being of the army seem to have been uppermost in Cromwell's mind. For example, on 14 July 1646, in one of his earliest recorded parliamentary interventions since his return from active military duty, Cromwell reportedly 'made a long speech in vindication of Sir Thomas Fairfax his Army from an aspersion cast upon it'.[5]

In his letters to Fairfax of 1646-7 Cromwell repeatedly expressed his dismay at anti-army sentiments circulating in London. In August he commented, 'We are full of faction and worse', and in December, writing soon after City presbyterians had presented a petition to Parliament urging the army's speedy disbandment, he was even gloomier, though he sought comfort in the intervention of God:

> We have had a very long petition from the City. How it strikes at the army and what other aims it has, you will see by the contents of it; as also what the prevailing temper is at this present, and what is to be expected from men. But this is our comfort, God is in heaven, and He doth what pleaseth Him; His and only His counsel shall stand, whatever the designs of men, and the fury of the people be.

During the second week of March 1647, by which time Parliament was pressing on with plans for compulsory disbandment, Cromwell bewailed, 'there want not in all places men who have so much malice against the army as besots them' and went on to comment on the embittered spirits of men and the imminence of the devil, though he did not entirely despair, again seeking solace in divine intervention: 'The naked simplicity of Christ, with that wisdom He please to give, and patience, will overcome all this.'[6]

In late January 1647 Cromwell had fallen seriously ill with what one contemporary called an 'impostume of the head'. By 7 March he had recovered sufficiently to give Fairfax an account of his illness. Once more, Cromwell saw the hand of the Lord at work, testing him but at the same time supporting, strengthening and guiding him. God had passed 'the sentence of death' upon him, Cromwell wrote,

> that I might learn to trust in him that raiseth from the dead, and have no confidence in the flesh. It's a blessed thing to die daily, for what is there in this world to be accounted of. The best men according to the flesh, and things, are lighter than vanity. I find this only good, to love the Lord and his poor despised people, to do for them, and to be ready to suffer with them.[7]

Cromwell played a low-key role during March and April 1647, with little evidence of parliamentary activity. One source, not above suspicion, claims that around 20 March he did speak in the Commons, assuring his fellow MPs 'in the presence of Almighty God' that the army would obediently disband if requested by Parliament so to do.[8] But Cromwell's name largely disappears from the Commons *Journal* and his failure to act as a teller in divisions or to be nominated to committees may be an indication that he was physically absent from the chamber. If so, it may simply have been the result of his recent illness, but at least one newsletter implies that there was more to it than this, claiming that Cromwell and Sir Henry Vane 'often forbear coming to the House'.[9] Although the motives cannot be firmly proved and ill-health or its after-effects cannot be entirely discounted, an apparent trait of Cromwell's political career during the 1640s and 1650s was a physical withdrawal from the theatre of debate if he found the subject matter extremely distasteful or if he was clearly losing the argument.

Certainly, the parliamentary tide had turned strongly against Cromwell and his political allies. During March and April 1647 the presbyterian majority swept on with a series of resolutions unwelcome to the parliamentary army, laying plans for the enforced disbandment for most soldiers who did not agree to serve in Ireland but making little provision for the material and legal welfare of ex-soldiers and their families. Cromwell was not appointed to the Irish army and Parliament's twin resolutions, that – Fairfax aside – no officer serving in the drastically streamlined English army should rank higher than a colonel and that no MP was to hold military command in

England, seemed to presage the end of his military career. But by the spring, Parliament's plans were running into serious difficulties, for there were clear signs that the New Model Army regiments, many of them based in and around Saffron Walden, were expressing open opposition to the plans and there were fears of mutiny or direct military action against Parliament.

Accusations surfaced at the time that Cromwell welcomed the growing militancy of the army. During the winter of 1646-7, it is alleged, Cromwell and his political colleagues realized that they were outnumbered by the presbyterians and that a majority existed in both Houses to press ahead with a political and religious settlement not to Cromwell's taste. Recognizing that they could not block such a settlement by normal parliamentary means, Cromwell and his colleagues looked to military intervention. Thus in the late winter and spring of 1647 they did nothing to prevent the presbyterians pressing ahead with measures likely to antagonize the army; far from urging caution or opposing these measures, they remained silent, did not vote against them or even absented themselves from the chamber. If placed in this context, Cromwell's intervention of late March, assuring the Commons that the army would disband if ordered to do so, plus another speech of 21 May, reportedly repeating that assurance, albeit with some riders, take on a sinister hue. They appear to be the work of an *agent provocateur*, deliberately luring his political enemies on to rash actions which he believed would lead to the destruction of their constitutional and religious aspirations, wrecked upon the rocks of direct military intervention.

However, Cromwell's own words and actions during 1647 can be read very differently, presenting an alternative and probably more accurate image. Time and again during 1647, Cromwell appeared extremely anxious to avoid open conflict between Parliament and the army. Even after he had been forced to take sides of a sort in June, he continued to work for compromise and to restrain more radical military elements pressing for Parliament to be thoroughly purged or utterly ejected by the army. Even though Parliament's actions had disappointed him and he clearly viewed many of its members with growing suspicion, Cromwell felt that a binding political and religious settlement could be achieved only through normal parliamentary procedures. A settlement imposed by the army through naked military action was worthless and would not hold, he argued.

This attitude is first seen during May 1647. Disturbed by reports of military unrest, Parliament dispatched commissioners to Saffron Walden to assure the army of Parliament's goodwill and to urge the soldiers to enlist for service in Ireland. Parliament selected as commissioners the four officer MPs most likely to command respect in the army, namely Cromwell himself and three 'recruiter' members: Henry Ireton, Charles Fleetwood and Philip Skippon. They were in Saffron Walden from 2 to 20 May, consulting representatives of the various regiments and other officers. We have accounts of several of the more structured meetings, during which regimental representatives reported their grievances. None of these meetings took the form of a free-flowing debate and no new course of action was decided upon. The formal sessions were chaired by Skippon, and Cromwell's only significant recorded contribution occurred towards the end of the final session, when he sought to counter growing clamours that the regiments should send their own representatives to London to state their grievances to Parliament. Attempting to bring the meeting to a close, Cromwell suggested that most officers return to their regiments, leaving behind just three representatives from each regiment who would work with the commissioners to tabulate the list of grievances. Like Skippon, he urged those officers present to report to their regiments the recent votes in Parliament to grant indemnity and pay arrears:

> Truly, Gentlemen, it will be very fitt for you to have a very great care in the making the best use and improvement that you can both of the Votes and of this that hath been last told you, and of the interest which all of you or any of you may have in your severall respective regiments, namely, to worke in them a good opinion of that authority that is over both us and them. If that authoritie falls to nothing, nothing can followe but confusion.

The officers were to understand that the authority of Parliament was the only way forward and that if Parliament was undermined then a lasting settlement was impossible and 'confusion' would inevitably follow.[10]

On 21 May Cromwell presented to the Commons a clear and detailed account of the commissioners' inquiries in Saffron Walden. A contemporary newsletter reports that Cromwell went on to assure that House that the army 'will without doubt disband' if ordered so to do, though he hinted at problems likely to be encountered with a small minority of the soldiers: 'the greatest difficulty . . . would be to satisfy the demands of some (whom he had persuaded as much as he could possibly) but a great part of the army remitt themselves entirely to be ordered by the Parliament'. He also warned that, apart from those who had already enlisted voluntarily, the troops would not agree to serve in Ireland.[11] The speech repeated the assurance he had reportedly made in the Commons in March and is consistent with the sentiments he had expressed at Saffron Walden. In reality, many soldiers were coming close to open defiance of Parliament's orders to disband and, within a week, parliamentary votes for disbandment to go ahead during the first fortnight of June were to provoke the New Model Army into making a stand against Parliament. But it is more likely that Cromwell's assurances on 21 May genuinely reflected the position as he saw it than that they were part of a cynical plot to encourage Parliament to rush on to its Waterloo. Self-delusion and a lack of awareness of the strength and direction of the army's current mood – apart from his three weeks in Saffron Walden, Cromwell had had little direct involvement with the army for almost a year – rather than cynical duplicity probably lay behind his speech.

On 27 May, as soon as Parliament had laid firm plans for the disbandment of much of the army, Cromwell claimed and received nearly £2,000, the full arrears on his army salary. He may have done so because of an awareness that events were reaching crisis point and a resultant desire to settle his personal and financial affairs, or, less sinister, because he expected his own military career to be ended with the imminent disbandment. But the differing historical interpretations of what caused Cromwell to claim his military arrears at this time are as nothing when compared to uncertainties over the depth of his involvement in the army's seizure of the King.

A body of New Model Army cavalry, led by Cornet Joyce, which had been active in and around Oxford, moved north at the beginning of June and during the night of 2–3 June secured Holmby House in Northamptonshire, where the defeated King was being held by Parliament. There had been apprehensions that Parliament would move him to London or even to Scotland. Fearing a counter-measure by troops loyal to Parliament, on 4 June Joyce carried the King away, towards Newmarket, where most of the New Model Army, by now openly defying Parliament's orders to disband, was based. According to an account published towards the end of 1647, Cromwell became aware of the mission on the evening of 31 May, when Joyce visited him in London. If the account is accurate, it implies that at the very least Cromwell did not attempt to prevent the mission, though it is by no means clear that he actively encouraged, let alone initiated, the move. Joyce himself never claimed to have authority from Cromwell or any other senior officer. Instead, he repeatedly asserted that that authority rested with the troops themselves. Moreover, most contemporary accounts make clear that initially the plan had simply been for the guard posted at Holmby to be replaced, willingly or unwillingly, by Joyce's New Model detachment, and that not until 3 June did Joyce and his men decide to move the King. It is likely that on 31 May Cromwell had heard, and given implicit or explicit approval to, plans merely for a changing of the guard, not for the King's removal to Newmarket.

Whatever the depth of Cromwell's involvement in Joyce's venture, he was at least aware that Holmby was being secured by an army unit. Almost certainly he would also have been quickly informed of the decisions of Fairfax's Council of War of 29 May to resist enforced disbandments and to oppose parliamentary orders. Although Cromwell did not despair of finding a means by which Parliament and the army could work together to achieve a lasting settlement and still opposed direct military intervention in political affairs, he did appreciate that some sort of parting of the ways – temporary, he hoped – had been reached. His repeated assurances of the army's obedience, the most recent barely a fortnight old, had been shown to be unfounded and misleading, he probably realized that he would quickly be suspected of involvement in the army's seizure of the King, and it may well have appeared to him that, for the moment, he could do more to avoid a violent clash between Parliament and the army and to secure a settlement at the army's HQ than he could in the House of Commons. Sometime during 3 June or early on 4 June he left London and rode north. During the evening of 4 June he arrived at Newmarket, Fairfax's HQ and the venue for a grand, two-day rendezvous of the New Model Army. His departure from London marked a clear set-back to, but not the complete abandonment of, Cromwell's hopes of healing the rifts between Parliament and its army, a goal which he had been actively pursuing as a London-based politician for almost a year.

During the latter half of 1647 Cromwell remained with the parliamentary army as it moved around the home counties, entering London in early August to restore order following a mob attack upon the Palace of Westminster on 26 July, pulling back to bases close to, but outside, the capital once that had been achieved. Thereafter, he kept in close contact with the army HQ and he was frequently at Putney consulting with Fairfax and other senior officers. As part of the army's high command, he consulted Fairfax, Ireton and other senior officers as they drafted and redrafted of the army's own blueprint for a constitutional settlement, the *Heads of the Proposals*. He actively supported the attempt to impose significant new limitations upon the royal prerogative via the *Heads of the Proposals*, which would have given Parliament temporary control over key aspects of the executive, as well as allowing broad liberty of conscience for all who adhered to a Protestant faith. He played a leading role in attempts to persuade other individuals or bodies to accept a settlement upon these lines. On 7 June he met the King at Childerley, near Cambridge. Although they may have glimpsed each other from afar during ceremonies associated with the parliaments of 1628 and 1640, as well as on the battlefields of Edgehill and Naseby, this was the first face-to-face meeting of the two. Cromwell met both the King himself and Charles's close advisers on several further occasions during the summer and autumn, and he was one of a group of senior officers who entered into negotiations with the King, held in honourable captivity near the army HQ, in an attempt to win his firm commitment to the *Heads of the Proposals* or a set of terms arising therefrom. At some stage shortly after the army's temporary occupation of London in July, and certainly by September, Cromwell also resumed his seat in the Commons and during the remaining months of 1647 he was active in Parliament – he wrote in mid-October, 'I scarce miss the House a day, where it's very necessary for me to be'[12] – frequently serving as teller and playing a prominent role in having key elements of the *Heads of the Proposals* converted into parliamentary bills and steered through the House.

During the late summer and autumn Cromwell and some of his fellow officers attempted to steer a middle course between a generally unresponsive King, a potentially hostile Parliament and an army whose rank and file were losing patience with the officers' cautious and apparently stalled plans. There is no evidence that, as yet, Cromwell ever deviated from his line of showing respect for the institution of monarchy, of working to reach an agreement with Charles I and of resisting any suggestions that the army intervene directly. During the fourth week of September he was prominent in a Commons debate, arguing strongly in favour of a proposal to resume direct negotiations with Charles. On 20 October, stung by recent criticism of the King and anxious to distance himself from anti-royal radicals, he reportedly made a mammoth three-hour speech, reflecting 'very favourably' upon the King and 'concluding that it was necessary to re-establish him as quickly as possible'.[13]

Again, trying to hold a middle line, at a meeting of the General Council of the Army on 9 September, Cromwell may have stressed that he was working for liberty of conscience and had no wish to 'cast down the foundation of Presbytery and set up Independency'.[14] At or before another meeting of the Council on 16 September, Cromwell became embroiled in a furious row with Thomas Rainborough, one of the more radical officers, fuelled in part by their divergent views on the merits of continuing to negotiate with Charles on the basis of the *Heads of the Proposals*.

In steering this middle line, Cromwell found himself increasingly isolated and under suspicion. This underlies a letter which he wrote to Michael Jones, parliamentary commander in Ireland, on 14 September:

> Though it may be for the present a cloud may lie over our actions, to them who are not acquainted with the grounds of our t[ransactions?]; yet we doubt not but God will clear our integrity and innocency from any other ends we aim at but his glory and the public good.[15]

Although ostensibly Cromwell is writing about the army as a whole, he may also have been making oblique reference to his own position. Not only were both Charles and Parliament decidedly lukewarm towards the *Heads of the Proposals* but also there were growing signs that substantial elements within the parliamentary army, some now under Leveller influence, had lost faith in the senior officers and their plans and instead were urging a more radical constitutional settlement, imposed by the army in the wake of direct military intervention in national politics.

Cromwell and the other senior officers were willing to exert pressure on Parliament. The *Heads of the Proposals* themselves called for the Long Parliament to dissolve itself within twelve months, as well as envisaging future biennial parliaments of limited duration. Moreover, several times during the summer and autumn the army called for both Houses to impeach or otherwise expel undesirables, especially though not exclusively eleven named leading presbyterian MPs and others who had taken the lead on and after 26 July, when the presbyterian mob had been in virtual control of Westminster. But Parliament itself was to rid the Houses of such members; it was to be a self-purge, a purge of Parliament by Parliament, albeit urged on by the army, rather than a direct, external military purge. Cromwell and the other officer MPs might also take their seats in an attempt to win over the House via the normal process of debating and voting. For example, a dispatch written by a London-based diplomat reports that on 20 August Cromwell and Ireton took their seats and urged the House to declare null and void all votes passed under mob influence on and after 26 July.[16] But during this period Cromwell seems consistently and sincerely to have felt that Parliament alone could establish or guarantee a firm, stable constitutional settlement and that, whatever its legitimate interests and concern, the army should not subvert or overthrow Parliament.

Twice during the latter half of 1647 the senior officers – Cromwell included – sought to defend and explain their approach and to retain or regain control over the restless rank and file by formally debating the issues with regimental representatives, the 'agitators'. The first of these debates, a two-day meeting held at Reading on 16–17 July, focused on two conflicting proposals – that of the agitators that the army should immediately march on London in order forcibly to purge Parliament as a preliminary to the fulfilment of a range of other demands, and that of most senior officers and others that the army should instead enter into peaceful negotiations on the basis of the newly drafted *Heads of the Proposals*. The surviving record of the Reading debate is incomplete. Nevertheless, sufficient survives to demonstrate Cromwell's general line at Reading.

As befitted the army's second-in-command, Cromwell played a prominent part, particularly in the first day's debate, which concentrated on the agitators' paper. Cromwell accepted that their specific demands were valid. But as a means to achieving those ends, Cromwell argued passionately that an immediate march on London and enforced purge were unacceptable. Any concessions or settlement reached in this manner would be tainted and open to dispute:

> that great objection . . . will lie against us, that wee have gott thinges of the Parliament by force; and wee know what itt is to have that staine lie uppon us. Thinges, though never soe good, obtain'd in that way, itt will exceedingly weaken the thinges, both to our selves and to all posteritie.

He conceded that, if all other routes failed, it might eventually be necessary for the army to intervene directly in the manner envisaged – 'I doe nott knowe that force is to bee used, except wee cannot gett what is for the good of the Kingdome without force' and 'I thinke that possibly that may be that that wee shall bee necessitated to doe'. However, that time had not yet come, and instead, 'for our honour and our honesty', the army should persist with its own draft 'Treaty':

> whatsoever wee gett by a Treaty, whatsoever comes to bee setled uppon us in that way, itt will be firme and durable, itt will bee conveyed over to posterity, as that that will bee the greatest honour to us that ever poore creatures had . . . And itt will have this in itt too, that whatsoever is granted in that way itt will have firmenesse in itt.

The army was physically capable of imposing its will and forcing through measures to meet its material grievances and political aspirations, but that route would not produce a firm and durable settlement – 'Really, Really, Have what you will have, that [which] you have by force I looke uppon itt as nothing.' Far better, Cromwell argued, to continue to negotiate with the King and parliamentary representatives in the hope of securing both a long-term constitutional settlement and solutions to the army's more immediate grievances through normal, peaceful political channels. That which 'wee and they gaine in a free way, itt is better then twice so much in a forc't, and will be more truly our's and our posterities'.

During the day's debate, Cromwell repeated and elaborated upon this general line, several times trying to wrap up the arguments on the proposal that the army march on London with an implicit or explicit acceptance that it should not, and so move on to the presentation and consideration of the officers' draft treaty. He urged caution and unity within the army, he pleaded that they should not act with the rashness of which he was sometimes accused –

> I am very often judged for one that goes too fast that way, and itt is the property of men that are as I am to bee full of apprehensions that dangers are nott soe reall as imaginary, to bee always making hast, and more some times perhaps then good speede.

– and he stressed that any decisions should be taken on the basis of cool reason: 'I desire that nothing of heate or earnestnesse may carry us heere, nor nothing of affirmation, nor nothing of that kinde may lead us, butt that which is truly reason, and that which hath life and argument in itt.' Cromwell suggested that Parliament had recently shown some willingness to discipline its own 'guilty' members and he argued that there was a consistently pro-army group within Parliament, that it was 'uppon the gaining hand' and that it would 'gaine more' if the army pursued peaceful negotiations. Any sudden and violent action by the army would wreck these developments. Eventually, Cromwell and his colleagues carried the day. It was agreed that the agitators' specific demands should be put to Parliament and a speedy reply required, but that there should be no immediate march on London or any explicit threat of a military purge.

The second day's debate concentrated on the officers' draft settlement, the document soon to be named the *Heads of the Proposals*. Cromwell appeared to have only a hazy prior knowledge of the document and to have liaised only quite sketchily with Ireton, probably the main author of the document. Cromwell's suggestion that a Council of War should meet to receive and discuss possible amendments was unwelcome to Ireton, who was probably seeking nothing more than agreement in principle to the document as it then stood. Although the record of the day's discussion is brief and very incomplete, the General Council clearly did give this outline agreement at or before the close of the second day's debate.[17]

The second series of debates were held at Putney during the autumn and focused, in part, upon the desirability of abandoning the officers' plans and instead pursuing an alternative, more radical constitution, the *Agreement of the People*, which greatly downplayed the power and position of both King and House of Lords and which stressed the sovereignty and liberties of the people. The full General Council or smaller committees appointed by it met daily, Sundays excepted, between 28 October and 11 November, to discuss both criticisms of the existing army line and the new constitutional proposal. We possess detailed if incomplete transcripts of the first three days' debates, but only brief outlines of the contents and outcomes of the later debates. Cromwell was present almost every day and played a leading role in many of the debates; because Fairfax was unwell in late October, he also chaired the opening sessions.

During the first day Cromwell intervened to calm rising tempers, to encourage an open-minded approach and to clear himself of allegations that he had recently presented in Parliament as army policy arguments which in fact emanated from him alone. But the main thrust of Cromwell's speeches on 28 October was to urge his colleagues to approach the *Agreement of the People* with great caution. It envisaged 'very great alterations of the very Government of the Kingedome' and, although many of its proposals might be very worthy and 'plausible' if dealing with a clean slate, its imposition on to the existing political and constitutional situation would lead to dangers and divisions: 'There will bee very great mountaines in the way of this . . . Itt is nott enough to propose thinges that are good in the end, . . . itt is our duty as Christians and men to consider consequences, and to consider the way.' However good the ends of the proposal may be, the present circumstances might make those ends unattainable and the attempt to reach them both extremely divisive and ultimately futile, Cromwell argued. Whatever the merits of the proposed constitution, he doubted 'whether, according to reason and judgement, the spiritts and temper of the people of this Nation are prepared to receive and to goe on alonge with itt', a sentiment not entirely consistent with a view he had expressed during the Reading debates, three months before, where at one point he had snarled that the army should work for 'the generall good of . . . all the people in the Kingdome. That's the question, what's for their good, nott what pleases them.'

Cromwell followed this up with a proposal that a committee be established to determine how far the contents of the *Agreement of the People* were consistent with the declarations issued by the army over the preceding months. All too aware that they breached earlier army engagements, especially regarding the power of King and Lords and the need for the present Parliament peacefully to endorse a settlement, Cromwell and Ireton stuck to this line for the remainder of the day and eventually won the point. Cromwell also supported a proposal that they spend the following morning in prayer, seeking God's guidance, and expressed his hope that they would 'recover that presence of God that seemes to withdraw from us'. The record of the debate becomes increasingly disjointed, but the day seems to have closed with several participants urging that they come, on the morrow, with open minds and without prejudice, seeking a reconciliation born of God's guidance. Cromwell referred to the 'jealousies and apprehensions' of some that he and his fellow senior officers were 'wedded and glewed to formes of Governement' and held such firm and unalterable constitutional views that there was no 'hope for any agreement from us to you'. He stressed that such 'apprehensions' were false.[18]

Victory and expectation turned to defeat on the following day, 29 October, when the committee to consider existing army declarations duly met. As chairman, Cromwell tried to implement the previous day's decision, attempting to steer the committee towards drawing up a list of existing army engagements before moving on to an examination of the extent to which the *Agreement of the People* was consistent with them and so worthy of further consideration. But in the face of strong opposition, he was forced to abandon the attempt and instead to allow a broad, open-ended debate on the merits and demerits of the *Agreement of the People*. This quickly developed into a long series of increasingly angry exchanges on the proposals to widen the franchise, exchanges in which Cromwell played little part. He made occasional, rather limp interventions to support the retention of a restricted franchise, though he did agree that some limited extension of the existing arrangements might be advantageous and suggested that a committee be set up to discuss the franchise; his proposal was ignored. Although the transcript breaks off before the conclusion of the day's debate, it apparently ended in a clear majority in favour of a very substantial broadening of the franchise. Cromwell had been overwhelmed by the strength of feeling within the committee, he had been largely sidelined during the main debate and had failed to stamp his authority on the meeting.[19]

Although more progress was made at another committee meeting on 30 October, during which a list of constitutional proposals was agreed, Cromwell's chairmanship of the full General Council on 1 November was again rather poor. He allowed – indeed encouraged – an often rambling exposition of the different views held by members of the Council and of their differing interpretations of the will of God. Early in the day, he pleaded that the army had no right to press its case upon Parliament in a violent or improper way – 'Either they are a Parliament or noe Parliament. If they bee noe Parliament they are nothing, and wee are nothing likewise. If they bee a Parliament wee are to offer itt to itt.' – for Parliament alone had the right to settle the constitution. However, he did imply that the army might have a just interest in ensuring that the 'formes of Parliament' be improved, including the eradication of electoral malpractice. He also stressed that the Lord General's authority in military matters could not be questioned or undermined and again tried, rather limply, to steer the meeting to consider what conditions the army was already committed to by its earlier declarations. Once more, this suggestion fell on stony ground.[20]

After this poor start, Cromwell did try to focus the discussion by drawing together some general threads upon which they were all agreed – 'to deliver this Nation from oppression and slavery, to accomplish that worke that God hath carried us on in, to establish our hopes of an end of justice and righteousnesse in itt'. He even conceded that 'wee all apprehend danger from the person of the Kinge, and from the Lords' and that 'if itt were free before us whether wee should sett uppe one or other', they would all be of one mind in opposing their establishment. However, that was not the position, for King and Lords were in existence. Cromwell emphasized that some members of the Council, including himself, felt a duty to preserve and defend the existing system, complete with King and Lords, while others in complete contrast clearly believed that it should be swept away. Although this lay at the heart of differences within the General Council, Cromwell was stating the case in unnecessarily stark terms; it might have been better to avoid such deep issues and instead to concentrate on those areas of the future constitution on which agreement had already been reached in committee. Eventually, the meeting did get round to considering some aspects of the proposed future constitution, with Ireton again becoming involved in bitter arguments with some of the supporters of the *Agreement of the People*. According to the surviving transcripts, Cromwell took no part in these discussions and made no attempt to support Ireton, to calm rising tempers or to move the meeting on to more fruitful areas. Even allowing for the strong feelings which Cromwell was facing within the committee, it was not an impressive performance.[21]

The General Council and committees drawn from it continued to meet for a further week or so, though we possess only very sparse records of these sessions. Cromwell may not have been present at all of them, for by 5 November Fairfax had recovered sufficiently to chair the army debates, and Cromwell possibly resumed his seat in the Commons. But he certainly was present at the Council session on Monday 8 November, for on that day he played a leading role in winding up the series of military debates. As the more radical, Leveller-inspired elements had come to dominate the debates, so Cromwell and his colleagues had grown increasingly uneasy both with elements of the constitutional proposals which were emerging and with the anti-monarchical sentiments expressed. There was also smouldering unrest in several regiments. Thus on 8 November, almost certainly acting as spokesman for a group of senior officers, Cromwell delivered a long speech, highlighting 'the danger of their principles who had sought to devide the army', and specifically criticizing the proposal to extend the franchise as 'tend[ing] very much to Anarchy'. Although opposed at length by a captain-lieutenant, Cromwell's proposal that the current series of General Council meetings be wound up and that its members return to their regiments to prepare for a general rendezvous carried the day.[22] Cromwell's fruitless and often poorly conducted attempts to reach an acceptable consensus had been ended by a decisive blow, overpowering his opponents and restoring his own and his colleagues' authority. For neither the first time nor the last, Cromwell appeared far more successful when deciding an issue by swift confrontation rather than prolonged discussion and negotiation aimed at a compromise, however much he may have preferred the latter course.

There survives one further glimpse of Cromwell at Putney, at a final administrative meeting on 11 November. A fragmentary record indicates that a row flared up over the army's attitude towards King Charles and monarchy in general, precipitated by an outspoken attack upon both. Cromwell's response is interesting. He gave hypothetical and scriptural examples to show that it was not always justified to take vengeance upon, and to kill, a murderer and that, in any case, it was not clear that the army had the right to proceed against him, for it was 'the worke of others to doe itt'. Cromwell's line was far from being a ringing defence of the King and it may imply an acceptance of Charles's guilt and a realization that others could and might bring him to account.[23]

On that evening, 11 November, Charles escaped from Hampton Court. Although the true reason for his flight was a desire to be able to negotiate more freely with the Scots, he claimed that fear both of a plot against him and of the closer guard which might be placed around him at Hampton Court to protect him motivated his flight. There certainly were rumours that an attempt was to be made to seize or to assassinate Charles and sometime during that day Cromwell himself had written a hurried warning to the commander of the King's guards, requiring extreme diligence, 'for if any thing should be done, it would be accounted a most horrid act'.[24] In some ways the King's flight was very convenient for Cromwell and his colleagues. No longer were they under an obligation to negotiate with Charles, so risking division within the army, and the army could now more easily be reunited to meet the new threat. Yet in other ways, it presented a danger, for a king on the loose, perhaps heading for the Channel Isles or for the Continent, where he would be better placed to encourage renewed military operations, would present far more dangers than an unco-operative but neutered monarch under the army's control at Hampton Court. Despite stories which circulated at the time, there is no clear evidence to suggest that Cromwell encouraged or colluded in the King's escape and every reason to believe that it went against Cromwell's own hopes and plans. A slightly later account indicates that Cromwell was both surprised and relieved to learn that Charles had got no further than renewed military captivity at Carisbrooke Castle on the Isle of Wight.

On 15 November Cromwell accompanied Fairfax to Ware in Hertfordshire for the first stage of a threefold general rendezvous, held on Corkbush Field, outside the town. The senior officers were confronted with a clear if rather subdued mutiny, for two non-summoned regiments appeared on Corkbush Field; many of their soldiers had copies of the *Agreement of the People* in their hats, signifying their adherence to the radical, Leveller-inspired constitutional proposals. Both regiments submitted quite swiftly when confronted by the Lord General, though contemporary accounts reveal that Cromwell and other senior officers rode among their ranks, removing copies of the *Agreement* from the hats of the ringleaders and the diehards. The sources clearly indicate that Cromwell was not only present but also played a direct, personal role in the restoration of order. On the other hand, it is also apparent that the mutiny was half-hearted and that the presence and leadership of Fairfax had already done much to restore discipline before Cromwell and other officers rode through the ranks. The remaining rendezvous, at St Albans on 17 and Kingston upon Thames on 18 November, passed off without incident.

Cromwell gave an account of the triple rendezvous to the House of Commons on 19 November, and on 23 November he spoke again, defending his own and his colleagues' actions during the recent weeks. Cromwell argued that they had allowed the more radical ideas to be debated at length only because they had believed that, through debate, 'their follies would vanish'. However, when the opposite occurred and the 'follies' had 'spread, and infected so much', he and other senior officers had decided that it was 'high tyme to suppress such attempts'. In particular, Cromwell clarified his attitude towards a broadening of the franchise, claiming that he allowed it to be debated because 'he saw many honest officers were possest with it' and, again, because he had felt that thorough discussion might 'perswade them out of the unreasonablenes'. But he had been shocked at suggestions that even those in receipt of alms should have the vote, for he foresaw 'a dangerous consequence' of allowing those who have 'no interest in estate at all' a say in choosing representatives; men without property would be in a majority and would probably elect 'those of their own condition'. Such a 'drive at a levelling and paritye' must be disclaimed and halted, Cromwell concluded, both because of the dangerous consequences which would follow the adoption of such a franchise and, more immediately, because merely discussing such ideas had destabilized the army and 'brought so many obloquies upon him and the officers'.[25]

From November 1647 to April 1648 Cromwell continued to divide his time between Parliament and the army. He was clearly attending Parliament quite regularly, for he was named to a string of committees; he was also appointed to Parliament's new Committee of Both Houses, set up during January 1648, and attended it regularly during the opening months of the year. But he was also frequently present at the army's headquarters in Windsor, attending meetings of the Council of Officers and further, rather low-key meetings of the General Council, taking part in prayer meetings and serving on various military committees.

Surviving sources afford several glimpses of Cromwell's growing disillusionment with the King, born out of several months' experience of fruitless attempts to negotiate with Charles and of the resulting military divisions, doubtless compounded by the King's flight. A much later account alleges that in late November 1647 Cromwell intercepted a letter from Charles to his Queen in which the King revealed that his negotiations with Parliament and the army were a sham and that he was determined instead to do a deal with the Scots.[26] Even if this tale is pure invention, Cromwell's hardening attitude towards the King at this stage is readily understandable. It can be seen in Cromwell's letter of late December to Robert Hammond, a distant relation by marriage, governor of Carisbrooke Castle and thus the King's gaoler, in which he urged Hammond to keep the castle well guarded and to dismiss any suspect servants, ending the letter with a typically religious exhortation: 'You see how God hath honoured and blessed every resolute action of these for Him; doubt not but He will do so still.' The King was not to be trusted and resolute action was necessary.[27]

Cromwell's wariness of the King emerged again a few days later, on 3 January 1648, in the course of a major debate in the House of Commons on the desirability of continuing negotiations with Charles I. Cromwell spoke strongly against further negotiation, acknowledging that in the past 'we declard our intentions for Monarchy', but adding the significant rider 'unles necessity enforce an alteration'. Necessity had enforced such a change, for the King had broken 'his trust', a reference to his flight from Hampton Court, his recently concluded Scottish alliance, and his rejection of four constitutional bills presented to him by Parliament during December. Cromwell urged his fellow MPs to be decisive – 'To say, there is a Lyon in the way, this difficulty, that danger, and dissatisfaction of the people, this becomes you not' – and to follow the will of God: 'A not owning of God in these troubles, hath caused a protraction of the war.' Parliament had a duty to protect the people, whom Parliament represented and who had placed their 'trust' in the Parliament – 'Expose not the honest party of the Kingdom, who have bled for you, and suffer not misery to fall upon them, for want of corage or resolution in you, els the honest people may take such courses as nature dictates to them.' Cromwell concluded by pointing out that the recent army unrest had been allayed, in part at least, by assurances that, if the King rejected the four bills, Parliament would seek an alternative route to secure 'the peace of the Kingdome'.[28]

Another strictly contemporary summary of the speech, published a few days later in a pro-royalist newspaper, claims that Cromwell was very animated throughout the delivery, spitting fire, 'the glow-worm glistening in his beak', quoting the biblical injunction that 'Thou shalt not suffer a hypocrite to reign', and ending by laying 'his hand upon the hilt of his sword'.[29] Whether this is accurate or merely royalist embroidery, Cromwell was clearly highly charged and buoyed by the outcome, for by a decisive majority the Commons voted to break off all negotiations with the King. Cromwell's sense of achievement is clear in his letter to Hammond that evening, full of references to God's mercies and providences. Alluding to the King's flight and subsequent developments, Cromwell wrote of them as 'a mighty providence to this poor Kingdom and to us all', for 'the House of Commons is very sensible of the King's dealings, and of our brethren's'.[30]

For the next few months Cromwell seems to have played his cards close to his chest. There are reports, often surfacing in royalist newsletters, that on several occasions during February he made Commons speeches strongly critical of monarchy, snapping at MPs who were more favourably inclined towards the Crown. For what it is worth, the published *Memoirs* of Edmund Ludlow claim that around this time Cromwell was hosting at his London house a series of meetings with fellow officers and senior MPs, including republicans. Cromwell and the officers reportedly 'kept themselves in the clouds' and refused to be drawn on whether they favoured 'monarchical, aristocractical or democratical government', instead commenting that there were virtues in each of them and leaving it to 'providence' to direct. When challenged directly by Ludlow, Cromwell supposedly resorted to jesting, throwing a cushion at Ludlow and then chasing him down the stairs. On the following day, Ludlow challenged him again in the more sober surroundings of Parliament, but Cromwell proved almost as evasive, answering that 'he was convinced of the desirableness of what was proposed, but not the feasibleness of it'.[31]

There were rumours both that Cromwell was actively exploring deposing Charles I in favour of one of his sons, and that, despite his speech of 3 January and the subsequent vote, he was surreptitiously reopening direct negotiations with the imprisoned monarch. Stories that at some stage during March or April he secretly travelled to the Isle of Wight, to meet the King face to face, cannot be substantiated and are probably false. He certainly did ride out of London in late March and was in Farnham, near the Surrey–Hampshire border, on 28 March. But the purpose was not, as rumoured, to negotiate with the King via Hammond, who was rumoured, equally falsely, to have travelled up to Farnham to meet him. Instead, Cromwell was in Farnham on completely different and more personal business, to negotiate the marriage settlement of his own son, Richard, to Dorothy Maijor, daughter of a Hampshire gentleman, Richard Maijor.

The preliminary negotiations, which had been under way for some weeks, had been conducted by Colonel Richard Norton. In a letter of late February Cromwell noted that he had received an alternative offer which was financially more lucrative, but he foresaw 'difficulties' here and 'not that assurance of godliness' which a Maijor match offered. In any case, he wrote, Mr Maijor's offer 'is more than I look for, as things now stand'. However, as usual, Cromwell looked to the Lord to decide the matter, noting his willingness

> to answer Providence ... If God please to bring it about, the consideration of piety in the parents, and such hopes of the gentlewoman in that respect, make the business to me a great mercy; concerning which I desire to wait upon God ... The Lord do His will: that's best.

That financial considerations were not uppermost was underlined in March, when Parliament completed an ordinance rewarding Cromwell with properties valued at nearly £1,700 per year. On 21 March Cromwell not only offered to subscribe £1,000 of this annually for the next five years to support the war effort in Ireland but also voluntarily waived the £1,500 owed him in back pay upon his army salary. Although Cromwell was clearly now a man of substance, he was still keen to secure a generous settlement of land and property from Mr Maijor before sanctioning his son's marriage. When Cromwell and Maijor met in Farnham on 28 March, Cromwell was not entirely satisfied by the latter's offer; Norton was given detailed instructions on future negotiations. For his part, Maijor had clearly held some reservations about Cromwell, for on that evening Cromwell wrote that 'some things of common fame did a little stick' with Maijor, though 'I gladly heard his doubts' and felt that he had satisfied him. Cromwell added: 'I know God has been above all ill reports, and will in His own time vindicate me; I have no cause to complain.' Lengthy further negotiations followed and the marriage did not take place until spring 1649.[32]

On 28 April the Commons voted by a substantial majority that government should remain by King, Lords and Commons. Cromwell made no recorded contribution to the debate and there is no evidence of how he voted. He may not have been in the House, for on that day the officers at Windsor began a three-day prayer meeting. Cromwell was certainly at Windsor on 29 April, when he made his only recorded contribution. According to an account of an officer who was probably an eyewitness, though one which was published and probably written many years later, Cromwell had urged all those present

> to a thorough consideration of our actions as an army, as well as our ways particularly as private Christians, to see if any iniquity could be found in them, and what it was, that if possible we might find it out, and so remove the cause of such sad rebukes which were upon us by reason of our iniquities.

In response, the officers searched their memories of recent events to discover the moment when the Lord had ceased to support the army. They concluded that this had occurred in 1647, when the army began negotiating with Charles I in the attempt to reach a settlement with him. Accordingly, the officers concluded that they should not repeat the mistake and cause God to continue his wrath. The third and final day ended with a resolution that, when opportunity presented itself, they should 'call Charles Stuart, that man of blood, to an account for that blood he had shed'. Even if we assume that the account is substantially accurate, it cannot be used to show that Cromwell had committed himself to regicide at this meeting. The resolution was vague and was certainly not an explicit call to regicide. Moreover, there is no indication that Cromwell was present on 30 April. He may already have been involved in more vital business, preparing to go into battle once more.[33]

On 30 April Cromwell was ordered to lead part of the parliamentary army westward, to put down a rebellion in South Wales. By the first week of May he was on the move, reaching Gloucester on 8 May and entering Wales via Monmouth on 10 May. By that time local parliamentary forces had already inflicted a crushing defeat over the rebel field army, and Cromwell's campaign in South Wales turned into a grand mopping-up operation. He smashed his way into rebel-held Chepstow on 11 May, marched along the coast unopposed and by 24 May was before the rebels' last stronghold, the walled town and castle of Pembroke. Cromwell settled down to a long formal siege, and eventually town and castle surrendered to him on 11 July. Because Fairfax and much of the army had become drawn into an even longer operation against royalist rebels in Kent and Essex, it then

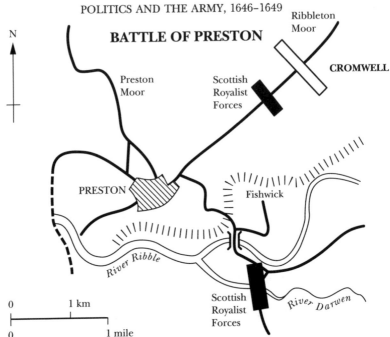

fell to Cromwell to command the parliamentary forces sent north to intercept and defeat the Scottish royalist army of invasion. Cromwell marched across the Midlands to Yorkshire, gathering supplies and reinforcements en route. Crossing the Pennines into Lancashire in mid-August, he fell upon and utterly destroyed a large part of the Scottish army outside Preston on 17 August. Over the following days, he pursued and overwhelmed remaining Scottish royalist units in and around Winwick and Warrington. After a brief respite, Parliament ordered Cromwell to march north, not only to ensure that the border towns of Carlisle and Berwick were recovered but also to enter Scotland itself, to encourage the disbandment of any remaining Scottish royalist forces and to bolster the new non-royalist government in Edinburgh. Cromwell was seeking merely to influence the workings of Scottish politics, not to impose English aspirations by force. He was in Scotland for barely three weeks, from late September until mid-October; he was in Edinburgh, as an honoured guest, from 4 to 7 October. The Scottish mission quickly concluded, Cromwell then settled down to a curiously protracted siege operation against Pontefract Castle, one of the very few isolated strongholds still in the hands of the broken royalists.

During the first civil war Cromwell had organized the defence of Cambridgeshire, commanded one wing of the cavalry in major battles and occasionally led detached units, up to four regiments strong, on brief campaigns around Oxfordshire and central southern England. But in 1648 Cromwell gained overall command of much larger forces. When he entered Wales in May, he was at the head of an army of over 6,500 men, horse and foot. At Preston, the first major battle in which Cromwell held overall command, he had an army of around 9,000 men. The scale and responsibilities of these campaigns were also new. Even if the rebellion in South Wales had already been broken by the time Cromwell arrived there, the threat from the Scottish royalist forces was enormous. Had Cromwell failed to engage them or, worse still, been roundly defeated by them, the whole parliamentary cause in England would have been in peril.

In reality, Cromwell had been victorious and emerged with greater experience and confidence and an enhanced reputation. It is impossible to read the account of Cromwell's speech to his troops at Gloucester on 8 May, reaffirming his support for the soldiers, reminding them of shared dangers and victories during earlier campaigns and pledging to 'live and die with them', without gaining a sense that Cromwell was more comfortable with the clarity and simplicity of military campaign than with the political intrigues of the preceding months.[34] He did, however, suffer frustrations before Pembroke, for he found the town strongly defended and, lacking ammunition and heavy artillery, he was forced to bide his time. His attempts to take the town by storm in early June failed, not least because the ladders proved too short to carry the walls. 'We lost a few men', he admitted rather vaguely, though 'I am confident the enemy lost more.' His confidence that lack of supplies within the town would force its surrender by the end of June was misplaced, for not until 11 July did conditions within Pembroke and the tardy arrival of Parliament's heavy guns induce the defenders – 'a very desperate enemy, who, being put out of all hope of mercy, are resolved to endure to the uttermost extremity', noted Cromwell – to surrender on terms. From his base before Pembroke, Cromwell dispatched orders to ensure that the remainder of South Wales was secure and that dangerous men were watched or arrested, threatening one royalist sympathizer: 'I will cause your treasonable nest to be burnt about your ears.'[35]

The restoration of order in South Wales served as a prelude to the greater victory at Preston. By approaching the town from the north-east, Cromwell interposed his forces between the Scottish army and their home country, so blocking their natural line of retreat and forcing the issue. By swooping down on the dangerously strung-out Scottish army and ensuring that at no stage did his own forces face anything like the full strength of the opposing host, he was able to break, scatter and crush an army which outnumbered his own by more than two to one. If he had engaged the Scots in a more orthodox campaign, with the full strength of both armies drawn up to face each other, the Scots' superior numbers may well have been decisive. His tactics in August 1648 had secured a surprisingly convincing and easy victory against a much larger army. As usual, Cromwell saw 'the great hand of God in this busines'; 'Give glory to God for this unspeakable mercy.'[36]

In the course of the campaigns of the second civil war, Cromwell detected God's hand at work far more clearly and deeply than in the war of 1642–6, and he drew from the events of 1648, both on and off the battlefield, important and far-reaching conclusions about the will of the Lord. On 28 June Cromwell was still unsure, hoping that God would teach the nation 'what the mind of God may be in all this, and what our duty is'. But Cromwell was already forming some hesitant conclusions about their God-given duty:

Surely it is not that the poor godly people of this Kingdom should still be made the object of wrath and anger, nor that our God would have our necks under a yoke of bondage; for these things that have lately come to pass have been the wonderful works of God; breaking the rod of the oppressor, as in the day of Midian, not with garments much rolled in blood, but by the terror of the Lord; who will yet save His people and confound His enemies, as in that day.[37]

The great victory at Preston caused Cromwell to appreciate once more the power of God and His ability to 'pull . . . down' anything in this world which 'is exalted, or exalts itself'. He feared that God's 'outward dispensations' might spill over into pride, vanity and mortal ambition, and warned against such temptations:

> Let us all not be careful what use men will make of these actings. They shall, will they, nill they, fulfil the good pleasure of God, and so shall serve our generations. Our rest we expect elsewhere: that will be durable. Care we not for tomorrow, nor for anything.

But more than this, Preston seemed to clarify for Cromwell something of the message which God was seeking to convey. Toward the end of a long letter which he wrote to the Speaker of the Commons of 20 August, three days after the battle, Cromwell advised him on 'what use should be made of this':

> Pray you, and all that acknowledge God, that they would exalt Him, and not hate His people, who are as the apple of His eye, and for whom even Kings shall be reproved; and that you would take courage to do the work of the Lord, in fulfilling the end of your magistracy, in seeking the peace and welfare of the people of this Land, that all that will live quietly and peaceably may have countenance from you, and they that are implacable and will not leave troubling the Land may speedily be destroyed out of the land. And if you take courage in this, God will bless you, and good men will stand by you, and God will have glory, and the Land will have happiness by you in despite of all your enemies.

As usual with Cromwell, some of the words and phrases are unclear, vague or ambiguous, perhaps deliberately so. But the overall message is apparent. Possibly by allowing the renewed civil war to happen in the first place, but certainly by giving the forces of Parliament such a crushing victory in that renewed war, God was not merely protecting His chosen people but utterly condemning those 'implacable' men who persisted in causing 'trouble'. To complete this work, God required that those who held power in the land – the 'magistracy' – should protect His chosen people by destroying 'out of the land' all who had caused the renewed disturbances of 1648. All who had disturbed God's people, 'even Kings', were to suffer reproof.[38]

In Cromwell's eyes it was God's will that the royalists had been defeated in 1648 and that all who had renewed the war should suffer just punishment. In mid-July, when Pembroke at last surrendered, Cromwell had picked out the former-parliamentarians-turned-rebels as worthy of harsh punishment, 'because they have sinned against so much light, and against so many evidences of Divine Presence going along with and prospering a righteous cause, in the management of which they themselves had a share'. Those 'who had always been for the King', Cromwell felt, had at least remained loyal to their original beliefs and did not carry such a burden of guilt.[39] But by the autumn, the experience of Preston and his deeper understanding of God's message led Cromwell utterly to condemn all the royalist rebels, whatever their pre-1648 backgrounds. On 20 November he wrote a highly charged letter, bitterly criticizing the lenient treatment of one of the leading Welsh rebels. The 'fault' of the 1648 rebels was double that of those who had participated in the earlier civil war 'because it is the repetition of the same offence against all the winesses that God has borne'. 'I find a sense amongst the officers concerning such things as these, even to amazement; which truly is not so much to see their blood made so cheap, as to see such manifest witnessings of God (so terrible and so just) no more reverenced.' On the same day, Cromwell wrote to Fairfax in very similar vein:

> I find a very great sense in the officers of the regiments of the sufferings and the ruin of this poor kingdom, and in them all a very great zeal to have impartial justice done upon Offenders; and I must confess, I do in all, from my heart, concur with them; and I verily think and am persuaded they are things which God puts into our hearts.[40]

It is against this background that we need to place two remarkable letters which Cromwell wrote to Hammond during November 1648. In the first, dated 6 November, Cromwell was concerned to explain his apparent support for the Argyle party in Scotland and to defend himself from accusations that he had been over-generous towards the Scottish presbyterians. Not only had the Scots been shown their errors and had 'acknowledge[d]' them 'publicly by acts of state, and privately', Cromwell argued, but he also felt that, as godly people holding a godly faith, the Scots should be embraced within a brotherhood of 'understanding' – 'I profess to thee I desire from my heart, I have prayed for it, I have waited for the day to see union and right understanding between the godly people (Scots, English, Jews, Gentiles, Presbyterians, Independents, Anabaptists, and all).' In the second letter, dated 25 November, Cromwell sought to lift Hammond's spirits, showing him that the 'sad and heavy burden' of guarding the King was given by God and would be supported by God. But in both letters Cromwell laid out, in greater detail than in any other surviving writings, his thoughts on the treatment of the King and on the way forward.

Cromwell had little faith in the renewed parliamentary negotiations with the King, being undertaken at Newport on the Isle of Wight, and feared that too much might be given away in an over-zealous effort to reach a settlement. 'I fear lest our friends should burn their fingers,' he wrote, 'as some did not long since, whose hearts have ached since for it', probably a reference to his own and his army colleagues' attempts to reach an understanding with Charles in 1647. Hinting at his belief that during 1648 God had made clear His will that vengeance be exacted against His enemies, Cromwell noted that

> Peace is only good when we receive it out of our Father's hand, it's dangerous to snatch it, most dangerous to go against the will of God to attain it. War is good when led to by our Father, most evil when it comes from the lusts that are in our members. We wait upon the Lord, who will teach us and lead us whether to doing or suffering.

Warming to the theme, Cromwell became more explicit in condemning a possible deal with Charles, for, however tempting such a course might be, they should not deal with a man against whom God had so clearly 'witnessed' – 'having had such favour from the Lord, and such manifestations of His presence, and I hope the same experience will keep their hearts and hands from him, against whom God hath so witnessed, though reason should suggest things never so plausible'.

Cromwell also turned his thoughts to how such rigorous action might be achieved. He noted that in England 'the honest party (if I may without offence so call them) in my apprehension are the weaker, and have manifold difficulties to conflict withal'. Reviewing recent developments within the Scottish government, Cromwell hinted that a similar solution might be available to the minority 'honest party' in England: 'Are they not a little justified in this, that a lesser party of a Parliament hath made it lawful to declare the greater part a faction, and made the Parliament null, and call a new one, and to do this by force ... [?]' Attempting to calm Hammond's disquiet over rumours that the English Parliament might indeed be forcibly purged or dissolved, Cromwell argued that, while authority rested with God, human institutions, such as parliaments, were both mortal and fallible. If it became clear that an institution was not acting according to God's will – perhaps even be undermining God's will – then the godly had a right and a duty to resist and, if need be, to remodel or overthrow that institution. Cromwell posed Hammond a series of leading questions. He inquired whether the safety of the people was not supreme and whether the proposed Newport Treaty would ensure this safety or, alternatively and contrary to earlier engagements and the 'implicit covenants' with the soldiers who had ventured their lives in 1648, would throw away 'the whole fruit of the war' and leave the pre-war dangers unresolved. Crucially, Cromwell also inquired whether the army, called by God to fight and clearly imbued with God's support and God's word, had a right to use its power to bring about God's will, even if that meant turning against Parliament, the 'outward authority' which had originally summoned the army into existence:

Whether this Army be not a lawful power, called by God to oppose and fight against the King upon some stated grounds; and being in power to such ends, may not oppose one name of authority, for those ends, as well as another, the outward authority that called them, not by their power making the quarrel lawful, but it being so in itself?

Cromwell drew Hammond's attention to the consistent and overwhelming series of God's providences which had moved 'this poor Army, wherein the great God has vouchsafed to appear'. The path might not be easy, for 'difficulties' and 'enemies' would undoubtedly be encountered and it ran against a 'natural tendency' to desire ease and 'comforts'. Yet it was God's path and must be followed. In similar vein, Cromwell condemned those currently seeking to make a treaty with the King, misguided men seeking an unworthy peace, as too 'passive', some of them motivated by unrealistic fears of Leveller-inspired social overturning which might result from political changes. Cromwell asked Hammond whether such men had not 'overlook[ed] what is just and honest, and [to] think the people of God may have as much or more good the one way than the other? Good by this Man, against whom the Lord hath witnessed; and whom thou knowest.'[41]

The tone and content of these letters suggest that Cromwell's ideas had hardened and crystallized by November. In contrast to his stance during 1647, he now appeared to support both firm justice against the King and direct military force against the Long Parliament. In other letters of late November he stated that he and his northern forces supported the army's recent *Remonstrance*, calling for the Newport Treaty to be abandoned and the King to be brought to justice, and that he supported a batch of petitions, drawn up by his army, which called for the King to face trial. In several letters of the late summer and autumn, he also referred to the lessons to be learnt from the Book of Isaiah, especially those sections which stressed that God's wrath awaited any who did not obey His wishes, the implication apparently being that Parliament was 'stumbling' and ignoring God's messages in continuing to seek a treaty with Charles I. However, it would be dangerous to read too much into Cromwell's letters or to assume that he had, as yet, reached firm conclusions upon the future treatment of the King. Neither in his letters nor in the army declarations do we find an unambiguous commitment to regicide; the call is for justice, harsh maybe, but there is as yet no explicit commitment to the death penalty. In his letter of 25 November Cromwell also expressed some reservations about the timing of *Remonstrance*, commenting that 'we could perhaps have wished the stay of it till after the treaty'.[42]

Moreover, Cromwell's actions at this time do not suggest wholehearted support for direct military intervention. He apparently preferred to be well away from London, whiling away week after week in the fairly low-key siege of isolated Pontefract, no longer a serious threat to the safety of the nation. Cromwell did not come south until he received from Fairfax in late November a direct summons to do so. He was on the move by the end of the month and entered London on the evening of 6 December. Perhaps it was no coincidence that he thus arrived a few hours after the army had taken the decisive step of intervening directly in government by purging Parliament. His behaviour during this crucial period suggests a man still undecided, an accomplice after the fact to, rather than a committed supporter of, the army's coup.

The same caution and uncertainty continued during the remainder of December. He took his seat in the Commons on 7 December and his subsequent appointment to various committees suggests that he attended from time to time thereafter. Conversely, he was present only infrequently at the regular meetings of the army's council. But he was present on 15 December, when it was decided to bring the King to trial, though he was not appointed to the sub-committee formed to consider 'the best ways and grounds' for so doing. According to Bulstrode Whitelocke's *Diary* and other, rather vague rumours which surfaced at the time, Cromwell was still not convinced of the necessity for trial and execution, and during the third week of December he employed Whitelock and others to work for a peaceful settlement. Its goal may have been not only the reversal of the army's purge of Parliament but also the extraction of such concessions from the King that, even at this late stage, a confrontation could be averted. Perhaps this explains Cromwell's opposition to instructions passed in the army council on 23 December barring any 'private discourse' between the King and 'any other person',[43] as well as Cromwell's rumoured preference for trying Hamilton and the other royalist rebels before putting the King on trial. If an attempt was made to win the King's acceptance of a final offer, it had collapsed by the end of December, its failure underlined by Whitelocke's departure for the country on 26 December.

A contemporary newspaper alleges that at an army council meeting on Christmas Day, Cromwell was still opposing execution, arguing that 'there was no policy in taking away his life' and showing that it would be better to keep the King alive for, at the very least, he would serve as a sort of insurance policy should they 'at any time loose the day'. However, at some stage during the closing days of December or very beginning of January, Cromwell spoke in the Commons, condemning as traitors anyone who had 'carried on a design' to depose or execute the King, but conceding that, 'since the Providence of God hath cast this upon us, I cannot but submit to Providence, though I am not yet provided to give you my advice'. Although he may have regretted it and was not prepared to discuss the matter at length, he had come to see that providence was pointing towards regicide.[44]

Slowly, hesitantly and perhaps unwillingly, Cromwell came round to support both trial and execution, driven forward by the messages which he felt God was sending to him personally and to the army in general during 1648. In late November he was still writing that he and his colleagues 'were in a waiting posture, desiring to see what the Lord would lead us to'.[45] By January 1649 he believed that the Lord required Charles I's trial and execution, a belief fuelled by God's word vouchsafed either direct to him or to the army, and perhaps strengthened by yet another refusal by Charles to commit himself to terms acceptable to the army. There is no need to swallow all the colourful stories which first emerged after the Restoration, many in the regicides' trials of 1660–2 – stories of Cromwell cajoling men into signing the King's death warrant, verbally or physically abusing some, while jesting with others – to accept that Cromwell was one of a group of parliamentarians who in January 1649 actively supported the trial and execution.

Cromwell was one of the most assiduous members of the High Court, attending twenty-one of its twenty-three sessions, and his signature appears third on the death warrant. Moreover, on several occasions thereafter he clearly and unambiguously defended both trial and execution as the just will of God. On 23 March 1649, during a long speech in the army council, he commented that

> God hath brought the war to an issue here, and given you a great fruit of that war, to wit, the execution of exemplary justice upon the prime leader of all this quarrel into the three kingdoms, and upon divers persons of very great quality who did co-operate with him in the destruction of this kingdom.[46]

In September 1650 he was equally forthright, praising the purged Parliament which,

> true to the ends of the Covenant, did, in answer to their consciences, turn out a tyrant, in a way which the Christian in aftertimes will mention with honour, and all tyrants in the world look at with fear; and many thousands of saints in England rejoice to think of it, and have received from the hand of God a liberty from the fear of like usurpations.[47]

Just a month before, he had recommended to the Scottish Kirk *A Declaration of the English Army Now in Scotland*, which contained an explicit and outspoken defence of regicide.[48] But Cromwell's most graphic reference is contained within a letter he wrote to Lord Wharton in January 1650. Talking of Charles's execution, Cromwell told Wharton:

> Be not offended at the manner; perhaps no other way was left. What if God accepted the zeal, as He did that of Phineas, whose reason might have called for a jury? What if the Lord have witnessed his approbation and acceptance to this also, not only by signal outward acts, but to the heart also? What if I fear my friend should withdraw his shoulder from the Lord's work . . . through scandals, through false, mistaken reasonings?[49]

Cromwell was making startling reference to the biblical story of Phineas, who thrust a javelin through a sinfully copulating couple, thus saving the people of Israel from the wrath of God. In the end, only brutal, summary justice against the King had served to complete God's work, to save the nation from His wrath and to secure His continuing love.

By 1649 Cromwell had survived another period of testing, not only on the battlefield but also in the furnace of politics. He had emerged with his military reputation enhanced and with a growing political role, a man of great power and influence. He also emerged confident at last that he knew the way forward, a way chosen by God and revealed to him during 1648. But the process of understanding and following this path had been painful. The attempts to keep Parliament and its army working together in constructive harmony had failed. The repeated attempts to prevent the army intervening directly in politics and government had not merely failed but, Cromwell now believed, had been fundamentally misguided and against God's will. The attempts to preserve the existing political system and to reach a firm settlement with Charles I had failed. In the wake of this, Cromwell had actively sanctioned or acquiesced in sweeping military interventions in civilian government, the harassing and wholesale purging of the duly elected Parliament, the execution of the divinely appointed, anointed monarch and, in its wake, the abolition of monarchy, and the overthrowing of many of the accepted procedures of government and constitution. If the protagonists remained convinced that in doing all this they had been following God's commands and if these actions duly opened the way to the achievement of God's will and purpose, namely the creation of a godly nation and the salvation of its people, then for Cromwell, and for those who shared his views, it would be an acceptable and a necessary price to pay. If the vision failed and the assurance of God's sanction faltered, the burden of guilt might prove unbearable.

5

ENEMIES AND DIVISIONS,
1649–1653

The five years which separated the execution of the King in January 1649 and the establishment of the Protectorate in December 1653 can, for Cromwell, be divided into two, roughly equal portions. Down to September 1651 he remained a soldier, campaigning briefly in England and then in Ireland and Scotland, leading operations to subdue those two nations. From September 1651 onwards, he became a London-based politician, devoting himself to national politics. He deployed his political skills, strengthened by the army backing upon which he could call, to play a central role, culminating in the events of 1653, when he intervened directly in an attempt to create new constitutions and political systems which he believed would be more in tune with God's will and the nation's needs.

During the mid- and late 1640s Cromwell had worked for a durable settlement within the existing political framework, retaining both Charles I and monarchy. Very late in the day but then unswervingly, he supported Charles I's trial and execution. At the time, his views on monarchy, formally abolished in March 1649, were not so clear, but in several later speeches, particularly those of spring 1657, Cromwell indicated a belief that God had spoken against monarchy. But Cromwell had also supported the army's sweeping purge of the House of Commons, leaving behind a small rump of more radical MPs, for although he had returned to London just after it had occurred and so avoided direct involvement in the physical process, he accepted and worked within the new situation, the purge permitted what he now believed to be the correct course of action to proceed and he seemed to have been exploring the idea of a purge in letters written less than a month before the event. Having struggled for years to work within the normal parliamentary arena and to prevent military intervention, Cromwell had been forced to reverse his stance. This involved breaking with many long-standing friends and colleagues and being a party to violent, unconstitutional action and the destruction of the existing political and governmental system.

Cromwell worked for the remainder of his life to achieve two goals, crudely but not unfairly labelled 'conservative' and 'radical'. The conservative goal was to heal the breach of the winter of 1648–9, not by restoring monarchy or the Stuarts, but by conserving or restoring as much as possible of what remained of the traditional political structure. Central to this was to entrust legislative power to a representative assembly, preferably elected by the people and free from external interference. In this way, the nation might be reconciled to the events of 1648–9 and, on a more personal note, Cromwell might be able to rekindle old friendships and alliances and to resume working through the normal processes of civilian politics. This goal was consistent with Cromwell's usually cautious and conservative political and social views. Cromwell referred to this goal repeatedly, though obscurely, in his letters and speeches of the 1650s, perhaps most notably in his first speech to Parliament of September 1654 in which he made 'healing and settling' a keynote.[1] The radical goal was more complex, for although it can be succinctly described as a desire to push ahead with godly reformation, in reality this involved a broad programme embracing several overlapping elements. There was to be liberty of conscience for the various Protestant faiths, groups and sects, in the belief that they all contained elements of God's truth and would eventually coalesce to reveal the whole essence of God's message. The nation was to be reformed to extirpate sin and encourage godliness, by means of legislation and spiritual leadership. The most inhumane elements of the legal, judicial and social systems might also need to be modified. In pursuing this goal, Cromwell looked for support from the godly minority who had already received God's message and had modified their own lives accordingly. He saw the army as a reservoir of support for this programme, not only because many within the army shared these beliefs but also because it was through the army, via the series of military victories of 1642–6, 1648 and beyond, that Cromwell's providentialist God had revealed His will. In pursuing this second, more radical goal, Cromwell believed that he was doing the work of God.

It is clear that these two goals might not always be compatible, and that the pursuit of one might render the achievement of the other more difficult or completely impossible. For example, no Parliament elected and assembling in a traditional manner would be likely to implement the programme of godly reformation, for the godly accepted that, in the still-imperfect nation, they constituted a minority. Again, although the army might be seen as the embodiment of godly aspirations and the instrument of the Lord, it would be difficult to contain such a large, expensive and politically aware element within a more traditional, civilian regime. Even the policy of broad toleration, so dear to Cromwell's heart, might serve as a cover for the dissemination of social, economic and political ideas so radical that even the godly, Cromwell included, would be alienated. Cromwell was no fool and he could see perfectly well that the achievement of both goals would be a difficult task and that, in the short term at least, measures to pursue one might impair the achievement of the other. Cromwell's life and career, not only in the period 1649–53 but also right through to his death in September 1658, can be viewed as a struggle to achieve these twin objectives, trying to contain the tensions created, juggling priorities, at different times apparently focusing on one or other of his goals. Biographers of Cromwell have also laid stress on different goals and produced different interpretations of this dichotomy. Some see Cromwell as in retreat from the political radicalism forced on him in winter 1648–9 and portray the 1650s as a period of growing conservatism, with Cromwell steadily abandoning many of the aspirations and allies of the 1640s and reverting to traditional forms, policies and personnel. Others argue that he never lost his zeal for godly reformation and that, for all the outward trappings and periodic reverses of the 1650s, right to the end he held true to his reforming aspirations, even where their promotion would undermine traditional forms and a newly won air of stability.

These conflicting aspirations became visible within weeks of the regicide. Cromwell had played a leading role in the regicide and apparently supported the abolition of monarchy. In contrast, he seems to have had no quarrel with the House of Lords and was personally or politically close to some of its members. Cromwell reportedly spoke out against the abolition of the Lords, on the grounds that it was a needlessly divisive and provocative act, and years later, he criticized the Rump for 'assuming to itself the authority of the Three Estates that were before', though the comment may well have been coloured by hindsight.[2] Similarly, Cromwell accepted Pride's Purge, but during the opening months of 1649 he perhaps strove, with some success, to persuade many MPs who had 'voluntarily' withdrawn to return – though such efforts surface only as vague rumours – during February he was instrumental in watering down the oath of the Rump's new councillors, and in April he may have made an unsuccessful attempt to persuade fellow MPs to allow all their purged colleagues to return. Despite his support for the revolutionary moves of December 1648 and January 1649, his stance over the subsequent months was often cautious.

The Commons *Journal* reveals that Cromwell was active in the Rump during the first half of 1649. In February he was also appointed to the Rump's first Council of State, attending frequently and regularly nominated to committees. Until early March Cromwell served as the first chairman or 'President' of the Council. In these capacities, Cromwell helped to handle a mass of business, much of it routine, some of greater import. For example, during the late winter Cromwell was reportedly one of those who, in both the Rump and the Council of State, urged tough action against the Levellers in general and John Lilburne in particular. Some historians see Cromwell's changing attitude to Lilburne as indicative of a broader shift in his political outlook. In 1640 and again in 1645 Cromwell had supported and defended Lilburne in the Long Parliament.

But in March 1649, worried perhaps as much by signs of unrest within the army as by Lilburne's published works attacking the new regime, Cromwell may have taken a very different line. On 28 March Lilburne was examined by the Council. As the Councillors then debated what action to take, Cromwell reportedly warned them:

> I tell you . . . you have no other way to deal with these men but to break them or they will break you; yea and bring all the guilt of the blood and treasure shed and spent in this kingdom upon your heads and shoulders, and frustrate and make void all that work that, with so many years' industry, toil, and pains, you have done, and so render you to all rational men in the world as the most contemptibilest generation of silly, low-spirited men in the earth, to be broken and routed by such a despicable, contemptible generation of men as they are . . . I tell you again, you are necessitated to break them.[3]

However, the story appears in an account written by Lilburne himself to blacken the new regime, and other details within the same account are suspect or clearly erroneous. Once more, a colourful insight into Cromwell may rest on nothing more than malicious invention.

During May Cromwell acted to help quell growing army unrest born out of Leveller agitation and political disillusionment as well as the more materialistic concerns of arrears of pay, enforced service in Ireland or disbandment. At a muster of loyal regiments in Hyde Park on 9 May, Cromwell spoke to the troops, allaying these fears and assuring them that Parliament would attend to their needs. The troops then marched off to crush an army mutiny, moving westward through Alton and Andover, where on 12 May Cromwell again addressed each regiment, using the emotional tie of their old camaraderie to bolster continuing loyalty – 'that he was resolved to live and die with them, and that as he had often engaged with them against the common enemy of this nation, so he resolved still to persist therein, against those revolters which are now called by the name of Levellers'.[4] They then turned north, into Oxfordshire, and crushed the mutinous troops in a largely bloodless swoop on Burford on the night of 14–15 May. After briefly being entertained at Oxford, where on 19 May he received an honorary Doctorate in Civil Law, he returned to London and on 26 May reported to the Rump that, 'by God's providence', the 'very dangerous and destructive' disturbances had been crushed.[5] On 7 June Cromwell was one of a group of senior officers entertained by the City during a day of thanksgiving for the restoration of order.

Twinned with his reported outburst against Lilburne and his ilk, some historians see Cromwell's role during the Burford campaign as further indication that the high tide of his radicalism had passed and that, by spring 1649, Cromwell was becoming reactionary. However, Cromwell had consistently encouraged tight military discipline and opposed any developments, either inside or outside the army, which seriously threatened that discipline, and his role at Burford was consistent with the line he had taken during 1647-8. Moreover, the entire Burford operation was under the direct control not of Cromwell but of his superior, Lord General Fairfax. It was Fairfax who oversaw and directed all the crucial stages of the operation, including the execution of three ringleaders in the churchyard at Burford. They were sacrificed by Fairfax to the cause of army discipline, not by Cromwell to an alleged conservative reaction.

The Burford interlude aside, two developments dominated much of Cromwell's time during the first half of 1649. One was entirely personal – resumed negotiations with Richard Maijor to agree terms for the marriage of Richard Cromwell to Dorothy Maijor. As in the abortive negotiations of 1648, Cromwell's correspondence, with Maijor and intermediaries, stressed both the role of God in the match – 'the dispensation of Providence' – and the need for a satisfactory financial and property settlement: 'I may not be so much wanting to myself nor family as not to have some equality of consideration towards it.'[6] On this occasion, the negotiations were successful and Cromwell's elder surviving son married Dorothy at the end of April. The other development was a much more weighty matter of state business. The first half of 1649 saw plans being laid for a military expedition to Ireland to put down a nation never fully pacified since the Catholic rising of autumn 1641 and most of whose inhabitants, many

Protestants as well as native Catholics, were strongly antagonistic towards the new English regime on political as well as religious grounds. As widely expected from the moment the expedition was first mooted, in mid-March 1649 the Rump's Council asked Cromwell to lead the expedition. Although he initially hesitated, he accepted the appointment at the end of the month and thereafter directed much of his energy to ensuring that the expedition was thoroughly prepared and well supported.

Cromwell's initial thoughts on Ireland were expounded at the General Council on 23 March, after he had been invited to lead the campaign but before he had accepted. It is the earliest really substantial speech of Cromwell for which we have something approaching a full transcript. After outlining the reasons for his hesitation – spiritual (the need to seek the Lord's guidance and to discover 'how God would incline my heart to it') as much as material ('to be well satisfied concerning a just and fitting provision' for the expedition) – Cromwell fleshed out some of his ideas. He repeated his belief that the army had been God's instrument 'to serve His own turn' and that what needed to be established was not which mortal figure should command in Ireland but, rather, whether they could be certain that the Irish campaign would advance God's will and be assured of His support. In attempting to answer this, Cromwell pointed out that all that God had hitherto achieved through the army might yet be undone by the 'strong combination of Scotland and Ireland'. The Scots, who had recently declared Prince Charles king and who had many potential allies within England, displayed 'a very angry, hateful spirit there against this Army, as an Army of Sectaries . . . And although God hath used us as instruments for their good, yet hitherto they are not sensible of it, but they are angry that God brought them his mercy at such an hand.' However, a greater danger came from Ireland, where many thousand 'Papist' troops were 'ready in conjunction to root out the English interest in Ireland'. English control over, and interests in, parts of Ireland were in great danger and, short of a 'miracle from heaven', only prompt military action could save them. Failure to do so would inevitably lead on to Irish attacks upon the English mainland, something which Cromwell dreaded:

I had rather be over-run with a Cavalierish interest than a Scotch interest; I had rather be over-run with a Scotch interest than an Irish interest; and I think of all, this is the most dangerous, and if they shall be able to carry on this work they will make this the most miserable people in the earth. For all the world knows their barbarism, – I speak not of any one religion, almost any of them but in a manner are as bad as Papists, – and you see how considerable they are at this time.

Just as it had been God's will that the army should prevail in the English war, so it must be God's will that the army save those English gains from the threats posed by Scotland and, even more pressing, by Ireland. For Cromwell, the same reasoning and motivation which had led him to pursue military victory and regicide at home caused him to see the Irish campaign as a just and necessary war. If they shared these beliefs, Cromwell argued, a sense of 'love to God and a duty to God' should motivate the soldiers and instil within them a desire to do God's service in Ireland, regardless of who might be appointed commander. If that was their cause, they would be assured of success:

if we do not depart from God and disunite by that departure and fall into disunion amongst ourselves, I am confident, we doing our duty and waiting upon the Lord, we shall find He will be as a wall of brass round about us till we have finished that work that He has for us to do.[7]

Having formally accepted command of the Irish expedition at the end of March, Cromwell spent much of the following three months preparing for the operation. Satisfied with progress, he left London on 10 July, halting for over a week in Bristol as men, money and other provisions came in, and reaching south-west Wales by the end of the month. As ships and men began gathering at Milford Haven, Cromwell shuttled between Swansea, Tenby and Milford itself, overseeing final preparations. He also received some unexpected but very welcome news.

The situation in Ireland was complex. Although the majority of the population opposed the English regime, there were deep religious, tribal, regional and personal divisions. One

IRELAND

of the largest armed cliques, a substantial royalist army under Ormonde, seemed to be threatening English control over Dublin itself. But on 2 August it was engaged and destroyed at Rathmines by the English forces based in Dublin, commanded by Colonel Michael Jones. When he received the news a few days later, Cromwell was justifiably elated, writing to Richard Maijor on 13 August, just a few hours before he sailed to Ireland:

> This is an astonishing mercy; so great and seasonable as indeed we are like them that dreamed. What can we say! The Lord fill our souls with thankfulness, that our mouths may be full of His praise, – and our lives too; and grant we never forget His goodness to us. These things seem to strengthen our faith and love, against more difficult times. Sir, pray for me, That I may walk worthy of the Lord in all that He hath called me unto.

Writing to his new daughter-in-law at the same time, Cromwell added: 'The Lord is very near, which we see by His wonderful works, and therefore He looks that we of this generation draw near Him. This late great mercy of Ireland is a great manifestation thereof.'[8] Just as locally based units had broken the rebellion in Wales before Cromwell arrived, so Jones's victory at Rathmines had made his task in Ireland much easier. He would now be assured an unopposed landing, would have a secure base in Dublin and would face a weakened enemy. As it turned out, none of the enemy forces in Ireland felt able or willing to face Cromwell in the field. His Irish campaign of 1649–50 would be marked, not by battles, but by operations against castles and fortified towns.

Cromwell landed near Dublin on 15 August. He made a brief speech, stressing that he and his forces were there to do God's work, to establish truth, peace and the 'Gospel of Christ', and to execute 'the great work against the barbarous and bloodthirsty Irish, and the rest of their adherents and confederates'.[9] He remained in Dublin for a fortnight, issuing proclamations for the strict enforcement of laws against 'profane swearing, cursing and drunkenness', prohibiting his troops from robbing, pillaging or doing 'any wrong or violence' towards the Irish population unless they be 'in arms or office with the Enemy', and assuring any who supplied his army and garrisons with provisions that they would receive cash payment and protection.[10] Cromwell's insistence that the expedition be properly funded was designed to reduce disorder and Irish ill-feeling.

On 30 August Cromwell moved north with a force of at least 12,000 men. His first target was Drogheda, formerly one of Ormonde's principal strongholds and a key point on the main road to Ulster. It was defended by walls, a stretch of the River Boyne, some steep ravines on the south side and by a largely Catholic garrison of a little over 3,000 men led by an experienced Catholic English royalist, Sir Arthur Aston. Cromwell's main force arrived before Drogheda on 2 September, but not until 10 September were his heavy guns in place. At that point he summoned the town, warning Aston 'if this be refused you will have no cause to blame me'.[11] When Aston scorned the summons, a heavy bombardment began which by the next day had opened at least two breaches in the southern wall. The first attempt to take Drogheda by storm was violently repulsed

– the defenders had dug earthworks behind the breached wall – and only a second assault, led by Cromwell in person and involving almost all his reserve, carried these defences. At this stage, some of the defenders sought and obtained quarter. However, many of Aston's men continued to resist, both in the northern half of the town, over the Boyne, and at the southern strongpoint of Mill Mount. Such resistance was overwhelmed and henceforth no further quarter was given. In the heat of battle, the defenders of Mill Mount, Aston included, all perished, and many more were killed in the street and in St Peter's Church. Others were killed on the following day, as remaining pockets of resistance fell. Of the 3,100 soldiers who had attempted to hold Drogheda, around 2,800 were probably killed; several hundred inhabitants of the town also died, especially members of Catholic orders. By Cromwell's own reckoning, all the officers bar one and all the rank and file soldiers bar about thirty had perished, as had all the friars found within the town.

The events at Drogheda have become notorious, divide opinions and arouse intense emotions. It is clear that the order to give no quarter, largely obeyed, came directly from Cromwell – 'our men getting up to them, were ordered by me to put them all to the sword. And indeed, being in the heat of action, I forbade them to spare any that were in arms in the town, and, I think, that night they put to the sword about 2,000 men.'[12] – and that although the majority of deaths occurred in the heat of battle, some killings continued in a cold, calculated way for a further day or two. It is clear, too, that the scale and nature of the bloodletting were very different from Cromwell's usual practice and from the civil war norm. As usual, Cromwell was sure that he was doing God's work and that credit for the victory belonged to the Lord, not to mere mortals. But in his letters Cromwell also explained why the bloodletting had occurred. Firstly, he felt that it was just revenge for the murder of Protestant settlers by Catholic Irish during the Irish rebellion of 1641 – 'I am persuaded that this is a righteous judgment of God upon these barbarous wretches, who have imbrued their hands in so much innocent blood' – though in reality Drogheda had never been a strong Confederate Catholic town and it is unlikely that many of the civilians had been involved in the atrocities of 1641; in any case, many of the soldiers who died there were English, not Irish, and at least one regiment was overwhelmingly Protestant. Secondly, and perhaps more plausibly, Cromwell felt that by letting loose such terror at Drogheda, the Irish would be in fear and less inclined to resist, strongholds would be more likely to surrender at the first summons and overall, therefore, English and Irish lives would be saved – 'The enemy were filled with much terror. And truly I believe this bitterness will save much effusion of blood, through the goodness of God.' As it turned out, Irish resistance did not crumble and many more lives were lost, though Cromwell's reasoning was not entirely faulty. A clutch of strongholds were abandoned or swiftly surrendered in the wake of Drogheda, including Dundalk, to which Cromwell sent a written summons on 12 September:

> I offered mercy to the garrison of Treedagh [Drogheda], in sending the Governor a summons before I attempted the taking of it, which being refused brought their evil upon them. If you, being warned thereby, shall surrender your garrison . . . you may thereby prevent effusion of blood.

Cromwell hoped that the events at Drogheda 'will tend to prevent the effusion of blood for the future, which are satisfactory grounds to such actions, which otherwise cannot but work remorse and regret'. Aware that something terrible had occurred, he felt that, in the long term, Drogheda's fate would lead to a reduction in bloodshed.[13]

Furthermore, as many military historians have pointed out, under the rules of war at that time Cromwell was quite justified in his actions, for a besieged garrison which rejected a summons to surrender and then inflicted casualties on the besieging force had no right to quarter if it subsequently fell to that force. Even at Drogheda, the slaughter was not complete or indiscriminate. There are few indications that women or children died, and unarmed male civilians who were not playing any active role in the defence of the town seem in general to have survived. Once the heat of battle had subsided, even soldiers in arms might escape death. When one of the mural towers subsequently fell to Cromwell's men, all the officers within it and one in ten of the common soldiers were killed on the spot, but only because, before it fell, some of Cromwell's troops had been killed and wounded by shots fired from that tower. When the other towers fell to Cromwell, 'the soldiers . . . were all spared', though they were destined to be shipped to Barbados.[14]

After the fall of Drogheda, Cromwell headed south and returned with much of his army to Dublin, for rest and recuperation. The mopping-up operation within Ulster was left to others. Instead, from late September onwards, Cromwell turned his attention to the south-east coast, campaigning to secure not only the coastal routes but also a swath of territory many miles inland, taking in much of Leinster and Munster. In the process, Cromwell's army would be severely depleted by illness, particularly dysentery, by the need to man newly established garrisons and by his decision from time to time to divide his forces, with units splitting off to capture a particular stronghold or to subdue a locality.

Cromwell's first target in the south-east of Ireland was the town of Wexford, defended by strong stone walls and, on the south side, by a medieval castle. Cromwell and his main force arrived before the town in early October, having secured as they marched south from Dublin a string of bases, abandoned or promptly surrendered to them. Drogheda was still having an effect. In his formal summons of 3 October, Cromwell stressed that he wished to avoid the 'effusion of blood' but that, if the summons was rejected, 'innocent persons' might well suffer with the guilty; 'I hope it will clearly appear where the guilt will lie.'[15] The governor played for time, but Cromwell's patience was soon exhausted and on 11 October a bombardment began, quickly opening up breaches in the castle walls. At this point negotiations resumed, Cromwell promising life and liberty to common soldiers and non-commissioned officers, life only to commissioned officers, 'no violence' to the civilian inhabitants and freedom from plunder. Hastily and apparently without liaising with the town's governor, the commander of the castle surrendered his fortress and its swift occupation by Cromwell's troops induced panic among the soldiers and civilians within the town. Cromwell's men perceived this and took the opportunity to pour into the town itself, initially almost unopposed, but later meeting, in Cromwell's words, 'stiff resistance' in the market place and along several streets. There the soldiers 'put to the sword all that came in their way', including the military and civilian defenders of Wexford and friars; more, including some women and children, drowned when trying to flee by water in overloaded boats. According to Cromwell's own estimate, almost 2,000 died, including around 300 drowned.[16]

The bloodshed at Wexford is often likened to that at Drogheda a month before. But there were clear differences. At Drogheda the order to allow no quarter was given by Cromwell himself as a matter of policy, albeit one issued in the heat of battle, and the killing continued in cold blood for at least twenty-four hours after the capture of the town. At Wexford the killings were not clearly undertaken on Cromwell's orders. The parliamentary soldiers who secured the castle seem to have acted on their own initiative in seizing the opportunity to storm the town and what followed was the result of unplanned and uncontrolled chaos. Equally, however, there is no evidence from the surviving sources that Cromwell deplored the killing or attempted to stop it. In his letter of 14 October to the Speaker, he portrayed the event as the fruit of unexpected divine intervention:

> And indeed it hath not without cause been deeply set upon our hearts, that, we intending better to this place than so great a ruin, hoping the town might be of more use to you and your army, yet God would not have it so; but, by an unexpected providence, in His righteous justice, brought a just judgment upon them, causing them to become a prey to the soldier, who in their piracies had made preys of so many families, and made with their bloods to answer the cruelties which they had exercised upon the lives of divers poor Protestants.[17]

Although, in both scale and circumstances, the killings at Drogheda and Wexford were not repeated, the operations there set the tone for the remainder of the campaign in Leinster and Munster through the winter and spring of 1650. The unusually mild and dry autumn weather broke in November, and thereafter heavy rain hindered the campaign. For example, Cromwell was unable to bring his artillery up to strengthen the siege of Waterford. He described 2 December, when he abandoned the siege, as the most 'terrible a day as ever I marched in, in all my life'.[18] Illness among the army further hindered the campaign. Cromwell himself seems to have enjoyed reasonable health in Ireland, saving only a bout of illness in late October and early November. Of this period, he wrote that 'I have been crazy in my health, but the Lord is pleased to sustain me', commenting later that he had been 'very sick' while staying at Ross.[19]

Cromwell's usual procedure in Ireland was to surround a stronghold, summons it, offering freedom from violence if surrendered but suffering if resistance continued, and then either accept a surrender or proceed to bombard and, if possible and necessary, to storm the stronghold. Some operations ran very smoothly, as in mid-October, when New Ross was surrendered on terms with nothing more than a brief bombardment. In February 1650 Fethard, Cashel and Cahir surrendered just as promptly, and in March Gowran Castle submitted, though only after the initial summons had been rejected and the bombardment had breached the wall; in consequence, Cromwell had all but one of the officers shot and a Catholic priest hanged. In contrast, Duncannon and Waterford both put up stiff resistance during November and early December, and Cromwell was forced to abandon the somewhat half-hearted operations against both towns. Sometimes success was achieved, but at a price. Thus in March 1650 Kilkenny surrendered on terms following a siege and bombardment, but only after Cromwell's attempts to take the town by storm had been repulsed with significant losses, so that at one point his troops refused to charge once more. Some operations went disastrously wrong. In late April and May 1650, in the last significant operation of his Irish campaign, Cromwell attempted to take the town of Clonmel. After a two-week bombardment, several breaches had been opened in the town wall, but repeated attacks were beaten off with heavy losses. The last, on 16 May, a four-hour operation, intended as a full-scale storming of Clonmel, proved to be an utter failure, leaving wave after wave of parliamentary dead. Although Clonmel was subsequently evacuated by the enemy troops and then surrendered on terms, the parliamentary losses were enormous – estimated at anything between 1,000 and 2,500 men. At Clonmel, as on a lesser scale at Pembroke in summer 1648, Cromwell's desire quickly to conclude a siege operation may have led him prematurely and unwisely to order an all-out assault.

Cromwell repeatedly stressed that he wished to avoid destruction of property and loss of life. His summons to New Ross included a claim that he always offered a chance to surrender, that 'the people and places where I come may not suffer except through their own wilfulness'.[20] He assured Waterford that he had come, 'not to destroy people and places, but to save them, that men may live comfortably and happily by their trade, (if the faults be not in themselves)'.[21] Accordingly, he generally offered generous terms to a surrendering town or castle and maintained tight discipline among his own troops, taking particular care to prevent his army plundering or disrupting Irish agriculture. On the other hand, he firmly rebuffed the governor of New Ross when he sought to include freedom of worship for Catholics within the terms of surrender:

> For that which you mention concerning liberty of conscience, I meddle not with any man's conscience. But if by liberty of conscience you mean a liberty to exercise the mass, I judge it best to use plain dealing, and to let you know, where the Parliament of England have power, that will not be allowed of.[22]

But he looked forward to a time when Ireland would be more settled and free from war, for just as God was rightly punishing the Irish for their sins, so there would come a time when they would share His grace:

> That a Divine Presence hath gone along with us in the late great transactions in this nation, I believe most good men are sensible of, and thankful to God for; and are persuaded that He hath a further end; and that as by this dispensation He hath manifested His severity and justice, so there will be a time wherein He will manifest grace and mercy, in which He so much delights . . . and that we live in hope to see

Him cause wars to cease, and bringing in that Kingdom of glory and peace which He hath promised . . . cannot but hope that goodness and mercy intends to visit this poor Island.[23]

As ever, Cromwell saw the hand of God at work in the Irish campaign. The successes in Ireland had been the work of the Lord, not of unworthy mortals:

The Lord is pleased still to vouchsafe us His presence, and to prosper His own work in our hands; which to us is the more eminent because truly we are a company of poor, weak and worthless creatures. Truly our work is neither from our brains nor from our courage and strength, but we follow the Lord who goeth before, and gather what He scattereth, that so all may appear to be from Him.[24]

Again, writing to the Speaker, Cromwell asked:

Sir, what can be said to these things? Is it an arm of flesh that doth these things? Is it the wisdom, and counsel, or strength of men? It is the Lord only. God will curse that man and his house that dares to think otherwise. Sir, you see the work is done by divine leading. God gets into the hearts of men, and persuades them to come under you.[25]

This letter was written just before the setbacks at Duncannon and Waterford, but even they could be interpreted as the work of God, giving men cause to ponder His message:

the Lord in wisdom and for gracious ends best known to Himself, hath interlaced some things which may give us cause of serious consideration what His mind therein may be; and we hope we wait upon Him, desiring to know and to submit to his good pleasure.[26]

Above all, the successes in Ireland should be seen as confirmation that God approved of and supported the new regime in England, while at the same time placing greater responsibility upon the regime and the nation to strive together with renewed vigour to fulfil God's will:

I beg of those that are faithful, that they give glory to God. I wish it may have influence upon the hearts and spirits of all those that are now in place of government, in the greatest trust, that they may all in heart draw near to God; giving Him glory by holiness of life and conversation, that these unspeakable mercies may teach dissenting brethren on all sides to agree, at least, in praising God. And if the Father of the family be so kind, why should there be such jarrings and heart-burnings amongst the children? And if it will not yet be received that these are seals of God's approbation of your great change of Government, which indeed was no more yours than these victories and successes are ours; yet let them with us say, even the most unsatisfied heart amongst them, that both are the righteous judgments and mighty works of God; that He hath pulled down the mighty from his seat, that calls to an account innocent blood, that He thus breaks the enemies of His Church in pieces.[27]

Cromwell left Ireland on 26 May 1650, at last answering urgent orders from the Rump to return to England in order to guard against the growing threat from Scotland. He never went back. The achievements of his nine-month campaign were mixed. He had not met an enemy army in the field, he had been rebuffed at Duncannon and Waterford, the towns of Drogheda and Wexford had been won at the expense of much enemy blood, and Kilkenny and – more so – Clonmel at the expense of much parliamentarian blood. Above all, Cromwell had not attempted to conquer the whole island. Duncannon and Waterford, plus the fortified town of Limerick – which Cromwell had not even approached – were secured only after his departure and there followed several years of bitter guerilla warfare. On the other hand, the campaign had broken the back of Irish resistance. By diplomacy as much as by military conquest, Cromwell had brought low the morale of his enemies and driven rifts between the various enemy factions. Thus much of southern Munster, including the towns of Cork and Youghal – where Cromwell passed the depths of winter – Kinsale and Bandon, had passed to him by diplomacy. By the end of 1649 Cromwell had even been able to turn his thoughts to the future civil administration of the country, envisaging the

the Rump had decided to send the English army north, to forestall invasion and to crush hostile moves within Scotland itself. Initially, the hope was that Lord General Fairfax would lead the expedition, with Cromwell present as second-in-command. But Fairfax, although willing to defend England against a Scottish invasion, would not undertake command of an English invasion. Cromwell and others were sent to persuade him to change his mind. Some contemporaries felt that Cromwell genuinely sought to win over his commander and colleague, others that his arguments were half-hearted, barely concealing his ambitions to replace Fairfax. Either way, the delegation failed and the Rump swiftly passed an Act relieving Fairfax of his command and appointing Cromwell in his place. Although he had led the Irish campaign and had been created Lord Lieutenant of Ireland, until this time Cromwell had been Lieutenant General of the Horse – in effect, second-in-command – of the parliamentary army. The commission appointing Cromwell Lord General of the army was dated 28 June, the very day he left London and headed north.

The Scottish campaign was marked by some significant victories and achievements, but they were occasional successes against a background of disappointment and problems. The main source of difficulty was the reluctance of the Scottish army to give battle in the field, preferring to lie in wait behind well-prepared defences. Thus Cromwell's 16,000–strong army initially entered Scotland unopposed, and swiftly occupied Dunbar, Haddington and Musselburgh during late July and early August, but were not strong enough to break the Scots' heavily defended line from Leith to Edinburgh and, despite some sparring in the Pentland Hills during August, were unable to tempt the Scottish commander, David Leslie, out into the open to give battle on reasonable ground. At the same time, Cromwell tried diplomacy, writing to the Scottish 'saints' in general and the Assembly of the Kirk in particular, attempting to persuade them to abandon their animosity. He defended regicide and the abolition of monarchy and the House of Lords, and argued that morally and politically the Scots were wrong to support Charles Stuart. But he focused on religion, stressing his toleration of Scottish presbyterianism and arguing that there was no cause for them to oppose the English regime. For example, an army declaration of July stressed:

> we do and are ready to embrace so much as doth, or shall be made appear to us to be according to the Word of God. Are we to be dealt with as enemies, because we come not to your way? Is all religion wrapped up in that or any one form? Doth that name, or thing, give the difference between those that are the members of Christ and those that are not? We think not so. We say, faith working by love is the true character of a Christian.[29]

In a letter to Leslie, written on 14 August, Cromwell repeated the theme:

> we continue the same which we have professed ourselves to the honest people of Scotland, wishing to them as to our own souls; it being no part of our business to hinder any of them from worshipping God in that way they are satisfied in their consciences by the Word of God they ought (though different from us), but shall therein be ready to perform what obligation lies upon us by the Covenant.[30]

Most famously of all, on 3 August, he had attempted to persuade the members of the General Assembly of the Kirk that they were misinterpreting God's word in pursuing their present line:

> Your own guilt is too much for you to bear: bring not therefore upon yourselves the blood of innocent men, deceived with pretences of King and Covenant, from whose eyes you hide a better knowledge. I am persuaded that divers of you, who lead the people, have laboured to build yourselves in these things wherein you have censured others, and established yourselves upon the Word of God. Is it therefore infallibly agreeable to the Word of God, all that you say? I beseech you, in the bowels of Christ, think it possible you may be mistaken.[31]

Just as these attempts to win over some of the Scots did not

BATTLE OF DUNBAR

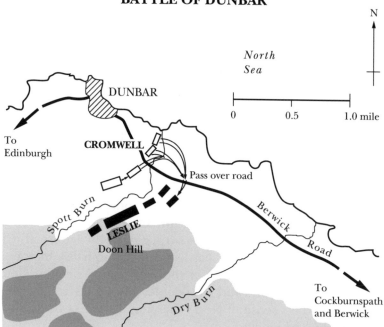

produce immediate results, so the military side of the campaign fared badly. Having failed to tempt Leslie to give battle, the English trudged back to Dunbar at the end of August. Shortage of supplies, bad weather, disease and desertion were lowering morale and depleting the army. By 1 September Cromwell thought that he had just 11,000 soldiers fit for service. The Scots saw their chance and pursued the English, bottling them up within Dunbar, their army of up to 22,000 men occupying Doon Hill above the town and also blocking the road south to Berwick, so breaking their enemies' line of retreat. Probably expecting nothing more than a desperate attempt by the English cavalry to cut their way out, Leslie's army moved down to the lower hillside on 2 September. But to Leslie's horror and surprise Cromwell decided on an all-out attack. He deployed his army under cover of darkness on the night of 2–3 September, and as dawn broke he threw his forces at the Scottish army. Instead of attacking along the entire front, Cromwell focused his assault on the Scots' right wing, with wave after wave of English attacks eventually causing that wing to collapse, leaving the Scots' centre exposed. The centre and the left wing were in turn engaged and overwhelmed, and the remains of Leslie's army were soon in chaos and flight. The Scots lost 3,000 dead and 10,000 captured, the English just twenty dead, most of them in a preliminary manoeuvre.

Cromwell had shown courage in committing his army to engage an enemy which outnumbered it by around two to one. Taking advantage of the lie of the land and a suspected lack of manoeuvrability among his enemies, he had displayed great skill in attacking only part of the Scottish army at a time. In this way Cromwell had avoided at any one time or point engaging the full strength and front of the Scottish army. It was, perhaps, Cromwell's greatest military victory, all the sweeter for being unexpected, and it was one of the few battles of the civil war where a numerically inferior army defeated a numerically superior force. Not surprisingly, the letters which Cromwell wrote after the battle were triumphalist in tone, referring to Dunbar as 'one of the most signal mercies God hath done for England and His people, this war'.[32] To his wife, he expressed his sense of God's mercies, as well as worries of a more physical type:

> The Lord hath showed us an exceeding mercy: who can tell how great it is. My weak faith hath been upheld. I have been in my inward man marvellously supported; though I assure thee, I grow an old man, and feel infirmities of age marvellously stealing upon me. Would my corruptions did as fast decrease. Pray on my behalf in the latter respect.[33]

But most tellingly of all, and not for the first time, in his letter to the Speaker, imparting news of a great military victory, he went on to give fairly specific and pointed advice to Parliament about how it should act, in this case a request for social and judicial as well as religious and moralistic reform:

> It is easy to say, the Lord hath done this . . . But, Sir, it is in your hands, and by these eminent mercies God puts it more into your hands, to give glory to Him; to improve your power, and His Blessings, to His praise. We that serve you beg of you not to own us, but God alone; we pray you own His people more and more, for they are the chariots and horsemen of Israel. Disown yourselves, but own your

authority, and improve it to curb the proud and the insolent, such as would disturb the tranquillity of England, though under what specious pretences soever; relieve the oppressed, hear the groans of poor prisoners in England; be pleased to reform the abuses of all professions; and if there be any one that makes many poor to make a few rich, that suits not a Commonwealth. If He that strengthens your servants to fight, pleases to give you hearts to set upon these things, in order to His glory, and the glory of your Commonwealth, besides the benefit England shall feel thereby, you shall shine forth to other nations, who shall emulate the glory of such a pattern, and through the power of God turn into the like.[34]

There might be a warning here for the future.

In the wake of Dunbar, both Leith and the town of Edinburgh fell swiftly and without further resistance, though Edinburgh Castle held out until Christmas. With Lothian and much of the central lowlands secured, Cromwell spent the autumn and winter based in Edinburgh, but with frequent journeys around the region. He now devoted himself more to diplomacy and to attempting to win hearts and minds than to campaigning.

He attended presbyterian services in Edinburgh and Glasgow, and repeatedly stressed his respect for both the Scots and their religion. He saw the people as basically good and potentially godly, though sadly led astray by political naivety, by personal and racial prejudices, and by the 'evils' of a few incendiaries. In October 1651, after the campaign was over, he wrote that 'we have had to do with some who were (I verily think) godly, but, through weakness and the subtlety of Satan, involved in interests against the Lord and His people.'[35] He stressed that he would allow presbyterian ministers to preach, though, as in England, not 'to rail, nor, under pretence thereof to overtop the civil power, or debase it as they please'.[36] Because he had time on his hands, he also conducted a long correspondence with the governor of Edinburgh Castle, trying to win him over by showing him the errors of his ways. In the process Cromwell again defended regicide and the abolition of the monarchy, and argued that the recent successes of the English regime and army revealed that God was with them, not the Scots. Once more, he also stressed his respect for the presbyterian faith, though he was critical of some aspects of the that church, especially its refusal to allow any but the approved to preach:

> Approbation is an act of conveniency in respect of order; not of necessity to give faculty to preach the Gospel. Your pretended fear lest error should step in, is like the man that would keep all the wine out of the country lest men should be drunk. It will be found an unjust and unwise jealousy, to deny a man the liberty he hath by nature upon a supposition he may abuse it. When he doth abuse it, judge.[37]

Edinburgh Castle was eventually surrendered on generous terms, though only after Cromwell had applied pressure by bombarding and undermining. Fine words needed physical reinforcement.

The period from September 1650 to July 1651 was marked by inactivity. This was due to more than the need to rest and bring up reinforcements in the wake of Dunbar and the subsequent onset of the Scottish winter. Two other factors played a part. Firstly, Leslie was able to regroup around Stirling and rebuild his army. Although the geographical location had changed, Cromwell found himself facing a familiar problem, for although he approached Stirling several times, he was neither able to tempt Leslie out into the field to give battle nor strong enough to launch a direct attack upon the new Scottish royalist HQ. One such manoeuvre in bad weather in early February had disastrous consequences, for Cromwell fell seriously ill. This illness, the second factor explaining the prolonged military inactivity, lasted until early June, and was marked by several relapses. At some points, especially during May, he was dangerously ill with recurrent fever and dysentery, and doctors were dispatched from London to minister to him. In late March, when Cromwell believed himself to be recovering from the first bout, he wrote to the President of the Council that 'I am a poor creature, and have been a dry bone, and am still an unprofitable servant to my Master and you. I thought I should have died of this fit of sickness, but the Lord seemeth to dispose otherwise.'[38] On 3 June, at last on the mend, he told the President of the Council:

> I shall not need to recite the extremity of my late sickness: it was so violent that indeed my nature was not able to bear the weight thereof. But the Lord was pleased to deliver me, beyond expectation, and to give me cause to say once more, 'He hath plucked me out of the grave!'[39]

By July 1651 Cromwell was fully recovered and his army, recently reinforced, now numbered over 21,000. He dispatched around 4,500 of these troops, under the command of Overton and Lambert, across the Firth of Forth, in an attempt to secure Fife and thus not only threaten Stirling from the north but also break Leslie's supply lines with northern Scotland. Cromwell, meanwhile, led the bulk of the army along the south bank of the Firth of Forth, towards Stirling. Alive to the threat, Leslie responded by dispatching around 4,000 men to rebuff the English incursion into Fife. However, on 20 July this Scottish force was engaged and destroyed at Inverkeithing. Although the victory was Lambert's, Cromwell had initiated the manoeuvre. As was now usual, Cromwell's letter to the Speaker, giving news of victory, carried a pointed political message

> I hope it becometh me to pray that ... you whom we serve, as the authority over us, may do the work committed to you, with uprightness and faithfulness, and thoroughly, as to the Lord; that you may not suffer anything to remain that offends the eyes of His jealousy; that common weal may more and more be sought, and justice done impartially. For the eyes of the Lord run to and fro; and as He finds out His enemies here, to be avenged on them, so will He not spare them for whom He doth good, if by His loving kindness they become not good.[40]

Leaving just eight regiments south of the Forth, Cromwell

BATTLE OF WORCESTER

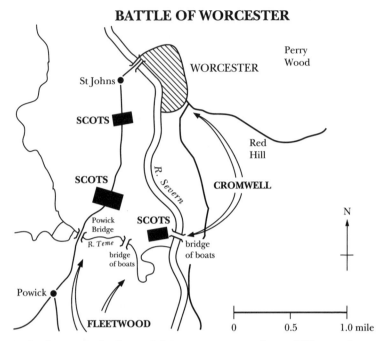

led the remainder of his army over into Fife at the end of July and on 2 August Perth was swiftly surrendered to them. Cromwell was undoubtedly aware that, with most of his army now north of Stirling, there was a strong possibility that Leslie would drive south, deep into the Scottish lowlands and probably into England. However, it is not entirely clear whether Cromwell merely viewed that as a risk worth taking as the price of severing Stirling's supply lines to the north or whether he positively hoped that the Scots would march south, more confident of destroying them in the open than of defeating them in and around Stirling. His letter to the Speaker of 4 August suggests the latter, for while he acknowledged that a Scottish march southward 'will trouble some men's thoughts, and may occasion some inconveniences', that would be better than allowing matters to drag on and so 'occasion another winter's war, to the ruin of your soldiery'.[41]

When he wrote this letter, the Scottish royalist forces, now led by 'King' Charles, were already marching south, through lowland Scotland and northern England, shadowed but not challenged by parliamentary forces. By 23 August they had entered Worcester and there they halted, strengthening the town against the inevitable parliamentary attack. Cromwell and part of his army had followed them south, leaving Scotland on 9 August and arriving in Worcestershire on 27 August. The Scottish royalist forces numbered fewer than 16,000, and perhaps not much above 12,000. By the beginning of September, Cromwell commanded an army of well over 30,000, comprising regular troops and militia forces. With such a huge advantage, he decided to attack rather than lay siege, planning a two-pronged attack on 3 September from the south-east and up the west bank of the Severn, communication between them maintained by a bridge of boats across the Severn. Rather than wait within Worcester, the enemy came out to engage Cromwell's army around the town. The battle was long, but eventually numbers told and the Scottish royalist force was broken. Worcester itself fell and by nightfall the Scottish royalist army had been destroyed, with 3,000 dead, over 7,000 prisoners and the rest, including Charles himself, in full flight.

Worcester was the last military action in which Cromwell was personally involved. Thus, less than fifteen months after being appointed Lord General, he had fought his last battle. Although he retained that office until his death, active command was delegated to others and thereafter Cromwell became a full-time politician and statesman. Overwhelming as it was, the success at Worcester was not unexpected, for Cromwell's forces had a huge advantage in terms of numbers, equipment, provisions and morale. It is also noticeable that the parliamentary forces could easily have been deployed on 2 September but that Cromwell chose to hold them back until the next day. What we would call superstition probably played a part, with Cromwell deliberately giving battle on the first anniversary of Dunbar. Although he sent the Speaker a hurried report of the outcome on the evening of 3 September, a fuller, more considered account followed on 4 September. Once more, Cromwell felt that God's will, as revealed on the battlefield, also encompassed broader concerns, to which Parliament should respond:

The dimensions of this mercy are above my thoughts. It is,

for aught I know, a crowning mercy. Surely, if it be not, such a one we shall have, if this provoke those that are concerned in it to thankfulness, and the Parliament to do the will of Him who hath done His will for it, and for the nation; . . . I am bold humbly to beg, that all thoughts may tend to the promoting of His honour who hath wrought so great salvation, and that the fatness of these continued mercies may not occasion pride and wantonness . . . but that the fear of the Lord, even for His mercies, may keep an authority and a people so prospered, and blessed, and witnessed unto, humble and faithful; and that justice and righteousness, mercy and truth may flow from you, as a thankful return to our gracious God.[42]

Fulfilling those supposedly divinely sanctioned aspirations would absorb Cromwell's time as the conquering hero returned to London and the political arena a week or so after Worcester.

An account of Cromwell's role during the remaining months of the Rump, from September 1651 to April 1653, is necessarily somewhat brief, for the sources are thin. In contrast to the informative letters which Cromwell wrote from Ireland and Scotland, his surviving correspondence once back in London becomes little more than a selection of official letters, military proclamations and directives to garrison commanders, pleas in support of petitioners and letters arising from his recent appointment as Chancellor of the University of Oxford. He was certainly active in central government, present in the Rump and its Council of State, and on committees of both. Apart from a very brief trip to Kent in May 1652 upon naval business, there is no evidence that he left the capital during the period and plenty to suggest that he was now an active London-based politician.

Apart from the angry tirade with which he eventually dismissed it, there survive no full or reliable versions of any speeches which Cromwell made in the Rump during this period. However, Cromwell did serve as teller in some of the key divisions and from this and his later statements we can reconstruct something of his beliefs. Like many of his fellow officers, he wanted the Rump to set a date for its own dissolution and to give way to a more stable, secure constitutional system. He supported a policy of reconciliation following the divisions of civil war, to be achieved through legislation granting broad indemnity or pardon to former royalists. Above all, he wanted the Rump to press on with a policy of 'reformation', to launch a rolling programme which would cure many of the nation's moral and social ills and would bring about many of the reforms which Cromwell had listed in his earlier letters to the Speaker. In all these areas, Cromwell was to be disappointed by the Rump's inability or unwillingness to make real progress.

Years later, in a speech of September 1654, Cromwell spoke of how his optimism after Worcester turned to intense disappointment and disillusionment with the Rump:

> after Worcester fight I came up to London to pay my service and duty to the Parliament that then sat. And hoping that all minds would have been disposed to answer that which seemed to be the mind of God, (viz.) to give peace and rest to his people, and especially to those who had bled more than others in the carrying on of the military affairs, I was much disappointed of my expectation, for the issue did not prove so.[43]

In another speech of September 1654, he portrayed the period after the end of the civil wars as one of confusion and chaos, with the fabric of the country tottering, God's interests ignored, blasphemies abounding, enemies at work at home and the nation needlessly embroiled in expensive wars abroad. 'Was not everything almost grown arbitrary?' he asked. 'What a heap of confusions were upon these poor nations.'[44]

However, the fullest account which Cromwell gave of his disappointment at the Rump's performance in the period after Worcester was contained within a speech of July 1653, delivered just a few weeks after the Rump's demise:

> coming with my fellow officers and soldiers, we expected, and had some reasonable confidence that . . . the mercies that God had shewed, the expectations that were in the hearts of all good men, would have prompted those in authority to have done those good things, which might by honest men

have been judged a return fit for such a God and worthy
of such mercies, and indeed a discharge of duty to those
for whom all these mercies have been shewed, that is, the
interest of the three nations, the true interest of the three
nations . . . That upon our return, we came fully bent in our
heart and thoughts to desire and use all fair and lawful
means we could, to have had the nation to reap the fruit
of all that blood and treasure that had been expended in
this cause.[45]

By summer 1652, Cromwell claimed, it had become clear to
him and his fellow officers that the Rump was achieving little,
whereupon they petitioned the House. Cromwell was referring to a petition of mid-August, which called for measures
to spread the gospel, the removal of ignorant and scandal-
ous ministers and the encouragement of godly ministers,
reform of the law, thorough inquiries into alleged financial
irregularities, provision to end begging and vagabondage,
payment of military arrears and provision for ex-soldiers and
military widows and orphans, and speedy consideration of
'such quallifications for future and successive parliaments, as
tend to the election only of such as are pious and faithfull
to the interest of the Commonwealth'.[46] The last request was
vague and did not call for an immediate dissolution. The
petition was in the name of the Council of Officers, but it is
probably safe to assume that at the very least it had Cromwell's
tacit approval; in his July 1653 speech he referred favourably
to this petition. In the same speech Cromwell claimed that Parliament's response brought no real satisfaction, merely 'a few
words given us'. Accordingly, 'finding the people dissatisfied
in every corner of the nation, and bringing home to our doors
the non-performance of those things that had been promised
and were of duty to be performed, we did think ourselves
concerned'.[47]

There is no doubt that one of Cromwell's principal concerns
at this time was that the Rump should dissolve itself and be
replaced by a better system of government. Equally, there is no
doubt that it was this matter which finally triggered the crisis
of spring 1653 and prompted Cromwell, with army support,
forcibly to dissolve or eject the Rump. But the precise nature

of Cromwell's political aspirations at this time is as uncertain as the detailed circumstances of the spring crisis. For the former, we have no clear evidence from Cromwell's own pen, and accordingly we are thrown back on a variety of other sources. In particular, much is often made of Bulstrode Whitelocke's accounts of two meetings he had with Cromwell around this time and which appeared in his published *Memorials* of 1682. The first, during the closing months of 1651, was a formal meeting of senior army officers and senior MPs, convened by Cromwell to discuss the future constitution. Cromwell sought opinions on whether it would be best to continue a republic or to seek 'a mixed Monarchical Government' and, if the latter, to suggest 'in whom that power shall be placed'. Most MPs favoured the restoration of monarchy in the person of one of Charles I's children, most officers strongly opposed this and preferred a republic. Near the end of the discussion Cromwell expressed his guarded support for 'a settlement with somewhat of the Monarchical power in it', though only if it 'may be done with safety, and preservation of our rights, both as Englishmen and as Christians'; he also recognized that 'that will be a business of more than ordinary difficulty'.[48]

The second meeting was a chance encounter in St James's Park one evening in November 1652. Cromwell confided to Whitelocke that he felt that the nation was in a 'dangerous condition', drifting away from God, with divisions growing within the army and between the army and the Rump. Cromwell clearly shared the army's low opinions of the MPs, who were full of

> pride, and ambition, and self-seeking, ingrossing all places of honour and profit to themselves and their friends, and their daily breaking forth into new and violent parties and factions; their delays of business, and designs to perpetuate themselves, and to continue the power in their own hands; their meddling in private matters between party and party, . . . and their injustice and partiality in those matters, and the scandalous lives of some of the chief of them . . . Nor can they be kept within the bounds of justice, law or reason; they themselves being the supreme power of the nation

and so uncontrollable. Cromwell had abandoned any hope that the Rump would produce a just, godly settlement and was fearful that they

> will destroy again what the Lord hath done graciously for them and us; we all forget God, and God will forget us, and give us up to confusion; and these men will help it on, if they be suf-fered to proceed in their ways; some course must be thought on to curb and restrain them, or we shall be ruined by them.

Cromwell then floated the idea of a return to monarchy – 'What if a man should take upon him to be king?' – and picked Whitelocke's brain about the implications. Whitelocke was cool, pointing out the difficulties and suggesting that, if a return to monarchy was envisaged, it would be better to reach some sort of arrangement with Charles Stuart. This was clearly not what Cromwell wanted to hear and he politely ended the conversation.[49]

Whitelocke's accounts are interesting and, where quoting Cromwell, they contain phrases found in Cromwell's letters and speeches. If true, they indicate that by autumn 1651 he was toying with the idea of re-establishing some sort of monarchical system and that by autumn 1652 he had clearly written off the Rump, convinced that no good could come of it and that the MPs were imperilling God's work. But there is little to corroborate Whitelocke's account, and certainly nothing in Cromwell's surviving letters of 1651–2 to prove that by then he had abandoned all hope of the Rump, still less that he was contemplating a monarchical restoration. What we do find in one of very few personal letters to survive from this period is a feeling of loneliness. Writing on 1 September 1652 to someone now unknown, but who was clearly a trusted friend, Cromwell felt that

> instead of pitying you I can a little bewail myself. Have I one friend in our society to whom I can unbowell myself? You absent; Fleetwood is gone; I am left alone – almost so – but not forsaken. Lend me one shoulder. Pray for me. The Lord restore you.[50]

But he did not go into greater detail or explain why he felt the need to 'unbowell' himself and the colourful tales related by Whitelocke in his published *Memorials* remain unproven. Equal mystery surrounds the precise reasons for Cromwell's ejection of the Rump in spring 1653. There is no reason to doubt the narrative which he gave in the speech of July 1653. Deeply worried by the train of events and by the failure of the Rump to push through reforms or to make proper provision for the future constitution, from October 1652 onwards he and other senior officers had held a series of meetings with MPs to discuss their worries, beseeching them 'that they would be mindful of their duty to God and man, and of the discharge of the trust reposed in them'. At length, in spring 1653, the Rump had leapt into action, suddenly pressing ahead with a bill to settle the constitution, in particular to provide for a new 'representative' or parliament; various proposals and bills to this end had hitherto been considered only intermittently and without enthusiasm. Cromwell and his fellow officers, however, strongly disliked something in this bill and now attempted to prevent its passage in its present form. Not only did they press for further discussion but they also wanted consideration given to their own very different proposal – that the Rump dissolve and make way, not for another elected parliament, but for an interim unelected body, with power for the time being entrusted to 'persons of honour and integrity that were well known, men well affected to religion and the interest of the nation'. On 19 April, at a late-night meeting between army officers and over twenty MPs held in Cromwell's lodgings and chaired by him, Cromwell and the officers thought that he had won a firm agreement that progress on the Rump's constitutional bill would be suspended pending further discussions between them. When, therefore, word was brought to Cromwell on the following morning, 20 April, that the Rump was pushing ahead with its constitutional bill as fast as possible and that it was likely to be passed that day, he reacted swiftly.[51] In scenes which Cromwell always passed over very briefly in his own letters and speeches but which other eye-witnesses described in lurid detail, Cromwell arrived at the House on the morning of 20 April, sat listening to the debates for a few minutes, then got up and, in a speech of much passion and bitterness, dismissed the House, calling in some musketeers to clear the chamber. The Rump's Council of State was ejected later that day.

Why did Cromwell act in this way? He was, after all, usually very cautious and very respectful towards constitutional government. He had certainly restrained the army from striking at the Long Parliament during 1647 and he was reportedly taking much the same line during the winter of 1652–3, resisting growing calls in the army for the ejection of the Rump. Yet on 20 April he took the lead in doing just that. Clearly, the immediate cause of Cromwell's actions was something contained within the Rump's constitutional bill, or at least something which Cromwell believed – possibly wrongly – to be in the bill. It is not known what that was and Cromwell's subsequent explanations, in speeches of July 1653, September 1654 and later, are vague, ambiguous and contradictory.

After his return from Worcester, Cromwell had consistently pressed the Rump to set a firm date for its own dissolution and by 1653 he had become convinced that the MPs no longer commanded much support or respect in the country:

> I pressed the Parliament, as a member, to period themselves, once, and again, and again, and ten and twenty times over. I told them, – for I knew it better than any one man in the Parliament could know it, because of my manner of life, which was to run up and down the nation, and so might see and know the temper and spirits of all men, the best of men, – that the nation loathed their sitting; I knew it.[52]

Accordingly, down to spring 1653 Cromwell had consistently and successfully rejected periodic suggestions that by-elections be held to fill those seats effectively made vacant by Pride's Purge, for they would strengthen the Rump, partly renew its mandate and imply a longer life-span. In his speech of 4 July 1653 Cromwell hinted that the Rump's constitutional bill had contained just such a provision, alleging that it was designed 'to recruit the House the better to perpetuate themselves'.[53] In one version of the 4 July speech Cromwell reportedly claimed that, at the meeting on 19 April with leading Rump MPs, 'we found from their own mouths that they did intend a perpetuation of themselves'.[54] Elsewhere in the same speech and in those of September 1654 he spoke of the 'just fear of the Parliament's perpetuating themselves'.[55] Cromwell was here hinting at a charge made explicit in some other contemporary attacks upon the Rump in the wake of its ejection, that the constitutional bill guaranteed that the existing Rump MPs would continue to hold their seats without facing fresh elections and that only vacant seats would be contested in the coming round of elections – in effect, a reversion to the old by-election scheme. Until recently, this interpretation of events was widely followed and accepted by historians.

More recently, however, historians have re-examined the contemporary sources and suggested other, very different interpretations. Indeed, Cromwell himself indicated that there was more to it than this. His speeches point towards two, perhaps interrelated fears. The first, which comes out most clearly in the speech of 12 September 1654, was that the constitutional bill would establish a succession of 'perpetual' parliaments, not in the sense that a sitting MP would be guaranteed a seat for life, but because one parliament would hand over to its successor without a break:

> when one Parliament had left their seat, another was to sit down immediately in the room thereof, without any caution to avoid that which was the danger, (viz.) perpetuating of the same Parliaments; which is a sore now that will ever be running, so long as men are ambitious and troublesome, if a due remedy be not found.

He went on to assert that such an arrangement, with a 'legislative power always sitting', would lead to 'arbitrary' power, pose a threat to the legal and judicial systems and provide insufficient protection for property and liberty.[56] It later became clear that Cromwell favoured a constitution in which legislative and executive powers were divided, and in which parliaments would exercise legislative power only and would sit from time to time, with substantial periods between the dissolution of one parliament and the summoning the next, when power would be vested in other individuals and institutions. Although these were Cromwell's views in September

1654, when he made this speech, they probably reflect and had been shaped by the events of May to December 1653. His explanation of the alleged deficiencies of the April 1653 constitutional bill may well, by then, have been coloured by subsequent events and hindsight.

Thus it is probably better to focus on the second alternative explanation advanced by Cromwell, for it appears in his speech of 4 July 1653, much closer to the events it describes. The new constitutional bill had lacked 'integrity' and 'caution', he said, for it failed to 'provide security' for the whole cause for which so much had been risked and sacrificed. Instead it would 'throw back the cause into the hands of them we first fought with'. Cromwell and the officers were worried that the constitutional bill contained insufficient 'qualifications', especially concerning both 'the rules of electors and elected' and 'who should execute' them. At the late night meeting on 19 April, Cromwell asked 'whether the next Parliament were not like to consist of all Presbyterians' or 'neuters'. He had intervened the following day not only because the MPs had gone back on their agreement not to proceed with the constitutional bill for the time being but also because he was informed that the MPs were 'leaving out the things that did necessarily relate to due qualifications', which would have 'thrown all the liberties of the nation into the hands that never bled for it'.[57] Although Cromwell could have been clearer, he was heavily implying that he believed that the constitutional bill was opening the doors to elections which were too free, with over-lax controls over who could vote, stand and serve as an MP; he also suggested that the mechanisms to ensure that such controls had been observed and to vet electors and elected before the next parliament assembled were somehow insufficient or undesirable. By 4 July, Cromwell's main charge against the bill was that it provided for elections which were too open, full and free and which, given public opinion, paved the way for a parliament antagonistic to the cause, as interpreted by Cromwell and the army officers. However, it is also possible that on 20 April Cromwell acted under a misapprehension, genuinely if mistakenly believing that the bill contained a crude recruiting clause, and subsequently shifted his arguments when he read the bill and became aware of his error. Most historians now interpret events along these lines, though the vagaries of contemporary accounts, not least Cromwell's own explanations, leave room for doubt.

There is a danger that historians' intense speculation about the precise contents of the Rump's constitutional bill and Cromwell's understanding of its contents when he acted on 20 April might obscure the fundamental reasons for his action, namely his broader dissatisfaction with the Rump. The constitutional bill was the catalyst which unleashed Cromwell's intervention, but there were much deeper and long-standing factors at work. Like most of his military colleagues, Cromwell had for some time been deeply dismayed by the Rump's performance, by its failure to do God's work through healing the rifts of the civil war years and through initiating a broad and far-reaching programme of reform. The Rump's failure to do this, just as much as its failure to make proper provision for the future government of the state and to work towards its own imminent dissolution, had led to rumours long before April 1653 that Cromwell and the senior officers would intervene abruptly to end the Parliament. We know that during the opening months of 1653 several army units were moved closer to London and that over the same period the Council of Officers was holding regular meetings, often chaired by Cromwell. There were contemporary reports that many of the officers were urging military intervention but that Cromwell repeatedly held back, arguing that the Rump deserved more time and that direct military intervention should be only a last resort. Cromwell's own speeches of July 1653 and September 1654 imply this. Certainly, Cromwell was absent from the House from 12 March until 14 or 15 April. Apart from a meeting on 27 March, he was also absent from the Council of State from 8 March until 7 April. There are no indications that he was unwell at this time and it seems more likely that these absences are another example of Cromwell withdrawing from the fray when he was both highly dissatisfied with a turn of events and seemingly unable to alter them from within. Although, in his later speeches, Cromwell discussed the constitutional bill and its shortcomings at some length, albeit often in a rather vague or contradictory way, he also made clear that much more deep-seated problems had given rise to the events of 20 April. For example, in July 1653 he spoke of the failure of Rump MPs to effect godly reformation and to work for the good of the nation and its people, and on other occasions he also accused Rump MPs of personal shortcomings. Through their actions as well as their inaction, they had risked 'the judgment and displeasure of God against them, the dissatisfaction of the people and the putting things into a confusion'.[58] A declaration issued by Cromwell and the Council of Officers on 22 April spoke, in similar terms, of the Rump's failure 'to give the people the harvest of all their labour, blood and treasure, and to settle a due liberty both in reference to civil and spiritual things'. It had become clear, the declaration alleged, that the Rump 'would never answer those ends which God, his people, and the whole nation expected from them'.[59]

In several later speeches Cromwell suggested that, with the departure of the Rump and its Council, he was the only legitimate power left in the land, pointing to the parliamentary statute which had appointed him Lord General of the army. Whatever the legal and constitutional validity of that interpretation, it is clear that, in practice, power had passed to Cromwell. He took certain steps on his own initiative. For example, on 25 April he wrote a letter to the commissioners for propagating the Bible in Wales, advising them 'to go on cheerfully in the work as formerly', even though the Rump had let lapse the statute which had established the commission, another signal of that Parliament's lamentable lack of reformist zeal.[60] However, both Cromwell's own actions in the weeks after the ejection of the Rump and his accounts of this period presented in later speeches suggest that, although his was the guiding hand, he did not act alone. Indeed, he went out of his way to stress that he had shied away from the exercise of 'boundless' power, unlimited and undivided. He suggested that he had been uneasy when the army had effectively seized political power and that he and his colleagues had been anxious to relinquish that power to a civilian government, emphasizing that the army had intervened 'not to grasp after the power ourselves, to keep it in a military hand, no not for a day'. Instead, Cromwell reflected in July, they had 'voluntarily and out of sense of duty divested themselves of authority and devolved the government into the hands of others'.[61] But more than this, Cromwell expressed a sense of personal unease at his own position, stressing his sense of relief when a new form of government was devised and when he was able to divest himself of the power which had fallen to him in April:

> I say, that as a principal end in calling that assembly was the settlement of the nation, so a chief end to myself was, that I might have opportunity to lay down the power that was in my hands. I say to you again, in the presence of that God who hath blessed and been with me in all my adversities and successes, that was as to myself my greatest end. A desire perhaps, and I am afraid sinful enough, to be quit of the power God had most providentially put into my hand, before he called for it, and before those honest ends of our fighting were attained and settled.[62]

Almost as soon as the Rump and its Council had gone, Cromwell began working with two bodies to reconstruct government. During the last week of April, he consulted a small number of confidants. On 29 April this group, now called a Council of State, began holding more formal and recorded meetings. Designed as a temporary body, to help keep governmental and administrative affairs running until a long-term government could be devised and established, it was in existence for around nine weeks, until 4 July. It comprised at first ten, later thirteen members, a mixture of senior army officers and leading civilian politicians, many formerly Rump MPs. Cromwell himself was an active member, attending roughly half the 106 recorded meetings. Moreover, most of the other members seem to have been personally or professionally close to him and it is notable that the published declaration, dated 30 April, which announced the establishment of this new Council of State, was issued in Cromwell's name alone; the text implies that the initiative was largely Cromwell's. The Council of State proved to be a very active body, handling a broad range of domestic business, important and routine. In contrast, it had only a very limited role in diplomacy, foreign policy and military affairs and was not involved in the long-term constitutional settlement.

The constitutional settlement rested with a second body, the Council of Officers, the assembly of senior officers. There is some evidence that, at this stage, it comprised captains and above and that between thirty and forty officers generally attended meetings. As Lord General, Cromwell would have been in the chair. The Council of Officers did not keep formal records, few unofficial accounts of the meetings of April to June 1653 survive and we know of its activities only through brief references in newsletters. Accordingly, we cannot reconstruct Cromwell's role within the Council in any detail. We do know that the Council was debating the future settlement within a few days of the Rump's ejection and that, after some divisions, it resolved to establish an assembly possessing supreme power, executive as well as legislative. Although the members of this assembly would represent counties or groups of counties, they were to be nominated, not elected. However, the Council of Officers envisaged this as a medium-term arrangement, not a permanent solution, for it was hoped that this assembly or its nominated successor would then make way for a more traditional elected parliament at some future point, perhaps in the mid- or late 1650s. The 140 members of this assembly were chosen by the Council of Officers. In a much later speech, and one in which Cromwell made a number of dubious assertions, he claimed that he had personally nominated very few members. By early June the membership had been agreed and writs were issued. The assembly, called variously the Nominated Assembly, Barebone's Parliament, the Little Parliament or the Parliament of Saints, met on 4 July.

Cromwell formally opened the Nominated Assembly by delivering one of his great state speeches, a two-hour oration delivered in the uncomfortably hot and crowded Council chamber at Whitehall. He began by reminding his audience of 'that series of providences, wherein the Lord hitherto hath dispensed wonderful things to these nations, from the beginning of our troubles to this very day'. This entailed a fairly brief review of events from the outbreak of the civil war down to the battle of Worcester. Cromwell made 1648 the highlight of this review, referring to it as 'the most memorable year . . . that ever this nation saw'. Cromwell was undoubtedly using the old-style calendar, thus encompassing March 1648 to March 1649 by modern reckoning, the period of the second civil war and also of the trial and execution of the King and the establishment of the republic. Cromwell then moved on to discuss in more detail the shortcomings of the Rump in the period after September 1651, providing a very long justification for his own and the army's stance during this period and their intervention in April 1653. Finally, and more briefly, he outlined in general terms the role which the Nominated Assembly was to play. Here Cromwell was at his most emotional, speaking in tones of exaltation, intensely aware of God's hand at work – 'truly you are called by God to rule with him and for him, and you are called to be faithful with the Saints, who have been somewhat instrumental to your call'. It was, he felt, 'a day of the power of Christ', a day when 'Jesus Christ shall be owned', and suggested that 'something is at the door. We are at the threshold', phrases redolent with millenarian enthusiasm. He told the new members that they had been selected on the basis of their 'faith in Jesus Christ and love unto all his Saints and people' and that they were 'as like the forming of God as ever people were'. He urged them to observe the truth and mercy of God, to propagate the Gospel and to be tolerant of and 'respect' all the 'Saints', even those 'of different judgments'. Indeed, at this point, Cromwell issued another eloquent plea for liberty of conscience:

> Therefore I beseech you ... have a care of the whole flock. Love all the sheep, love the lambs, love all, and tender all, and cherish all, and countenance all in all things that are good. And if the poorest Christian, the most mistaken Christian, should desire to live peaceably and quietly under you, soberly and humbly desire to lead a life in godliness and honesty, let him be protected.

Cromwell closed by stressing that the Assembly was now 'the supreme authority', for not only was he relinquishing all political power to it but also the existing Council of State was at its disposal. On the other hand, he stressed both in his speech and in a written 'Instrument' which he had signed on behalf of the Council of Officers, that the Assembly was to be of strictly limited duration and was to work toward a time when the people had imbibed God's message sufficiently to permit a return to elected parliaments.[63]

The Assembly was designed to sit until 3 November 1654, a life-span of sixteen months. In reality, it survived little more than five, until December 1653. One of its earliest decisions was to co-opt a handful of senior army officers, including Cromwell, as members. Equally, Cromwell was appointed to the Assembly's first Council of State, which absorbed and superseded the Council established at the end of April, and to its short-lived second Council, appointed in November. In practice, Cromwell chose to sit neither in the Assembly nor in its Council, reportedly giving a cool answer to an unofficial delegation of members which urged him to attend. Indeed, Cromwell seems to have played a very low-key role during this period, avoiding direct involvement in government and politics. As Lord General, he remained in charge of army business, though his active campaigning was over. He appears to have remained in London, from where he wrote or signed a stream of official letters springing from his offices of Lord General and Chancellor of the University of Oxford. There are indications in newsletters and some diplomatic dispatches that Cromwell was continuing, behind the scenes, to take an active interest in diplomacy, trying to speed and to smooth the ending of hostilities with several European states and to conclude further alliances. The self-important Whitelocke, for example, recorded in his published *Memoirs* several meetings with Cromwell during the early autumn, during which Cromwell flatteringly and at length successfully sought to persuade Whitelocke to serve as ambassador to Sweden.

Although Cromwell seems to have left the work of governing to the Assembly, he was certainly well aware of political developments. To Cromwell, as to many inside and outside the army, the Assembly soon proved to be a grave disappointment, and the euphoria of Cromwell's speech of 4 July turned to dust. Although some solid reforms were accomplished, the Assembly became riven by factionalism. In the process, some much-needed reforms were lost or become hopelessly bogged down, while other very radical or ill-thought-out measures were pushed through. A sense of unease, dejection, even personal failure, comes out very clearly in Cromwell's letter to Fleetwood of 22 August, though his disappointment with the Assembly was tempered by hopes that God would give him strength:

> Truly I never more needed all helps from my Christian friends than now! Fain would I have my service accepted of the saints (if the Lord will), but it is not so. Being of different judgments, and of each sort most seeking to propagate their own, that spirit of kindness that is to them all, is hardly accepted of any. I hope I can say it, my life has been a willing sacrifice, and I hope, [word missing] for them all. Yet it much falls out as when the two Hebrews were rebuked: you know upon whom they turned their displeasure. But the Lord is wise, and will, I trust, make manifest that I am no enemy. Oh, how easy is mercy to be abused: Persuade friends with you to be very sober. If the day of the Lord be so near (as some say), how should our moderation appear. If every one (instead of contending) would justify his form of judgment by love and meekness, Wisdom would be justified of her children. But, alas, I am, in my temptation, ready to say, Oh, would I had wings like a dove, then would I, &c. but this, I fear, is my haste. I bless the Lord I have somewhat keeps me alive, some sparks of the light of His countenance, and some sincerity above man's judgment. Excuse me thus unbowelling myself to you: pray for me, and desire my friends to do so also.[64]

Dismayed by the ability of the radicals during November and early December to push ahead with quite sweeping changes, especially to the ministry, the moderate members of the Assembly decided to end proceedings. By a prearranged plan, on 12 December they brought the Nominated Assembly to an end via a written resignation, soon bearing the signatures of a clear majority of members, which returned their power and authority to Cromwell as Lord General. According to a contemporary report, Cromwell was surprised at the arrival of the delegation of members and their resignation, and in the following September he assured the next Parliament, 'and I can say it in the presence of divers persons here, that do know whether I lie in that, that I did not know one tittle of that resignation, until they all came and brought it, and delivered it into my hands'. In the same speech, he spoke ruefully but very briefly of the Nominated Assembly, which gave 'such a disappointment to our hopes'; 'it hath much teaching in it, and I hope will make us all wiser for the future'.[65] In another speech, delivered a few days earlier, he had been much fuller in outlining the Assembly's shortcomings. He was almost certainly referring to the Assembly, when he spoke of the legal and social chaos which over-zealous idealism would unleash:

> Notions will hurt none but them that have them. But when they come to such practices, – as to tell us, that liberty and property are not the badges of the kingdom of Christ, and tell us that instead of regulating laws, laws are to be abrogated, indeed subverted, and perhaps would bring in the Judaical law instead of our known laws settled amongst us, – this is worthy every magistrate's consideration, especially where every stone is turned to bring confusion.[66]

In an angry outburst to the army officers in 1657, Cromwell was reportedly very bitter about the Assembly, alleging that its main concern was to 'fly at liberty and property', that the members, though 'honest', 'could not governe' and were likely to destroy 'ministry and propriety' – 'if one man had twelve cows, they held another that wanted cows ought to take a share with his neighbour. Who could have said any thing was their own, if they had gone on?'[67] A few months later, in April 1657, Cromwell was more measured in his account, talking more in sorrow than in anger, referring to the Assembly as 'a story of my own weakness and folly'. The Assembly had been established in good faith, but the system proved imperfect and the situation too complex – 'the issue was not answerable to the simplicity and honesty of the design'.[68]

Cromwell's claim that he had no hand in the Assembly's decision to resign or any prior knowledge of it was probably strictly true, though some historians are sceptical and see this as another example of duplicity. Cromwell had been involved in discussions during the autumn about the possible form of a new government. These discussions were highly confidential, but the evidence of newsletters and diplomatic dispatches suggests that, dissatisfied with the Assembly and aware that it might collapse well before November 1654, a group of senior officers began drafting a new written constitution which might replace the Assembly. Although not involved in the drafting process – 'I was not privy to their councels', Cromwell later claimed[69] – as the document took shape, he was consulted on one or more occasions, probably in the latter half of November. According to a few contemporary and slightly later reports, at this stage the draft constitution envisaged making Cromwell king. However, unwilling to accept the crown or to be a party to the destruction of the Assembly, Cromwell rejected the proposals. But the existence of the draft constitution enabled events to move swiftly in the wake of the Assembly's resignation, for in the days immediately thereafter, the draft constitution was amended, accepted by Cromwell and agreed upon as the foundation for a new government. On the afternoon of 16 December Cromwell was inaugurated as Lord Protector under the terms and conditions of the new written constitution. The obscure country gentleman of 1640 had become head of state.

The five years from 1649 to 1653 had, for Cromwell, been marked by mixed fortunes. In military terms, he had led broadly successful campaigns in Ireland and Scotland, been promoted to Lord General of the army and had, unwillingly perhaps, used his military power to eradicate flaws in the political system. On the other hand, neither the Irish nor the Scottish campaign was faultless, for both had at times failed in their objective or been very expensive in parliamentarian as well as enemy blood, and in both countries there were signs of age and illness taking a toll on Cromwell. In the political sphere, neither of Cromwell's two goals, the achievement of healing and settling and the promotion of godly reformation, had made much headway, and high hopes had repeatedly turned to dust. Yet, although at times he was depressed, Cromwell had not lost faith in God, in his desire to do God's will and in the belief that he had the power and the understanding to execute the Lord's wishes. If mortal frames of government proved imperfect and unable to promote the cause, they must be and were replaced, if necessary through the regrettable but – he hoped and expected – ultimately beneficial process of direct military intervention. Each time,

Plate 1 The bronze statue of Cromwell, sculpted by Sir Hamo Thornycroft and completed in 1899, the tercentenary of Cromwell's birth, stands on a grand plinth in front of the Palace of Westminster. *A. F. Kersting.*

Plate 2 A contemporary engraving of the richly dressed wax and wood effigy of Cromwell which lay in state at Somerset House in autumn 1658. Notice that a crown rests on a chair beyond the effigy's head. *Fotomas Index.*

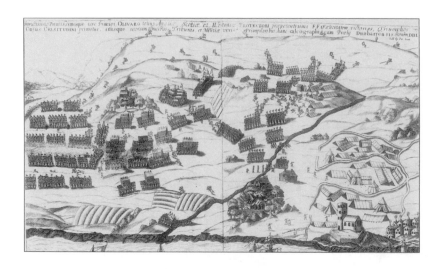

Plate 3 A somewhat stylized contemporary representation of the battle of Dunbar of 3 September 1650. Cromwell's camp is shown on the right, on low ground close to the town. Having crossed the small valley and burn, the parliamentary cavalry and infantry are engaging and breaking the Scottish army on the slopes of Doon Hill. *Fotomas Index.*

Plate 4 Basing House, the strongly fortified medieval and Tudor Palace, as it appeared towards the end of the parliamentary siege, with parts already rendered semi-ruinous by the parliamentary bombardment. The buildings were sacked and burned after Cromwell successfully stormed them in October 1645. *Fotomas Index.*

Plate 5 Perhaps the grandest Elizabethan house in England, Burghley House was the scene of one of Cromwell's earliest military actions. In July 1643 he bombarded the house and its small royalist garrison; when he then threatened to storm the place, the King's men surrendered the house on terms. *A. F. Kersting.*

Plate 6 The coinage of the Protectorate featured an imperial bust of Cromwell, complete with a laurel wreath about his head, engraved by Thomas Simon. On the reverse, the lion rampant, the insignia of the Protector's family, appears between the cross of St George, the Scottish saltire and the Irish harp. *Reproduced by kind permission of the trustees of the British Museum.*

Plate 7 Cromwell's personal powder flask, richly inlaid with ivory, amber and mother of pearl, and decorated with astronomical images. *Cromwell Museum, Huntingdon.*

Plate 8 Cromwell's large dark felt hat. This was probably the hat which he wore to Parliament on 20 April 1653 and which he removed when he rose and dismissed the Rump. *Cromwell Museum, Huntingdon.*

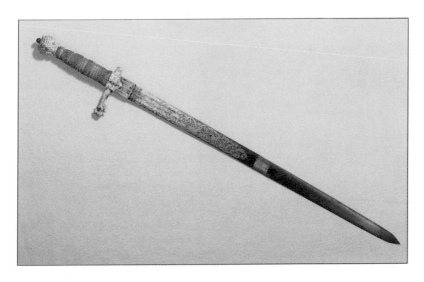

Plate 9 The ornate sword of state, probably made during the Protectorate and perhaps dating from 1654. *Cromwell Museum, Huntingdon.*

Plate 10 A full length portrait of Cromwell, probably by Robert Walker and dating from the late 1640s. Although Walker more often showed Cromwell three-quarter length, the general stance of the figure and appearance of the face here are very similar to those of the more familiar Walker portraits.
Cromwell Museum, Huntingdon.

Plate 11 Samuel Cooper's water-colour miniature, perhaps the most striking likeness of Cromwell to survive, was probably painted in the early 1650s. It appears unfinished, and may have served as a 'master' from which numerous copies and derivatives were taken. *The Duke of Buccleuch and Queensberry/Bridgeman Art Library.*

Plate 12 In one of the most attractive surviving likenesses, Cromwell is shown on horseback with London and the Thames in the background. An inscription which accompanies the painting suggests that it is a representation of Cromwell in the early 1650s, when he was both governor of Ireland and chancellor of Oxford University.
Cromwell Museum, Huntingdon.

Plate 13 Robert Cromwell, father of Oliver, who died in 1617. In his will he wrote that he had been 'taught by large experience in others that man's life in his sound and perfect health is like a bubble of water'. *Cromwell Museum, Huntingdon.*

Plate 14 Elizabeth Cromwell, mother of Oliver, seems to have remained very close to her only surviving son during her long widowhood. She died at Whitehall in autumn 1654, in her ninetieth year. Artist unknown. *Cromwell Museum, Huntingdon.*

Plate 15 Elizabeth Cromwell, wife of Oliver, a portrait attributed to Sir Peter Lely. The 'Lady Protectress' survived her husband and spent her last years living quietly in Northamptonshire. *Cromwell Museum, Huntingdon.*

Plate 16 Richard Cromwell, the elder of the two sons of Oliver who survived him, ingloriously succeeding his father as Lord Protector. His eight months in power were followed by more than half a century in exile on the Continent and (from 1680) in retirement in England. He died in Cheshunt, Hertfordshire, in 1712, only two years before the end of the Stuart dynasty. *Cromwell Museum, Huntingdon.*

Plate 17 In May 1647 Cromwell and other senior officer MPs conferred with officers of the New Model Army at the Sun Inn, Saffron Walden. The late medieval building, extended in the seventeenth century, is decorated with elaborate plasterwork known as pargeting. *A. F. Kersting.*

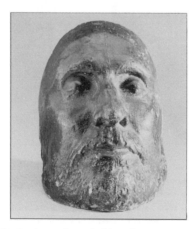

Plate 18 Cromwell's death mask probably taken on or soon after 3 September 1658 and used to create the wax face of the effigy which subsequently lay in state during the autumn and which played a central role during the state funeral of November. *Cromwell Museum, Huntingdon.*

rely very largely upon the string of speeches which he gave during the Protectorate, usually on formal state occasions, and often to his two Protectorate Parliaments. That historians draw so heavily upon them reflects the limited nature of the alternative, bureaucratic and impersonal, sources.

Secondly, and in part arising from this, it becomes difficult to focus upon Cromwell himself. We know where he lived, a little about his private life, health and family, but a purely personal picture would omit many key issues and questions concerning Protector and Protectorate. Cromwell was now head of state, and to understand Lord Protector Cromwell, it is essential to explore the operation of central government. Twin dangers lurk. The governmental sources are oblique and it is difficult to discover precisely the role which Cromwell played in government and to reconstruct the degree to which he initiated and moulded policies. It is tempting simply to assume that the Lord Protector and the Protectoral central government were one, and that all policies and developments of these years stemmed from Cromwell himself. Based upon that assumption, it would be possible to explore the last years of Cromwell's life via accounts of the key policy areas of the period 1653–8. However, that would shift the emphasis away from biography and toward impersonal political history. Moreover, the assumption upon which it is based – that, as Lord Protector, Cromwell exercised vast political and governmental power and personally ran the state – may not be accurate.

From the inauguration ceremony to his state funeral, the Protector was consistently projected as the conspicuous figurehead of government, ensconced in palaces, surrounded by an increasingly elaborate court, appointing many officials and distributing honours, receiving ambassadors and other dignitaries, opening and closing parliaments and presiding on state occasions. He was invested with much of the pomp, trappings, duties and ceremonials of an early modern monarch. Although Cromwell always retained an air of simplicity and modesty which contrasted sharply with many Stuart monarchs, as Protector he did adopt more formal, ceremonial ways. In February 1651 he had reacted with horror to a proposal that his likeness appear on a medal commemorating the victory at Dunbar, 'earnestly beseech[ing]' that an image of Parliament appear in place of his own.[1] During the Protectorate, however, a head and shoulders profile with an imperial air, complete with a laurel wreath, featured on coins and medals.

Although several former royal residences were placed at Cromwell's disposal, as Protector he lived in just two palaces: Whitehall and Hampton Court. In April 1654 he and his immediate family took up residence in a newly decorated and refurnished suite of rooms in the heart of Whitehall Palace, which remained his principal residence throughout the Protectorate. Hampton Court was used only intermittently at first, but as the Protectorate wore on Cromwell travelled there with increasing frequency and regularity, often spending weekends at this semi-rural retreat. Again, he and his family made use of the principal rooms, and much of the furnishings and works of art which adorned them were drawn from the former royal collection; other pieces were newly acquired or commissioned. At both palaces Cromwell and his family were attended by an expanding household, structured along regal lines, with departmental heads and subordinate officers and departments, some largely honorific, some functional. Both palaces were the venue for formal state occasions, especially entertaining and granting audiences to foreign diplomats, as well as less formal, family occasions, including wedding entertainments for his two youngest daughters in 1657. Cromwell occasionally visited the City and probably viewed naval vessels on the Thames, but there is little indication that he left the London area during the Protectorate.

As well as undertaking state duties at Whitehall Palace and Hampton Court, Cromwell also played a central role in many of the ceremonies held in London during the Protectorate. He opened and closed parliamentary sessions, and from time to time he was richly entertained by the lord mayor and aldermen. On such occasions, he travelled by coach in some style. Perhaps the most important ceremonies were those held to inaugurate the regime. That of 16 December 1653, formally opening the Protectorate, was quite simple, and Cromwell attended dressed in a plain black suit. In June 1657, when the Protectorate was formally re-inaugurated, the ceremony was more elaborate. Cromwell, dressed in an ermine-lined 'mantle of estate' and wearing a richly jewelled sword, headed a stately procession comprising gentlemen of the bedchamber and other household officers, as well as the Speaker and clerk of the House, MPs, the lord mayor and aldermen, members of the Council, a few of the old nobility, a handful of foreign envoys and a range of civic and judicial officers. The principal ceremony took place on a raised dais in Westminster Hall and featured a canopied chair of state – probably the coronation chair used at regal coronations since the fourteenth century – a richly gilt bible, several swords of state and a golden sceptre. Most of the traditional elements of a regal coronation were present in June 1657, save only the anointing and the crowning. It is possible that a new crown was made around this time but played no part in the ceremony. A crown did, however, feature in the funereal ceremonies of autumn 1658.

There were other signs of Cromwell's enhanced status. Immediately upon becoming Protector, he ceased using his surname as part of his signature and – even on personal letters – signed himself 'Oliver P', standing for 'Oliver Protector', clearly copying the style used by the reigning monarch. He also possessed and used a Protectoral seal. It quickly became the established practice to address Cromwell as 'His Highness' or 'Your Highness' and those admitted to his presence generally approached him with due deference and respect, a courtesy returned in full measure. By 1655–6 it was becoming common to refer to the Protectoral Council of State as the 'Privy Council', a style formalized in the 1657 constitution, which spoke of 'the Privy Council of Your Highness'. Throughout the Protectorate, though with increasing frequency in 1657–8, Cromwell created new knights, over thirty of them in total. In the last two years of the Protectorate, he also created a dozen new baronets and two new hereditary peers. In 1657 he nominated over sixty people to the new parliamentary second chamber, though these positions did not carry a formal title of honour.

Cromwell served as head of state with some aplomb, and even critics of the man and the regime tended grudgingly to concede that he bore himself with dignity when performing his official duties. He was by far the most visible and prominent element of the Protectoral regime and it is understandable that many contemporary commentators assumed that in all important matters Cromwell was the government. Accordingly, there has been a tendency to ascribe to him almost unlimited powers and to assume that virtually alone, or at least with no more than pliant servants about him, Cromwell ran the Protectoral regime. How far is this interpretation valid?

The starting point must be the written constitutions. The Instrument of Government established a permanent, well-defined and powerful executive and an assured and regular succession of parliaments entrusted with wide legislative powers. In an attempt to avoid renewed conflicts between the two, the constitution also laid out a series of checks and balances to encourage co-operation and to prevent one arm exercising too much power in isolation from, or against the wishes of, the other. The two arms were drawn together by the Lord Protector, who was to oversee and work with both. Although the Humble Petition later modified certain elements and placed more emphasis upon the role of parliament, in essence the structure of government established in December 1653 remained unaltered until spring 1659.[2]

Cromwell's image as a powerful and at times dazzling Lord Protector was not entirely without constitutional foundation. Under the Instrument, he was appointed for life and could be removed only by death; there was no provision for forcible dismissal or voluntary resignation. Similarly, he was guaranteed a modest annual income, safe from reduction or interference by any other institution, parliament included. All government documents were to run in the Protector's name and all magistracy and honours were 'derived' from him. He had extensive powers of pardon, could delay and veto parliamentary bills and had power to dissolve parliament once a set minimum period had expired. The final choice of a new Councillor would be his, though from a shortlist of two selected by others. Existing public lands were 'vested' in him and his successors. Possibly because of a drafting error, the Instrument also gave him sole power to 'dispose and order' the regular armed forces when no parliament was sitting. The revised constitution of 1657 modified some of these provisions. As Protector for life, Cromwell gained the right to name his successor, to command the county militias and trained bands, to declare war and make peace, and to select the founder members of the new parliamentary 'other House' and of the Privy Council – though thereafter he had only a limited voice in filling vacancies – and he gained greater freedom in deciding when parliaments should be summoned. Crucial as some of these powers were, many vital areas of government, particularly finance, new taxation, appointment to senior offices of state and command over the armed forces, lay outside the reach of the Lord Protector acting alone.

On paper, Cromwell was forced to work with other institutions to establish a powerful central government. Clause after clause of both constitutions laid down that the Protector could exercise certain key powers only with the advice and consent of parliament or Council. Alone, Cromwell could do little, but Protector and parliament or Protector and Council together were given wide powers and would be able efficiently and effectively to run the country. Alone, both parliament and Council were themselves vested with limited powers. Parliament was to meet every three years at most, to remain in session for at least a set minimum period, to exercise apparently extensive legislative functions, and also to play a prominent role in filling vacancies in the Council and in its own 'other House'. However, the Protector was given effectively an unlimited power to veto parliamentary bills and a completely free hand to dissolve parliament once the minimum period had elapsed. Under the Instrument, the Council, too, was given certain powers of its own – to examine and possibly exclude MPs, to reduce a shortlist of candidates for Council vacancies and to elect a new Protector on the death of the old – which it lost under the revised constitution of 1657. But throughout the Protectorate, the real power of parliament and Council lay in their role as a check upon the Protector, their ability to prevent the Protector acting unless he first obtained their advice and consent, and their authority to work with the Protector to oversee vital areas of government. How did these provisions work in practice?

As Protector, Cromwell worked with two Parliaments, the first from September 1654 to January 1655, the second from September 1656 to June 1657, with a brief second session in January to February 1658. Relations between Protector and Parliament were not always harmonious and these Parliaments were often divided over specific issues and developments, as well as over the constitution and constitutional revision. None the less, there is evidence that Cromwell did abide by the terms of the Instrument in seeking Parliament's advice and consent. For example, Cromwell presented to the first Protectorate Parliament the names of those recently appointed to senior offices of state for approval or rejection. For their part, MPs approved the list swiftly and without a murmur. Again, in autumn 1654, Cromwell's agents in the House raised foreign policy, particularly the preparation of the so-called 'Western Design', an expedition to attack and seize Spanish colonies in the West Indies. MPs expressed no disapproval and instead respectfully agreed to leave the matter to Protector and Council. By 1656, this had flared up into a naval and colonial war against the Spanish, a matter which Cromwell laid before his second Protectorate Parliament, inviting MPs to debate the situation. Once more, the sitting MPs were supportive and approved the Spanish war *nemine contradicente* after a brief debate in which hardly a word of criticism was apparently uttered. Cromwell laid detailed accounts of state finance before both Parliaments. He generally did not raise money other than in the ways and for the purposes approved in the written constitution, and instead turned to Parliament to grant additional sums, especially in 1656–7 to help finance the Spanish war. In his dealings with the legislature, Cromwell only rarely exceeded the powers given him under the constitution, and in practice he generally sought Parliament's advice and consent where required to do so.

However, it is more valuable to explore Cromwell's relationship with the Council. For most of the Protectorate, no parliament was sitting, and under the constitutions Cromwell was required to share power with, and to be supervised by, the Council. It is difficult accurately to assess the role and relationship of Protector and Council, for the Councillors conducted their business in strict secrecy. Commentators and diplomats knew little about the Council's work and the personal papers of the Councillors are disappointingly discreet. Historians are forced to rely heavily upon the official conciliar documents, principally a series of order books giving a rather dry and clearly incomplete record of meetings held and decisions reached. They do not contain records of debates and there survives a single account of a Council debate, a paper of dubious veracity relating a highly stylized and probably atypical discussion – principally an exchange between Cromwell and John Lambert – on foreign policy. From these sources, it is possible to reconstruct something of the relationship between Protector and Council, but it is a difficult task.

From the order books, we know that Cromwell was present for part or all of 332 (or around 40 per cent) of the 813 recorded meetings. His attendance was surprisingly poor during the first year of the Protectorate and fell away markedly from mid-1657 onwards, presumably because of ill-health. Conversely, he attended well over half the recorded meetings of 1655 and his attendance fell only slightly during 1656. In addition, some newspapers and commentators reveal that unminuted, informal meetings were held at Whitehall or Hampton Court with Cromwell invariably present. That Cromwell frequently attended meetings and consulted Councillors is a sign that he was working closely with the Council, but not that he accepted or acted upon its advice, still less that he was seeking conciliar approval or experiencing conciliar restraints.

In contrast to this general pattern of the Protector's fairly regular attendance at Council meetings, from time to time Cromwell missed most or all recorded sessions for periods of a month or more. Very occasionally, important business was clearly deferred until his return. Usually, however, Cromwell's prolonged absences had no perceptible impact on the range or quantity of business transacted by the Council. Important Council directives had to gain the Protector's assent and Cromwell would thereby retain ultimate control. Key decisions taken in his absence were ineffective until so approved and he would return to find a backlog of orders awaiting him. But the Council nevertheless pressed on, examined an undiminished range of business and took important decisions, apparently unhindered by Cromwell's long absence; such decisions were almost always approved by the Protector upon his return, without renewed discussion or amendment.

Some of Cromwell's own comments on his constitutional position and the efficacy of conciliar restraints have been preserved. On several occasions during the Protectorate, he alluded to his unease in December 1653, when the departure of the Nominated Assembly had left total and potentially corrupting power in his hands – 'I was arbitrary in power, having the armies in the three nations under my command.' In his speeches to Parliament in September 1654, he claimed that he had welcomed the advent of the Protectorate, not only because it clarified his position but also because it included a constitution which limited and carefully defined his powers as Protector, thereby lessening the perceived dangers. He stressed the tight restrictions placed upon him by the written constitution, which 'limited me and bound my hands to act nothing to the prejudice of the nations without consent of a Council until the Parliament met'. He was emphatic that these provisions had been strictly observed during the opening months of the Protectorate – 'This government hath been exercised by a Council, with a desire to be faithful in all things' – and he underlined the crucial role which the Council played, particularly when Parliament was not sitting:

the Council are the trustees of the Commonwealth, in all intervals of Parliaments; who have as absolute a negative upon the supreme officer in the said intervals, as the Parliament hath whilst it is sitting. It cannot be made use of, a man cannot be raised nor a penny charged upon the people, nothing can be done without consent of Parliament; and in the intervals of Parliament, without consent of the Council it is not to be exercised . . . there is very little power, none but what is co-ordinate, in the supreme officer . . . he is bound in strictness by the Parliament, out of Parliament by the Council, that do as absolutely bind him, as the Parliament, when Parliament is sitting.

In his speech opening the second Protectorate Parliament, Cromwell consistently used the first person plural when reviewing government actions, not in this case the royal 'we', but an almost unconscious recognition of the Councillors' close co-operation. Halfway through the speech he suddenly realized that his audience may not have understood the reference – 'We did find out – I mean, myself and the Council.' In spring 1657, by which time Cromwell had become very critical of aspects of the Instrument, he commented, 'I was a child in its swaddling clouts. I cannot transgress by the Government. I can do nothing but in ordination with the Council.'[3]

Such statements could have been hypocrisy or deception, to impress MPs and others. Similarly, Cromwell's reported claims that he had been prevented from fulfilling certain promises, such as a pledge to abolish tithes by September 1654 – 'for his part, he could not do it, for he was but one, and his Councel alledge it is not fitt to take them away'[4] – may have been false images to cover his own failure or disinclination to act. If so, the duplicity ran very deep. Two of the most important conciliar restraints imposed upon the head of state by the revised 1657 constitution were not contained within the Humble Petition passed by Parliament in May. Instead they sprang from a 'paper of objections', a list of suggested amendments to the constitution, submitted to Parliament, accepted by the House and embodied in the Additional Petition of June. The paper is in the hand of Secretary of State John Thurloe, but it carries many corrections and additions penned by the Protector himself and Cromwell was probably the driving force behind the entire document. It is inconceivable that such fundamental changes would have emanated from a secretary of state alone. Thus it was almost certainly Cromwell himself who suggested that, during the intervals between parliaments, the Protector should require the Council's consent before making appointments to senior offices of state. Nowhere had the Humble Petition empowered the Council to supervise state finance and the Protector's use of the military budget, and it was Cromwell's paper which first suggested that 'the money directed to be for supply of the sea and land forces be issued by the advice of the Council.' On 21 April, in a speech to a parliamentary committee outlining his suggested revisions, the Protector spoke at length about state finance, commenting that 'it will be a safety to whomsoever is your supreme Magistrate, as well as security to the public, that the monies might be issued out by the advice of the Council.' Once more, Cromwell appeared uneasy, almost fearful, at the prospect of exercising wide, unsupervised and potentially corrupting power.[5]

Neither of Cromwell's Protectorate Parliaments seems to have viewed conciliar – or parliamentary – restraints upon the head of state enshrined within a written constitution as a worthless sham. Although strongly critical of the Instrument and keen to draft a revised constitution of its own, the first Protectorate Parliament retained the concept of an advisory and restraining Council within its own revised draft constitution, giving the Council temporary or permanent joint control over finance, appointment to senior offices, foreign policy, diplomacy, the conclusion of peace and command of the armed forces. Over two years later, the second Protectorate Parliament followed much the same lines, and Cromwell's amendments incorporated in the Additional Petition merely strengthened the already extensive supervisory role ascribed to the Council in the Humble Petition. The Council's role had already been enhanced during the early spring, as the House debated and revised the draft document. The diaries and other accounts of the two Parliaments reveal no sweeping attacks on the existing Council, scepticism about its role, or broad condemnation of conciliar restraints upon the Protector as an ineffective paper sham.

We can reconstruct something of the Council's role and relationship with the Protector in the handling of a few important items of business. For example, a variety of sources throw considerable light on the exclusion of MPs from the two Protectorate Parliaments. The Instrument authorized the Council to examine newly elected MPs and to exclude from the House those who fell outside the qualifications listed elsewhere in the constitution. This was one of the few powers given to the Council alone and, on paper, the Protector had no say. In 1654 the Council used their powers very sparingly. From mid-August until the eve of the Parliament, the Council considered up to twenty elections, though in the end, less than a dozen MPs were excluded, mostly indiscreet royalists, and in 1654 pre-session exclusions never became a major issue. Cromwell appears to have played little or no part in the process, for the Council's own records and contemporary reports suggest that the approval of MPs and the issuing of admission tickets was the work of the Council, and no mention is made of Cromwell's participation. Moreover, Cromwell was rarely present at the formal Council meetings at which this process must have been under way, attending just five of the twenty-five meeting recorded in the three weeks preceding the Parliament. He was absent on 1 and 2 September, when the Council committee examining specific cases presented its findings and when final decisions to admit or exclude were probably taken. In two cases we have more tangible evidence. Some of the inhabitants of Ely complained against the election of one of their MPs, initially in a petition addressed and presented to the Protector. Cromwell graciously received it but then merely referred it to the Council. It was as a consequence of a second petition, drawn up a week later and addressed directly to the Council, that the complainants secured a hearing before the Council's electoral committee and were able to have the MP excluded. Clearer still was the response to a petition from some of the inhabitants of Bristol, seeking to have both of the city's newly elected MPs disqualified. They first approached Cromwell, only to be told politely but firmly that he could do nothing in this matter and that they must address their complaints to the Council. They did so, though in this case without success. The pre-session exclusion of MPs in 1654 seems to have been handled by the Council alone, not by Protector and Council, and Cromwell was apparently anxious that others should know he had no hand in it.

In September 1656 the terms of the Instrument were employed to devastating effect to bar around one hundred political opponents and undesirables from the second Protectorate Parliament. Although the Council order books rarely mention exclusions, they do record a Council order of 15 September to exclude one of the Lincolnshire MPs and a request of 28 August that all Councillors attend to dispatch important – but unspecified – business concerning the forthcoming Parliament. The frequent and well-attended Council meetings of early and mid-September were probably given over to examining evidence against MPs. No one was better placed than Secretary Thurloe to know the truth. On 16 September he wrote that 'the councell, upon consideration of the elections, have refused to admitt of neare 100 of those, who are chosen', and in a separate, undated note he confirmed that the Councillors had fulfilled their constitutional obligation to examine and exclude MPs and stood 'ready to give an account of their proceedings thereupon, when they shall be required thereunto by his Highness or the parliament'.[6] Once the session opened, sitting MPs attacked the Council for the exclusions and called upon Councillors to explain their actions. In the course of defending exclusions in the House on 22 September, Councillor Nathaniel Fiennes repeatedly stressed that the action had been taken by the Council – the Council was empowered to do this, the Council had examined and excluded MPs, the Council had taken care to exclude no one unfairly – and made no mention of the Protector being involved in any way. Excluded members were subsequently directed to appeal to the Council for admission and in due course the Councillors did review and reverse several exclusion orders.

Cromwell seems to have played no part in the exclusions and to have been disturbed by their extent. On 9 September Thurloe directed Henry Cromwell to detain and thus exclude an Irish MP, calmly adding in passing, 'I have not had tyme to acquaint his Highness with it.'[7] In an angry outburst to army officers in February 1657, Cromwell was bitterly scornful of the mass exclusions and stressed that he had had no part in them, though surviving accounts of the speech have him ascribing responsibility to the officers themselves rather than to the Council. Perhaps George Courthope was more accurate when he reported Cromwell's declaration in spring 1657 that exclusion 'was an act of the Council's, and that he did not concern himself in it'.[8] Certainly, Cromwell had been absent from most Council sessions during September 1656, including all those held in the week before the opening of Parliament at which the exclusion orders had probably been issued. It is tempting to see Cromwell's poor attendance at Council during September – present at just four of the nineteen recorded meetings, compared to seventeen of the twenty-four held in July and August and fourteen of the seventeen held in October and November – as signs of his distaste for, and wish to distance himself from, the process of mass exclusion pursued by his Council.

The power to call the second Protectorate Parliament lay with the Protector, though under the constitution he was to act only 'with the advice of the major part of the Council'. Between them, they eventually decided to call a parliament in an attempt to stem the regime's growing debts, though only after several weeks of debate, during which alternative courses were probably explored. Cromwell was present at most of the frequent and well-attended Council sessions of the first half of May, and he and his Councillors also held a number of informal and unminuted meetings around this time. Despite the order books' silence, other sources suggest that Protector and Council were deeply divided over the various options available, with one group favouring summoning another parliament and laying the issue before the legislature, another – including Cromwell – fiercely opposed to it and advocating purely financial measures, such as an increase in assessments, to solve the problem. The arguments raged for over a month and although the Venetian ambassador's colourful tales – of Cromwell crying in Council and at one stage decamping to Hampton Court with his allies on the Council in order to get away from other members with whom relations were 'not quite cordial'[9] – may owe much to imagination, it seems that feelings were running high, for both Secretary Thurloe and Councillor Charles Fleetwood speak of long and hot debates preceding the final decision. Although for several weeks Cromwell reportedly resisted an increasing conciliar majority in favour of calling a parliament, during the second week of June he was either won over or gave way, for he issued writs for a new parliament on or around 10 June. The Major-Generals were also meeting in London at the time and doubtless their confidence in controlling elections helped sway the argument, but Thurloe is quite specific that the decision to call a parliament had been taken by 'His Highness and the Counsell'.[10]

Once again, Cromwell's attendance record at Council may indicate something of his feelings towards the Councillors' decision. His repeated absences during June, missing seven of the ten meetings – in marked contrast to May, when he attended assiduously – may have been a response to the Council's rejection of his proposals for a purely financial solution and its insistence on a parliament. That Cromwell had initially opposed calling a parliament but had been pushed into it by others certainly comes across in his later angry outbursts. 'I gave my vote against it' and 'it was against my judgment, but I could have no quietness till [it] was done', he told the army officers in February 1657, though he again apparently laid the blame on the officers themselves.[11] But a year later, in February 1658, he was more accurate in ascribing responsibility – 'as also of his calling this Parliament, whereunto, being advised by his Council, he yielded, though he professed it, in his own judgement, no way seasonable'. Another version of the same speech reports him saying that 'He was against the calling of the late Parliament. But the Councell urged it soe.'[12]

There is, then, evidence that Cromwell abided by the restrictions which the constitutions placed upon his actions and powers. In key areas, including the making of war, state finance and appointment of senior state officers, he sought and obtained parliamentary consent. More importantly, perhaps, Cromwell worked with the Council and allowed it to play a substantial role in Protectoral central government, handling the highest matters of state as well as the day-to-day mass of routine and administrative business. There are indications that Cromwell sought and obtained the Council's consent where required by the constitution, that he respected the Council's independent powers, even where he disapproved of its use of them, and that occasionally he was deflected from his own preferred path by the Council's persuasion or prohibition. However, this image of Cromwell almost as a prisoner of the constitutions, railed in by restraints, cannot be taken too far, for there are indications that Cromwell was puppeteer far more than he was puppet.

Despite Cromwell's occasional claims to the contrary, it is most unlikely that the Protector was seriously or frequently ensnared by Parliament or Council. Certainly, the legislature had only a very limited capacity to control the head of state. Parliament need be in session for just a few months every three years, it could be dissolved at will as soon as its set minimum period had elapsed, and the Protector had effectively unlimited power to veto its legislation. The Instrument placed restrictions upon who could elect and be elected and it gave the Council sweeping powers to exclude MPs from the House. Both the Protectorate Parliaments were heavily purged by the executive at or near the start of the session. It is more difficult to assess the strength and independence of the Council. The written constitutions laid down complex procedures by which existing Councillors might be removed for alleged corruption and any vacancies arising from death or removal filled, procedures in which the Protector had little or no part. However, it is likely that Cromwell had played a significant role in the choice of the founder members of the Protectorate Council, named within the Instrument of Government itself, and in summer 1657 the Humble Petition left him entirely free to choose the founder members of his Privy Council. In fact, Cromwell chose to reappoint most of the existing Councillors, though he took the opportunity to remove from the Council John Lambert, probably the most powerful and independent member of the Instrument's Council, who had shown most capacity to oppose Cromwell on key issues. It would be unfair to characterize all the other Councillors as weak or second-rate, for they included some of the most senior army officers of the day as well as experienced politicians and administrators and a couple of minor peers. But Cromwell's Council lacked the powerful figures usually found among a Stuart Privy Council, perhaps because it contained none of the major peers of England, the great landed aristocrats who possessed power and sway of their own.

The overwhelming consensus of contemporary opinion, that Cromwell towered over the Protectorate and effectively controlled most aspects of central government, is almost certainly correct in essence. Ultimately, the Protectorate owed its very existence, and Cromwell his position as head of state, to military backing. Until Parliament's revised constitution was adopted in summer 1657, the only explicit endorsement given to the regime came from the army in general and its Council of Officers in particular. The security and survival of the regime depended upon the military, and Cromwell's command as Lord General of a large, experienced and potent standing army hugely enhanced his position, far beyond the powers given him by the paper constitutions. Although occasional ripples of discontent spread through parts of the army, it remained overwhelmingly loyal to Cromwell until his death. The army was deployed to control Scotland and Ireland and, via an active and at times aggressive foreign policy, to ensure that the regime was respected in Europe. Within England and Wales, the army generally played a lesser role, though the presence of up to 15,000 troops stationed in towns and garrisons throughout the country contributed to the domestic peace and order which generally prevailed, and at times the army was actively deployed to crush planned or actual royalist rebellion. The availability of the military arm doubtless encouraged a degree of respect and deference in Parliament and Council alike, though Cromwell only very rarely physically deployed troops to underline his authority in central government. Perhaps the only clear example is his employment of soldiers to ensure that the first Protectorate Parliament was briefly closed on 12 September 1654.

The military presence was not overplayed and it is hard to maintain that, as Protector, Cromwell was running a military dictatorship. With a few exceptions, the established process of law was observed, martial law was not imposed upon civilians, and few military men served as JPs or on central government committees. Even the rule of the Major-Generals, with the division of England and Wales into districts, each headed by a Major-General assisted by commissioners and commanding a newly raised or expanded horse militia, casts only a slightly darker light. The full system, established in October 1655 in response to royalist disturbances, ran for less than a year, for it fell into abeyance in September 1656, with the meeting of the second Protectorate Parliament, and was effectively inoperative long before its formal abolition in January 1657. Moreover, the Major-Generals and their commissioners worked with the existing local government and justice, especially the JPs, they did not supersede them. But these clear indications that, within England and Wales at least, Protector Cromwell flexed his military muscles only lightly and occasionally, should not disguise the fact that a vast military potential was available to Cromwell and that he had reserves of power which elevated him far above paper constitutions.

Many of the key decisions in Protectoral domestic policy seem to have been taken by Cromwell, acting largely or wholly alone. The power to dissolve parliament was his and there are strong indications that the timing and imposition of the dissolutions which ended the two Protectorate Parliaments were determined by Cromwell. In his long dissolution speech of January 1655, Cromwell at no point made explicit or implicit claim that this was a joint decision, reached after consultation with any other individuals or institutions. Instead, he implied that this was a personal response, albeit guided by his care for the welfare of the nation and its people. The circumstances surrounding the dissolution of the second Parliament in February 1658 are even clearer, for several contemporary commentators state that it was a sudden decision of Cromwell alone, which took many senior politicians, including Councillors Fiennes and Fleetwood, the latter by then probably the most prominent and influential member of the Council, completely by surprise. Again, the crucial and potentially very divisive issue of the title of the head of state seems to have been a matter decided by Cromwell. In late autumn 1653 Cromwell reportedly rejected a draft version of the Instrument in part because it then proposed that he be created king. In spring 1657 Parliament's revised constitution initially restored monarchy in the person of King Oliver. There followed several weeks of uncertainty, as Cromwell consulted his own conscience and his God, as well as coming under various external pressures, chiefly military and parliamentary. The final decision, however, was his alone and had a substantial impact upon the shape and nature of the regime. The establishment of the system headed by the Major-Generals was also a long-drawn-out affair, spanning the period August to October 1655. The Council was heavily involved, for the conciliar records indicate that the matter came before the Council several times and they also contain several drafts of the key documents, some of them bearing revisions made in Council. It is also likely that senior army officers were consulted. However, contemporary commentators indicate that Cromwell was closely involved in the process and the fact that – most unusually – the Council all but suspended consideration of the subject during his absence through illness, itself suggests that Cromwell was making a substantial, perhaps guiding, contribution to the business.

Informed contemporary comments about Cromwell's role in the formation of foreign policy are more numerous, though the evidence points in different directions. On the one hand, some diplomats certainly felt that Cromwell's was just one voice among many and ascribed to the Council a key role in foreign business. For example, when in March 1654 the Dutch representatives were presented with a paper agreeing to certain terms in the prospective peace treaty, signed by Cromwell alone, they returned it, 'not considering it valid, and insisting on having it signed in a clearer form by the Council of State'.[13] On several occasions diplomats reported that little progress was being made in foreign policy because the Council was meeting infrequently or had other demands upon its time. Cromwell reportedly told one diplomat that he played little part in the formation of foreign policy, 'that he himself without the council did not use to dispose of such affairs'.[14] Although by 1653 Cromwell was experienced in domestic politics, army politics and relations with Scotland and Ireland, he had had very little direct involvement in international affairs and foreign policy. In contrast, several of the Protectoral Councillors, including Walter Strickland and Secretary Thurloe, possessed far greater experience in this area. The Swedish representatives in London were frequently in contact with Protector and Council, and their surviving dispatches of 1655–6, particularly full and detailed, suggest that Cromwell was not as skilled or confident in negotiating with foreign diplomats as he was in debating with domestic opponents; occasionally, he reportedly appeared hesitant or uncertain, particularly if he had no Councillors or Council brief to guide him. The Swedes often found themselves nego- tiating with selected Councillors, who allegedly from time to time quietly corrected impressions erroneously conveyed by the Protector. It must, however, be noted that the Swedish dispatches, like those of most London-based diplomats, were not always accurate or reliable.

On the other hand, despite his initial inexperience, Cromwell does seem to have taken an active interest in foreign affairs, and during the Protectorate he appears to have devoted considerable time to foreign policy, not least to formal and informal meetings with diplomatic representatives in London. Diplomats not only found themselves frequently in contact with the Protector but also felt it worthwhile attempting to fathom his thoughts, to win his ear or to cultivate his affection. The only purported record of a Council debate to have survived, the highly stylized exchange of July 1654 between Cromwell and Lambert, the former supporting and the latter opposing the proposal to launch an attack on the Spanish colonies, is not above suspicion and may be very inaccurate. None the less, we know from subsequent reports that Cromwell felt personally responsible for the progress of this plan, and particularly shattered by its failure, the Swedish representative reporting that the outcome 'weighs most heavily on the lord protector' for 'he knows that he urged and insisted on this American venture singly, against the desire and consent of his whole council, and so can blame no one but himself'.[15] Cromwell defended and supported the resulting Anglo-Spanish war in his speech at the opening of the second Protectorate Parliament.

If the evidence about Cromwell's precise role and power in Protectoral central government leaves much uncertain, a number of sources, not least Cromwell's own speeches, are clearer about his overall aims and objectives. During the Protectorate, as during the 1650s as a whole, Cromwell seems to have had a number of broad but sometimes conflicting goals. In the wake of the chaos left by the Rump and the Nominated Assembly, Cromwell saw a need for healing and settling, a period of calm, order and good government, during which old wounds would heal, the nation would be united and so be strong, and its people would flourish. This involved the restoration of as many traditional forms as possible without imperilling the cause. Thus Cromwell favoured an assured succession of representative assemblies elected as freely and as widely as the security and survival of the regime would permit and possessed of the fullest measure of power possible without giving Parliament the ability to destroy the regime. As Protector, Cromwell was anxious that his position and the Protectoral constitution as a whole should receive the approval and sanction of the people, signified through Parliament. The failure of the first Protectorate Parliament to grant such approval was a grave disappointment, just as the willingness of the second to draw up an acceptable constitution was a source of considerable relief and satisfaction. Also consistent with this was the moderation and caution apparent during the Protectorate, Cromwell's repeated and patient attempts to win over critics of the regime or at least to secure their peaceful acquiescence, his desire to abide by the traditional processes of law, and the remarkably limited use of imprisonment without trial or of capital punishment against political enemies of the regime. Consistent with this, too, was the slow but steady reduction in the size of the standing army. Not only was the physical presence of the army reduced but so was the military budget, permitting the regime to reduce the high levels of direct taxation inherited in December 1653. Many historians argue that Cromwell's regal ways and court, and his apparent attraction to the offer of the crown in 1657, are also symptomatic of this conservative goal. Some historians have portrayed Cromwell as increasingly reactionary as the Protectorate wore on, progressively shedding the last vestiges of a radical past.

Against this, however, there are many signs that Cromwell held passionately and with barely dimmed enthusiasm to the goal of reformation, to a broad programme of spiritual, moral and social reform, even though that might well arouse opposition, run against traditional forms and thereby undermine the process of healing and settling. During the Protectorate this goal was complex, made up of overlapping elements and often obscurely enunciated in Cromwell's surviving letters and speeches, but it involved reform of the law and of the judicial system, the establishment of more just and efficient administrative machinery and cautious moves towards greater social justice. The overarching and dominant feature was spiritual, bringing the nation closer to God and God's will by ensuring liberty of conscience to all who possessed an element of God's truth, and by employing both civil and spiritual officers to extirpate sin and to promote outward and inward godliness. Cromwell continued to feel tied to the army and inclined closely to observe its mood, for the army had clearly been God's instrument during the civil war and was probably still being used to convey His wishes. This reliance on the army as a spiritual touchstone reinforced the dependence of Protector and regime upon a strong, reasonably large and therefore inevitably costly army as the ultimate guarantor of their survival. Together, this ensured that Cromwell was never able or willing completely to civilianize his regime, or to revert entirely to traditional means and forms. Similarly, and despite the scepticism of some historians, it is unlikely that Cromwell ever completely abandoned or seriously reduced his commitment to godly reformation, even though it, too, would hinder or prevent a return to traditional order and stability. Even in 1657–8 there is a radical edge to many of Cromwell's speeches. He was never satisfied with the status quo.

Yet there are indications that, as the Protectorate wore on, Cromwell lost some of his initial confidence and optimism, and became aware that the way was more difficult and would take longer to traverse than he had initially envisaged. During 1654 he and his Council achieved much in solving or reducing many of the regime's inherited problems and in instituting modest but useful reforms. The Moses-like efforts of Protector and Council were leading God's people out of the wilderness and approaching the Promised Land; one final effort by the first Protectorate Parliament might complete the process of reformation. Alas, the 1654–5 Parliament disappointed Cromwell and there is a sense in the surviving documents that thereafter Cromwell never fully regained a belief in the imminence of the Promised Land. He never abandoned hope and he continued to work for reformation, but the goal had retreated and remained elusive. Further disappointments during 1655 not only served as distractions but also might be interpreted as signs of God's rebuke, suggesting that the regime had gone astray and incurred God's wrath. As ever, Cromwell's response was to attempt to discover precisely how, when and why God's support had been lost, in order that those sins could be purged and the passage towards the Promised Land resumed. A sense of political harmony returned in 1657, with the achievement of more stable relations between Protector and Parliament and the passage of the parliamentary constitution, but the confidence in the imminence of attainment, apparent in 1654, was never fully restored. By the latter half of 1657 old age was taking a toll and during 1658 there were signs of physical decline and drift.

Under the Instrument of Government, there was to be a

period of almost nine months of government by Protector and Council, before the meeting of the first Protectorate Parliament on 3 September 1654, the anniversary of Dunbar and Worcester. The drafters of the Instrument recognized that these months would be particularly difficult, for Protector and Council would have to resolve many issues left unsettled in 1653 and to ensure that sufficient order had been restored by summer 1654 to permit elections to go ahead. At the very least, they would have to do something about a number of temporary parliamentary statutes, due to lapse before September 1654. Accordingly, if a little curiously, the Instrument gave the Protector 'with the consent of the major part of his Council' temporary power down to September 1654 to 'make laws and ordinances for the peace and welfare of these nations where it shall be necessary'.

The executive was certainly very active in these months, undertaking a wide range of business and achieving solid results. Treaties were negotiated with several foreign states, most notably the Dutch, thereby ending the increasingly desultory First Dutch War; attempts were made not only to provide for a strong military grip over Scotland and Ireland but also to reform their civil and judicial administrative structures and to tie them more closely to England; steps were taken to guard against royalist conspiracies and to strengthen the security of the new regime; the existing fiscal system was maintained, though attempts were made to make it more efficient and to reduce corruption; the government also announced a reduction in the main direct tax; a commission was set up to judge or 'try' the suitability of future appointees to the public ministry and another to eject incumbent ministers and schoolmasters deemed unworthy; and aspects of the judicial system, including the Courts of Chancery and Admiralty and the law dealing with creditors and poor prisoners, were revised. Over and above this, a surprising amount of time was devoted to quite minor business, much of it of a private or local nature. Protector and Council were flooded with petitions from individuals, groups or localities and they acted as supreme arbiters and co-ordinators. Most of this business was transacted in Council meetings. The order books record just over 200 Council meetings held in the period down to the opening of the first Protectorate Parliament; Cromwell attended part or all of a little over seventy – or slightly over a third – of them.

Peace treaties apart, most of the key decisions were issued by Protector and Council in the form of an ordinance. Over 180 ordinances were completed during this period, though almost half of them were 'private' in nature, settling local affairs or matters concerning an individual or small group. The remainder covered wider 'public' business and the majority of these were published at the time. Some made major policy advances, but most introduced worthy but lesser measures. It is clear that the Council played a large, perhaps dominant, role in the preparation of these ordinances, the passage of which was modelled upon parliamentary procedure. Having gone through three readings and a committee stage in Council, the ordinance then came before the Protector, who could pass it, refer it back for further amendment or veto it altogether. The records suggest that Cromwell almost always followed the first course and that on less than twenty occasions did he query an ordinance passed by his Council.

Only around a dozen ordinances were referred back to the Council by the Protector, often accompanied by the specific amendments which Cromwell was seeking. Although the majority were public in nature, the suggested amendments were usually very minor, often no more than alterations to the lists of county commissioners. Around half a dozen ordinances were apparently vetoed completely by Cromwell, for they disappear from the records after being presented to him, with no sign that they received the Protectoral consent vital if they were to have any standing or effect. However, almost without exception these apparently vetoed ordinances were minor private measures, dealing with specific individuals or localities. It is possible that the Protector applied his powers of referral back or veto so sparingly because he had played a substantial role earlier in the process, ensuring that his own ideas and wishes were incorporated within the draft document when it was still being debated and amended in Council. However, his modest attendance rate during this period and the intermittent pattern of those attendances – for example, he was present at just 26 of the 111 Council meetings recorded from January to May 1654 inclusive – indicate that he cannot always have had a direct voice in the preparation of ordinances by the Council. Cromwell's approval of the vast majority of the ordinances as they came to him, without referral back, may be revealing of the roles of, and relationship between, Protector and Council.

When he opened the first Protectorate Parliament in early September 1654, Cromwell devoted most of his speech to a long account of the chaos which the new regime had inherited in the previous December and to a briefer review of the order which he and his Council had re-established since then. Cromwell claimed that by late 1653 the interests of the nation, the authority of magistracy and the whole order of society had been under threat. He asserted that both the justly hierarchical social order and true religion had been in grave danger. The nation had also been in direct physical danger, Cromwell claimed, through the unchecked activities of the Jesuits within England, a weakening English grip upon, and growing unrest within, Scotland and Ireland, and unwise and unnecessary wars with a number of European states, which had also disrupted trade. However, in the months since December 1653, many of these problems had been alleviated or solved by the new regime; he highlighted reforms to the legal and religious systems, treaties with several Continental states and the new air of stability which permitted the Parliament to assemble.

Towards the end of his speech, Cromwell sought to focus the minds of MPs by emphasizing that the work was not yet complete, drawing attention to financial pressures, the condition of Ireland and the need to strengthen foreign alliances. At several points in the speech, he stressed the need for 'healing and settling', which he felt was 'the great end of your meeting'. There was a sense of joy and expectation – 'You are met here on the greatest occasion that, I believe, England ever saw' – bolstered by a belief that the tide had already turned and that the past few months had brought solid achievement: 'After so many changes and turnings which this nation hath laboured under, to have such a day of hope as this is, and such a door of hope opened by God to us, truly I believe, some months since would have been above all our thoughts.' Five months later, he referred to the day upon which the Parliament met as 'to my apprehension, the hopefullest day that ever mine eyes saw, as to considerations of this world'. At one point of his opening speech, he took up the theme of the sermon just preached to MPs, reminding them of the story of 'Israel's bringing out of Egypt through a wilderness, by many signs and wonders towards a place of rest: I say, towards it'. Cromwell argued that the Promised Land, although now within view, had not yet been reached:

> Truly, I thought it my duty to let you know, that though God hath thus dealt with you, yet these are but entrances and doors of hope, wherein through the blessing of God you may enter into rest and peace. But you are not yet entered. You were told today of a people brought out of Egypt towards the land of Canaan, but, through unbelief, murmuring, repining, and other temptations and sins, wherewith God was provoked, they were fain to come back again, and linger many years in the wilderness, before they came to the place of rest.
>
> We are thus far through the mercy of God. We have cause to take notice of it, that we are not brought into misery; but, as I said before, a door of hope is open. And I may say this to you; if the Lord's blessing and his presence go along with the management of affairs at this meeting, you will be enabled to put the top-stone to this work, and make the nation happy.[16]

At one point during the speech of 4 September, Cromwell peered into the abyss: 'if this day, that is this meeting, prove not healing, what shall we do?' It was a question which, by January 1655, he was forced to face, for his high hopes of the previous September had been dashed. Things went badly wrong from the outset, for during the first week of the session a band of republicans and implacable opponents of the regime launched sweeping attacks upon the whole Protectoral edifice, apparently hoping to destroy the system and the head of state. In consequence, Cromwell used troops temporarily to close the House on 12 September and summoned MPs to listen to a second speech. He began defensively, seeking to prove two points. Firstly, he sought to show that his elevation had not come about through personal ambition and calculation, stressing that he owed his promotion not only to God but also to mortal developments beyond his control, to the unexpected, unsought and largely unwanted actions of other individuals and institutions. Secondly, he attempted to demonstrate that a large number of individuals and institutions had already given 'implicit' or 'explicit' consent to the regime in general and to his office in particular through 'their good liking and approbation thereof', not least all who had taken part in the parliamentary elections over the summer. Indeed, Cromwell reminded MPs that, as required by the Instrument, the principal electoral officers and a sample of voters had signed and returned documents not only naming the duly elected candidates but also declaring that 'the persons elected shall not have power to alter the government as it is hereby settled in one single person and a Parliament'. This provided the turning point in the speech, at which defence turned into attack.

Cromwell repeated his earlier assurance that this was a 'free Parliament', but he indicated that there were limitations to this freedom. MPs were expected to reciprocate by respecting 'the government and authority that called you hither'. He had expected MPs to have 'understood that I was the Protector, and the authority that called you, and that I was in possession of the government by a good right from God and men'. He stated that he would not allow Parliament to attack the very roots of the existing government, for that would cause instability, undermine the will of God and wreck the desires of the people for 'peace, and quietness, and rest and settlement', as well as giving encouragement to the nation's enemies. Before returning to the House, MPs would therefore be required to sign a Recognition, a brief but formal document stating that they accepted the basic tenets of the Protectoral constitution. These 'fundamentals', which were not negotiable and were to be 'delivered over to posterity, as being the fruits of our blood and travail', Cromwell defined as government by a single person and parliament, liberty of conscience in religion, provision to prevent parliament perpetuating itself, and joint control over the armed forces. All other aspects of the constitution were 'circumstantials' and could be amended or omitted by Parliament 'as I shall be convinced by reason'. Cromwell stated that, in these non-fundamental areas, he was even prepared to consider amendments aimed at reducing or more closely binding the powers of the Protector, 'in anything that I may be convinced of may be for the good of the people, in preservation of the cause and interest so long contended for'. It was on these grounds, as well as on those of 'necessity' – 'necessity hath no law' – and 'counsel from God', that Cromwell claimed he had taken this regrettable action.[17]

Around eighty MPs – out of a House of 460 – felt unable on political or moral grounds to accept these terms and sign the Recognition. They were permanently excluded from the House after 12 September. But the majority of MPs soon resumed business, initially in a somewhat subdued and less openly hostile atmosphere. Most attention focused on the Government Bill, Parliament's draft constitution, designed to replace the Instrument of Government. Initially, the document appeared to accept Cromwell's four fundamentals, and much of it comprised sensible provisions, generally retaining the existing basic structure of government. As the session progressed, however, many supporters of the regime became seriously worried by the drift of events. The religious clauses within the Government Bill were rather loosely worded and there were fears that they might be used to reduce liberty of conscience and impose tighter restrictions via persecution. Those fears were heightened by Parliament's harsh treatment of James Biddle, for although Biddle himself – who in published works appeared to deny the divinity of Christ – elicited little sympathy, there was a fear among some that Parliament itself, or others employing Parliament's revised constitution, might take similar action against other alleged 'heretics' and 'blasphemers'. Equally, both via the Government Bill and other draft legislation, a majority in Parliament sought drastically to reduce the size of the army by slashing the military budget and to remove the guaranteed permanent joint control of the Lord Protector over the armed forces. Parliament became divided, as supporters of the regime sought to ward off or delay unwelcome developments. Growing signs of opposition brewing outside as well as inside Parliament added to the Protector's worries. Interpreting the Instrument's five-month minimum session as equalling twenty weeks, Cromwell dissolved the Parliament at the earliest opportunity on 22 January 1655, thereby killing the Government Bill.

From Cromwell's point of view, the Parliament had been a complete failure. In his dissolution speech, he roundly condemned MPs for turning the peace and harmony which they found in September 1654 into division and discontent, wittingly or unwittingly encouraging the activities of enemies at home and abroad, thus imperilling the divinely sanctioned cause and creating 'real dangers to the whole'. There had been no need for the Parliament to have embarked upon the thorough revision of the Instrument, he said, for the existing regime had proved its worth by healing divisions and dispensing law and justice, and thus was not only 'owned by God, as being the dispensation of His providence', but also 'sealed and witnessed unto by the people'. In addition, he condemned several elements of the draft constitution as unsatisfactory. Cromwell defended the Instrument, though he repeated his assurances that he would have considered limited amendments to non-fundamental elements. He also defended himself against accusations of ambition, asserting that he did not wish the office of Lord Protector to become hereditary in his family. Parliament had shown no inclination to make 'good and wholesome provisions for the good of the people of these nations', and it was, he concluded, 'not for the profit of these nations, nor fit for the common and public good', for the Parliament to continue any longer.[18]

The failure of Parliament to act as Cromwell had hoped can be ascribed to a number of factors. In large part, it was due to the strength of opposition to the existing system within the House itself, even among those who felt able to take the Recognition and resume their seats. But Cromwell, too, might share the responsibility. The Protector had failed to guide and control the session, both directly and through his agents within the House, principally the Councillor MPs. For example, he did not use his opening speech to provide a clear, tangible lead, choosing to give a grand overview rather than to focus on concrete proposals. He clearly misjudged the mood of the Parliament when it opened, taken by surprise and completely unprepared for the vehemence of, and the tactics employed by, the opponents of the regime during the first week of the session. Although Councillor MPs and others tried to regain control, it was too late, and Cromwell was forced to intervene directly on 12 September. It seems that Protector and Council had not worked out a programme of public legislation for the session, for there is no sign that the legislation considered over the following months sprang from Cromwell's Councillors or other agents within the House and several bills clearly arose from unplanned developments. At times, contemporaries were able to identify a group of Protectoral agents and supporters in the House, a loose amalgam of Councillor MPs, civilian office holders and army officers, but they do not seem to have constituted a unified, long-term, durable party, led and operated by the Protector.

That the Protector's attempts to control and manage the Parliament were so fitful and limited might itself be explained in several different ways. It might simply have been the consequence of bad planning, born of overwork during the summer – the desire of Protector and Council to complete as many ordinances as possible before that power lapsed on 3 September, together with the Council's examination of the election returns – and Cromwell's overconfidence that the MPs would share his own vision of the approach of the Promised Land and would therefore accept the existing regime and its achievements. In part, too, the explanation may lie in sheer ignorance, for Cromwell's personal experience of parliamentary affairs was drawn from the 1640s and early 1650s, a period of crisis, war and constitutional novelty, and he had no direct experience of the workings of a balanced constitution in which there were good relations between parliament and head of state.

However, the explanation for the Protector's handling of both his Parliaments probably goes deeper. Cromwell felt that, as Protector, he should not intervene directly or interfere with parliamentary affairs. He should be above and beyond the parliamentary fray, watching over events perhaps, but refraining from direct intervention or participation. Instead, he believed that his role as head of state was to look to the overall safety of the nation, thus ensuring that Parliament would be secure and unhindered. Cromwell made this a recurring theme of the dissolution speech, thereby stressing that the Parliament had been 'free'. He pointed out that, after 12 September, 'you have had no manner of interruption or hindrance of mine in proceeding to that blessed issue which the heart of a good man could propose to himself, to this very day.' He held back from further involvement in parliamentary affairs, for 'I did think it to be my business rather to see the utmost issue, and what God would produce by you, than unseasonably to intermeddle with you.' Rather unfairly, he went on to criticize the Parliament for not contacting him and seeking his advice: 'I do not know what you have been doing. I do not know whether you have been alive or dead. I have not once heard from you in all this time, I have not, and that you all know.'[19] It was a breathtaking assertion, and probably not accurate. In mid-November a parliamentary committee had approached Cromwell to confer with him on a religious clause in the draft constitution, only to be smartly rebuffed. Cromwell reportedly snapped that because they had already altered many parts of the existing constitution 'as they pleased, without his advice', he felt that 'it would not become him to give any advice at all, singly or apart, as to this article'.[20] Again, it seems that the Protector was deliberately refusing to become involved with parliamentary proceedings, preferring to stand aloof. Whether motivated by hopes of ensuring parliamentary freedom, as Cromwell claimed, or by a baser calculation that by so doing he would avoid being implicated in parliamentary failures and shortcomings, the attitude adopted by the Protector does much to explain the limited and patchy nature of parliamentary management during the Protectorate.

The dissolution of the first Protectorate Parliament formed one of the nadirs of Cromwell's rule. His feelings come across in a revealing letter to an old army colleague, Lieutenant-Colonel Wilks, written sometime during January, almost certainly before the dissolution. Cromwell talked darkly of the 'wounds' which he had received, even from 'such as feare the Lord', who were now under a 'sad dispensation . . . being divided in opinion and too much in affection ready to fall fowle upon one another'. Meanwhile, within the army and outside it, in England and in Scotland, enemies were uniting and plotting to destroy the godly. There is a distinct air of self-pity about the letter, Cromwell clearly referring to himself when he wrote 'that whosoever labours to walk with an even foot between the several interests of the people of God for healing and accommodating their differences is sure to have reproaches and anger from some of all sorts'. He had concluded that the people were 'unwilling . . . to bee healed and attoned'.[21] Many of these specific themes, as well as the underlying feelings of anger and bitterness, disappointment and dejection, leavened with a sense of personal rejection and betrayal, surfaced again in the dissolution speech.

However, Cromwell was not without hope, as ever seeking reassurance in the Lord. Writing to Wilks, Cromwell still felt certain that, whatever the present disappointments, 'yet the Lord will not let it bee always soe'. Regardless of the accusations of self-interest and ambition heaped upon him by his enemies, so long as he retained his 'innocency and integrity', so long as he was working to advance God's will and not his own mortal ambitions, the Lord would show 'mercy and truth, and will owne it' and 'will make His owne councils stand'. Warming to the theme, he added a warning – 'and therefore let men take heed least they be found feighters against Him, especially His owne people'. He felt sure that God would intervene to correct current errors: 'I am perswaded the Lord will not suffer His people alwayes to be deceived by such pretenders and pretences to Righteousness and Justice, and care not how unjustly and unrightiously they walke.' Already, the Lord 'hath appeared very gracious to us' by revealing the royalist intrigues, and Cromwell could look forward to a time when God would again 'make His people of one heart, and give them one lip'.[22] Again, these themes were repeated in the dissolution speech, when, amid his review of disappointments and dangers, Cromwell expressed his belief that God would not only rescue the nation and its people but also, more personally, continue to be a source of strength and comfort:

> But if the Lord take pleasure in England, and if he will do us good, he is able to bear us up; let the difficulties be whatsoever they will, we shall in his strength be able to encounter with them. And I bless God I have been inured to difficulties, and I never found God failing when I trusted in him; I can laugh and sing in my heart when I speak of these things to you, or elsewhere.[23]

The twenty months between the dissolution of the first Protectorate Parliament in January 1655 and the meeting of the second in September 1656 was a period of rapid developments at home and abroad. In foreign affairs, the military expedition against the Spanish island of Hispaniola met with a stunning defeat in March 1655, though the surviving forces were able to occupy the island of Jamaica; by autumn 1655 relations with Spain had deteriorated into formal war. At home, royalist rebellions during March 1655 were quelled without great difficulty, though in their wake a number of new security measures were imposed, above all from autumn 1655 onwards the system of more overtly military provincial administration in England and Wales under the Major-Generals. Growing financial problems, springing not least from the overseas war and from the failure of a new 'decimation' tax on former royalists fully to cover the costs of the system headed by the Major-Generals, led to the summoning of the second Protectorate Parliament. Cromwell's speech at the opening of that Parliament portrayed the preceding period as a time of danger and menace, of threats to the regime, the nation and its people at home and abroad. Cromwell felt that 'the very being and interest of these nations, these nations in general, and especially . . . the interest of the people of God in these nations', had been and remained under threat.[24]

Occasional illnesses apart, Cromwell played an active role in Protectoral central government over this period. The dispatches of London-based diplomats make frequent reference to formal audiences and informal discussions with the Protector, from time to time Cromwell chose to hold discussions with a number of political and religious opponents of the regime, and we know that the Protector and his Councillors were working together closely at this time, for 1655–6 were the years of Cromwell's most assiduous attendance at Council meetings. They no longer had power to produce their own legislation in the form of ordinances, but they did issue a variety of lesser orders, some dealing with specific crises – especially the royalist rebellions – others continuing routine administration. The ordinances of 1653–4 remained in force, and Cromwell went out of his way in his speech at the opening of the second Protectorate Parliament to praise the continuing work of the triers and ejectors. He also defended the policy of broad liberty of conscience:

> I will tell you the truth, that that which hath been our practice since the last Parliament, hath been to let all this nation see that whatever pretensions be to religion, if quiet, peaceable, they may enjoy conscience and liberty to themselves, so long as they do not make religion a pretence for arms and blood.[25]

It was in this spirit, and apparently at Cromwell's personal initiative, that a proposal formally to readmit the Jews into England had been discussed at length during the closing weeks of 1655.

Cromwell's confidence that he was doing the Lord's work, that regime and nation were assured of God's support, had been badly shaken by the failure of the first Protectorate Parliament. He was anxious thereafter to find signs of God's continuing support, keen to interpret further successes as evidence that the Lord had not turned his back on the nation. Thus in March 1655 Cromwell emphasized that the crushing of the royalist rebellions had been 'a blessing of God': 'We doubt not but you have heard before this time of the hand of God going along with us, in defeating the late rebellious insurrection.'[26] Again, in June Cromwell felt that the success of an attack on Tunis shipping had been given by God, telling Admiral Blake that 'we have great cause to acknowledge the good hand of God towards us in this action, who, in all the circumstances thereof . . . was pleased to appear very signally with you.'[27] In 1657 naval success in the Canaries was seen as a 'wonderful' sign of God's blessing, 'and according to the wonted goodness and loving-kindness of the Lord, wherewith His people have been followed in all these late revolutions; and call for on our part, that we should fear before Him, and still hope in His mercy'.[28]

These signs of divine support were all the more precious because, over the same period, there were also distressing signals that the Lord had deserted the cause. In May 1655 Cromwell was deeply affected by news of the massacre of several hundred Piedmont Protestants by the Catholic Duke of Savoy. In late July Cromwell received the shattering news that the Western Design had been torn to pieces by the Spanish in and around San Domingo. That the surviving members of the expedition had been able to occupy Jamaica was small comfort, for although a Protectoral proclamation of August spoke warmly of 'the good providence of God' in giving this island to the English, Cromwell's letters of autumn 1655 tell a very different story. The defeat at Hispaniola had been a 'sad loss' and a great 'discouragement', a rebuke by the Lord, 'who hath very sorely chastened us'. The Protector was convinced that the defeat was a sign of God's displeasure, and it triggered in Cromwell a new round of heart-searching. In the wake of the defeat, Cromwell wrote emotionally of the need 'to humble ourselves before the Lord', to 'lay our mouths in the dust'. As usual, Cromwell had not utterly despaired, for he felt sure that in time the Lord would restore His favour, especially to the righteous venture against the evil Spanish, telling Admiral Goodson:

> He would not have us despond, but I trust gives us leave to make mention of His name and of His righteousness, when we cannot make mention of our own. You are left there; and I pray you set up your banners in the name of Christ, for undoubtedly it is His cause ... And though He hath torn us, yet He will heal us; though He hath smitten us, yet He will bind us up; after two days He will revive us, in the third day He will raise us up, and we shall live in His sight ... The Lord therefore strengthen you with faith, and cleanse you from all evil: and doubt not but He is able, and I trust as willing, to give you as signal successes as He gave your enemies against you. Only the Covenant-fear of the Lord be upon you.[29]

Cromwell's immediate reaction to the defeat in Hispaniola was to attempt to discover how and why God's support had been lost and what dreadful sin had provoked this divine rebuke. 'No doubt but we have provoked the Lord, and it is good for us to know so, and to be abased for the same', he wrote in October 1655. He had already identified part of the problem as 'the extreme avarice, pride and confidence, disorders and debauchedness, profaneness and wickedness, commonly practised' in the expedition army. Accordingly, he urged stricter discipline, to remove 'all manner of vice' and to create conditions wherein 'virtue and godliness' could flourish.[30] In summer 1656 Cromwell was still complaining of the continuing failings of the surviving troops on Jamaica, pointing to their 'sloth and sluggishness of spirit' both as a sign that God had not yet fully restored his support and as a possible cause of the Lord's continuing disfavour.[31] However, not all the sins could be laid at the door of the combined naval and military expedition. In his letter of October 1655 to the commander on Jamaica, Cromwell expressed a belief that God's reproof had been administered 'upon the account of our own sins as well as others".[32]

In all three speeches to the first Protectorate Parliament, as well as in his letter to Wilks, Cromwell had repeatedly referred to accusations, common at the time, that he was an ambitious, self-seeking hypocrite, who had sought political power for his own and his family's ends. Repeatedly, he had denied them. He returned to this theme in a letter of late June 1655, to his son-in-law Charles Fleetwood in Ireland. He began by denying rumours that he was about to recall Fleetwood and replace him with his son Henry Cromwell, writing darkly of

> The wretched jealousies that are amongst us, and the spirit of calumny, turns all into gall and wormwood. My heart is for the people of God: that the Lord knows, and I trust will in due time manifest; yet thence are my wounds; which though it grieves me, yet through the grace of God doth not discourage me totally.

Cromwell then denied as 'malicious figments' rumours that he was about to take the crown, claiming at the same time that he had hoped that both his surviving sons would have lived privately in the country and asserting that only with great reluctance had he been persuaded to grant a commission to Henry. Clearly, Cromwell was worried that the accusations of self-advancement were gaining strength and some credibility. He looked for succour and support from the Lord:

> We, under all our sins and infirmities, can daily offer a perfect Christ; and thus we have peace and safety, and apprehension

of love, from a Father in Covenant, who cannot deny Himself. And truly in this is all my salvation; and this helps me to bear my great burdens . . . Pray for me, that the Lord will direct, and keep me His servant. I bless the Lord I am not my own; but my condition to flesh and blood is very hard. Pray for me; I do for you all.[33]

Even more explicitly and making direct reference to his own situation, in the following spring Cromwell warned his son Henry to

take heed of studying to lay for yourself the foundation of a great estate. It will be a snare to you: they will watch you; bad men will be confirmed in covetousness. The thing is an evil which God abhors. I pray you think of me in this. If the Lord did not sustain me, I were undone: but I live, and I shall live, to the good pleasure of His grace; I find mercy at need.[34]

At the very least, Cromwell was acutely aware that he was surrounded by great temptation and that he and his family must avoid using their positions for personal gain or private advancement. It is possible – though the surviving evidence no more than hints at this – that Cromwell was worried that he had overstepped the mark and succumbed to the temptation of mortal pride and ambition, that he suspected and feared that his own sins had contributed to the withdrawal of God's favour.

It is possible to interpret the establishment of the system headed by the Major-Generals as a further attempt to win back God's favour, seeking to tighten discipline at home and more vigorously to extirpate the sins and sinners to be found within England and Wales. The Major-Generals were certainly given powers to promote moral reformation. However, this is not the whole story, for the system had other roots. Firstly, in part it was a straightforward attempt to increase security in the wake of the royalist risings led by John Penruddock and others. Secondly, it sprang from the drive to reduce the size and costs of the standing army within England and Wales, for the Major-Generals were designed to command and oversee the militias which would replace the standing army in many areas.

Most of the long and complex instructions issued both to the Major-Generals and to the commissioners who assisted them were not directly concerned with moral reformation. Drafting and revising these instructions was certainly a protracted business, for although Protector and Council had produced one version by August 1655, the final enlarged version was not issued until October. It is likely that Cromwell played an important part in the process, for the progress of this matter in Council was delayed by his absence through illness. However, the surviving evidence does not reveal exactly how far or in what areas Cromwell was responsible for initiating or amending the instructions, and suggestions that he took a personal interest in initiating, enlarging or strengthening those parts relating to moral reformation are speculative.

It is clear that Cromwell supported the system headed by the Major-Generals, though in his recorded utterances he laid as much stress upon the security aspect as upon the element of moral reform. For example, in a speech of March 1656 to the mayor and corporation of London, he bracketed 'the security of the peace of the nation' with 'the suppressing of vice and encouragement of virtue' as 'the sole end of this way of procedure'.[35] Again, in his speech of September 1656 at the opening of his second Parliament, he went out of his way to praise and defend both aspects of the system. In reference to political unrest, he described his 'poor little invention' as a 'necessary' and 'honest' security measure designed to end the dangers and divisions being fomented by the royalists, 'the Popish party' and others. At the same time, he defended the decimation tax on former royalists as fair and necessary, even though 'I hear [it] has been much regretted.' He also praised the Major-Generals as 'persons of known integrity and fidelity' who had, by their efforts, given the nation a year or more of 'tranquillity'. Cromwell returned to the topic later in the same speech, again defending the system and praising the work of the Major-Generals in providing security and preserving the peace. Here he also made reference to their moral work, praising it as being 'more effectual towards the discountenancing of vice and settling of religion, than anything done these fifty years'. At this point in the speech, Cromwell seemed to be intertwining the moralistic and security elements of their work, suggesting that both were pleasing to the Lord and were likely causes of God's beneficent providences.[36] Even though Cromwell seemed unmoved when in January 1657 the second Protectorate Parliament formally rejected the decimation tax, thereby ending the whole system, he still felt that the experiment had been 'justifiable' and told an audience of army officers that 'your Major-Generals did your parts well'.[37]

On 17 September 1656 Cromwell opened his second Protectorate Parliament with another grand state speech, reportedly over three hours long. Much of it was devoted to a lengthy defence of the Spanish war. Cromwell claimed that the Spanish were the 'natural' enemies of England, citing historical, legal and biblical evidence, and that they were also aiding Charles Stuart, 'a captain to lead us back again into Egypt . . . returning to all those things that we think we have been fighting against and destroying of all that good . . . we have attained unto'. He also attacked the intrigues of closet royalists, republicans and Fifth Monarchists at home. These dangers at home and abroad justified the Spanish war, the Major-Generals and other recent security measures, including the imprisonment without trial of political opponents. As he rather ominously put it, 'if nothing should be done but what is according to law, the throat of the nation may be cut, till we send for some to make a law', though he was adamant that all the measures imposed by his regime had been vital 'in order to the peace and safety of the nation'. He called upon MPs to support and endorse the Spanish war and to go on without delay to supply the money urgently required to wage that war.

As well as 'security', Cromwell prescribed 'reformation' as a means to 'avert the present dangers' and as a 'worthy return for all the blessings and mercies which you have received'. In ringing phrases, he explained and defended the policy of allowing broad liberty of conscience to all who lived peaceably and did not disturb others, stressing once more that this was the main driving force of the whole cause, 'the peculiar interest all this while contended for'. He defended tithes and praised the continuing work of the triers and ejectors. He again urged Parliament to promote 'the reformation of manners', to eliminate 'those abuses that are in this nation through disorder', defending steps already taken by his regime, including the curbing or banning of organized cock-fights and horse-races, and argued that the most valuable work which MPs could undertake would be to continue these attempts to eradicate sin. In so doing, they would not only earn God's blessing but also 'be more repairers of breaches than anything in the world'. Cromwell also drew attention to 'the great grievance' which lay in the administration of justice and in some particular laws. Of the latter, Cromwell picked out especially those 'wicked abominable laws' under which a man could be hanged for stealing 'sixpence, thirteen pence, I know not what'. Conversely, through the 'ill framing' of the law it was possible for 'abominable murders quitted'.[38]

The first session of the second Protectorate Parliament proved remarkably productive and generally placid, and Cromwell allowed it to run on until June 1657. Many of the features noted in the Protector's handling of his first Parliament apply just as much to the second, above all the impression that Cromwell had laid few plans before the session began and made few attempts to guide the House once it had opened. For example, the opening months of the session were calm but rather empty, giving Councillor MPs and other Protectoral agents ample opportunity to launch a governmental legislative programme. But the 'courtiers' had no such programme to hand and instead MPs drifted along with a growing body of very varied and worthy legislation, much of it clearly springing from *ad hoc*, unplanned roots. From December 1656 until the end of the session, much of Parliament's time was devoted to three major issues – the Naylor case, the Militia Bill and the new constitution – all of which seem to have been largely unplanned and unexpected and none of which arose from attempts by Cromwell to manage the House.

Cromwell seems to have felt that he should not attempt to influence or interfere with the work of Parliament. In April 1657 he told assembled MPs that, although as a 'common person' he had inevitably heard reports that he was to be

offered the crown, 'I could not take notice of your proceedings therein without breach of your privileges.' He felt
that he should be outside and above the fray, acting like
'a good constable to keep the peace of the parish'.[39] This
approach was more fruitful in 1656–7 than it had been two
years before, for many of Parliament's actions were consistent
with the broad objectives which Cromwell had laid out in his
opening speech. The Spanish war was swiftly approved and in
due course extra funds were granted to cover the resulting
costs, and a steady stream of legislation was produced, much
of it covering the area of 'reformation'. Cromwell appeared
unmoved by the MPs' rejection of the Militia Bill, thereby
formally ending the system headed by the Major-Generals,
and positively welcomed Parliament's decision to revise and
replace the existing constitution. In contrast, Cromwell was
clearly angry and distressed when, during December 1656,
Parliament attacked and severely punished James Naylor, a
Quaker who had ridden into Bristol on a donkey, thereby
allegedly committing 'horrid blasphemy'. As in the Biddle case
two years earlier, Cromwell had little sympathy with Naylor's
actions – 'We detest and abhor the giving or occasioning the
least countenance to persons of such opinions and practices,
or who are under the guilt of such crimes as are commonly
imputed to the said person', as Cromwell put it in a carefully
worded letter of Christmas day[40] – but he feared that this
was the thin end of the wedge and would encourage the
persecution of other Protestant groups. However, Cromwell
took no direct and immediate action beyond sending the
Speaker a polite if somewhat sharp letter inquiring about the
legal grounds of Parliament's action.

In 1656–7 Cromwell welcomed constitutional revision, and
not merely because the production by MPs of an acceptable constitution would mean that his regime would, at long
last, rest directly upon the support of the people signified
through Parliament. The Naylor case had highlighted one of
the defects of the Instrument, for Cromwell now felt that
it had been a mistake to bestow legislative power upon a
single-chambered parliament. As he told a meeting of army
officers in the midst of an angry speech of late February
1657:

That it is time to come to a settlement and lay aside arbitrary proceedings, so unacceptable to the nation. And by the proceedings of this Parliament, you see they stand in need of a check or balancing power (meaning the House of Lords or a House so constituted) for the Case of James Naylor might happen to be your own case. By their judicial power, they fall upon life and member, and doth the Instrument in being enable me to control it?

Another version of the same speech has Cromwell condemning the Instrument as 'an imperfect thing which will neither preserve our religious or civill rights'.

You are offended at a House of Lords. I tell you that unless you have some such thing as a balance you cannot be safe, but either you will grow upon the civill liberties by secluding such as are elected to sitt in Parliament . . . ; or they will grow upon your liberty in Religion. I abhor James Nailor's principle, yet interposed. You see what my letter signified. This Instrument of Government will not doe your worke.[41]

This confrontation with the officers had occurred in the wake of the introduction in the House of a new draft constitution, which after much revision emerged as the Humble Petition and Advice. It contained a generally sensible series of provisions, modelled upon the Instrument of Government, most of which passed through the House swiftly and without causing great division. The constitutional fundamentals of Cromwell's speech of 12 September 1654 were retained and guaranteed. By restoring a second, nominated House of Parliament, the new system might provide greater safeguards, with each House acting as a check and balance upon the other, thereby making less likely a repetition of the Naylor case. When the Humble Petition was formally presented to Cromwell on 31 March, he immediately expressed both his gratitude to Parliament and his appreciation of the importance of the document, though he requested time 'to ask counsel of God and of my own heart' before making any reply. The search was brief, for just three days later, on 3 April, he was able to make a more considered response. He told MPs that their constitution answered 'the two greatest concernments that God has in the world'.

> The one is that of religion and the preservation of the professors thereof, to give them all due and just liberty, and to assert the truths of God, which you have done in part in this paper, and referred to be done more fully by yourselves and me hereafter . . . The other thing cared for is the civil liberties and interests of the nations, which although it be, and indeed ought to be subordinate to a more peculiar interest of God, yet it is the next best God hath given men in the world, and better than any words, if well cared for, to fence the people of God in their interest.

However, he told MPs, 'you have one or two considerations that do stick with me. The one is that you have named me by another title than that I now bear.' Although he was honoured to be offered the crown, he felt that he was 'unable for such a trust and charge'. 'I have not been able to find it my duty to God and to you to undertake this charge under that title.'[42]

These were the grounds of the settlement finally concluded in late May, when Cromwell accepted a revised version of the Humble Petition from which kingship had been dropped and which instead maintained Cromwell as Lord Protector, though with the right to nominate his successor. But this final settlement had emerged only after weeks of complex negotiations and uncertainty, principally repeated and prolonged attempts by the majority within Parliament to persuade Cromwell to accept the crown. In response, several times during April and early May the Protector met the whole House or a specially appointed parliamentary committee to respond to repeated offers of the crown and to explain his position. After apparently wavering during April, or at least giving a number of ambiguous and 'dark' responses, Cromwell firmly rejected the crown on 8 May.

Cromwell clearly found the offer of the crown disturbing. Even his closest political colleagues, such as Secretary Thurloe, did not know what Cromwell would decide and found the Protector unusually reserved. Many of his expressions during April – 'We must all be very real now, if ever we will be so',

and 'lifting up my heart to God, to know what might be my
duty at such a time as this, and upon such an occasion and
trial as this was to me' – attest to the pressure which Cromwell
believed himself to be under. He acknowledged that the office
of king had history and tradition behind it, and that the legal
system had long been based upon a king – 'And the law
knowing this, the people can know it also, and the people
do love what they know.' However, he also argued that the
office of Lord Protector had served perfectly well for over
three years, had gained 'almost universal obedience . . . from
all ranks and sort of men', and that the legal system had
continued to operate just as well as, if not better than, it
had done under a monarchy. Equally, he argued that he saw
his principal role as the prevention of 'mischief and evil', like
a 'good constable to keep the peace of the parish', and that
this could be performed just as well with the title of Protector
as with a crown. At one point, he even hinted that he saw this
as a temporary role – 'I have no title to the government of
these nations, but what was taken up in a case of necessity,
and temporary, to supply the present emergency' – and that
once his God-given work was done he would not seek 'the
continuance of my power or place, either under one title or
another'.[43]

Several arguments can be advanced to explain why Cromwell
eventually refused the offer of the crown. The simplest and
crudest rests on Cromwell's supposed fear that he would
lose control of the army if he accepted the title. In 1657
much of the rank and file as well as many senior officers
strongly opposed the restoration of monarchy. The latter
included John Lambert, probably the most powerful Councillor and hitherto a close colleague of Cromwell, and John
Disbrowe and Charles Fleetwood, both of them Councillors
and Cromwell's relatives by marriage. Perhaps fear that senior
officers of this calibre would actively oppose him if he took
the crown, or at least stand by in all-too-eloquent inactivity
as unrest spread among the rank and file, caused Cromwell
to reject Parliament's offer. However, Cromwell does not
come across as a man who stood in fear of army mutiny.
On several occasions during the Protectorate, he ruthlessly
but efficiently quelled military unrest, and he retained tight

control over the army until his death. In late February 1657 he had not minced his words to a gathering of senior officers, going out of his way to blame the officers for a whole litany of errors since 1653 – indeed, many of his accusations seem unfair, blaming the officers for decisions which were, in reality, taken by Protector and Council. In summer 1657 he stripped Lambert of his commission and dismissed him from the army, a bold move which caused barely a ripple in military circles. When Fleetwood tried to persuade the Protector to hold back from dissolving Parliament in February 1658, he was scornfully brushed aside as 'a milksop'. This was followed by a further, effective purge of disaffected officers and another powerful and outspoken speech to a gathering of senior officers. As Protector, Cromwell confronted and crushed army opposition and retained tight control. It would have been out of character for him to have backed away from kingship in spring 1657 through fear of the army.

A second, more plausible explanation would lie in Cromwell's political outlook in 1657. One of Cromwell's twin ambitions during the 1650s as a whole was 'healing and settling', and many supporters of kingship probably wanted Cromwell to accept the crown for this very reason, as it would pull him back towards traditional forms and away from constitutional novelty, particularly one bolstered by an army. Cromwell saw some attractions in this, for in his speeches at the time he repeatedly speculated that kingship might be a vehicle for achieving a deeper, more lasting 'settlement'. On 21 April he confessed to the parliamentary committee that

> I am hugely taken with the word settlement, with the thing and with the notion of it. I think he is not worthy to live in England that is not . . . Because indeed it is the great misery and unhappiness of a nation to be without it; and it is like a house, and much worse than a house divided against itself, it cannot stand without settlement.

He returned to the same theme later in the speech: 'Settlement is the general work now, that which will give the nation to enjoy their civil and religious liberties, that will conserve the liberty of every man and not rob any man of what is justly his.'[44]

However, Cromwell may at the last have held back because he also saw disadvantages here. The very process of accepting the crown and thereby moving further towards a traditional form of government may have brought closer his goal of 'settlement', but only at the price of undermining his other great objective, 'reformation'. It is noticeable that in the speech of 21 April, where he spoke at greatest length about the 'settlement' which the new constitution, complete with kingship, might bring, Cromwell moved on to address, in phrases just as ringing, the unfinished work of 'reformation'. He again urged Parliament to reform the laws and legal system, work 'acceptable to God upon many accounts, and I am persuaded it is one thing that God looks for and would have'. He also advocated 'reformation of manners', stressing the need both for the existing laws to be better enforced by JPs and for further measures to punish 'dissolute and loose persons'.[45] Whatever his attraction to settlement, reformation remained at least as important to Cromwell and it is possible that his rejection of the crown stemmed in part from his belief that its acceptance would undermine and put back the cause of reformation to an unacceptable degree.

However, another factor may have played a part in Cromwell's eventual refusal of the crown. Although he repeatedly made light of the title, referring to it several times as merely 'a feather in a hat',[46] he may have been uncomfortably aware that it would be seen as another sign of personal advancement. That it would fuel and strengthen the long-standing accusations that he was a self-seeking hypocrite was probably not his main concern. It is possible that Cromwell was having self-doubts, and that there were dark thoughts lurking somewhere at the back of his mind that the accusations of pride and ambition may contain an element of truth. He may have feared that, in accepting the crown, he would be falling into the mire of personal advancement and that, far from doing God's work, he would lose the Lord's favour. In his speeches of 1654–5 and in his letters and utterances of 1655–6, Cromwell had been very conscious of the accusations of self-advancement and personal

ambition and had occasionally hinted that he feared that
there may have been some truth in them, worrying that
this had caused God to desert the cause. However, in
his recorded speeches of 1657, as in his earlier writings and speeches, such feelings emerge only occasionally,
and then in dark and ambiguous forms. If self-doubt
about his own character and ambition did play a part
in Cromwell's rejection of the crown, it remained largely
internalized.

Instead, Cromwell's fullest and most eloquent explanation
for his refusal of kingship points to a similar but less personal
interpretation of God's wishes. In his speech of 13 April,
Cromwell emphasized that many good men, who appeared
to be godly and to be in tune with the Lord, were strongly and
openly opposing kingship. Cromwell had just spoken about
his military career, his promotion of godly men within the
army and the manifestations of God's support for the army,
and when he told Parliament that 'I cannot think that God
would bless me in the undertaking of anything, that would
justly and with cause grieve them', he was probably referring
largely, though perhaps not exclusively, to the feelings of his
military colleagues.

> But if that I know, as indeed I do, that very generally good
> men do not swallow this title, though really it is no part of
> their goodness to be unwilling to submit to what a Parliament
> shall settle over them, yet I must say that it is my duty and
> my conscience to beg of you, that there may be no hard
> thing put upon me, things I mean hard to them, that they
> cannot swallow. If the nation may as well be provided for
> without these things, . . . I truly think it will be no sin to you
> to there favour, . . . no grief of heart to yours that you have a
> tenderness, even possibly if it be to their weakness, to the
> weakness of those that have integrity and uprightness.

It would be far better, he argued, to drop the title which good
men so much opposed, thereby

> complying, indulging, and being patient unto the weaknesses
> and infirmities of men that have been faithful, and have bled

all along in this cause, and are faithful and will oppose all oppositions . . . to the things that are fundamental in your Government, in your settlement for civil and gospel liberties.

Moreover, although Cromwell claimed not to be 'scrupulous about words or names or such things', he had an intense belief in God's providence and felt that he should be guided by the Lord's hand. It was God who had been responsible for the regicide of 1649, and He had spoken as much against the title as against the person of Charles I and the Stuart family:

> Truly the providence of God has laid this title aside providentially. De facto it is laid as aside and this not by sudden humour or passion, but it has been the issue of a great deliberation as ever was in a nation; it has been the issue of ten or twelve years' civil war, wherein much blood has been shed . . . And God has seemed providentially not only to strike at the family but at the name.

Cromwell reiterated that, in his eyes, God 'hath not only dealt so with the persons and the family, but he hath blasted the title'. Regardless of mortal arguments in support of kingship, Cromwell felt that he could not go against the Lord's will, and the Lord had clearly spoken against monarchy – 'I would not seek to set up that that providence hath destroyed and laid in the dust, and I would not build Jericho again.'[47] When the Humble and Additional Petitions formally replaced the Instrument of Government on 26 June and Cromwell was inaugurated for a second time as head of state, he was enthroned as an ermine-clad Lord Protector. There would be no King Oliver.

The last year or so of Cromwell's life, from the second installation until his death, is often portrayed as a period of drift and failure, caused by old age and ill-health and, some historians suggest, by a lack of ideas attributable to the reactionary path which he was treading. Although this last point may well exaggerate the true position, it is undeniable that this period comes across as remarkably empty, at least in domestic terms. There were few new policy initiatives and Protector and Council appeared to be merely maintaining the regime and treading water in administrative matters. During the parliamentary recess of the latter half of 1657, the Protector selected the founder members of the new second House, advising with Councillors and others about his choice. The second session of the second Protectorate Parliament, which opened on 20 January 1658, proved to be both brief and divisive, for many MPs spent their time attacking the regime and the new second chamber. Cromwell's intervention of 25 January, attempting to direct their energies into more fruitful and necessary matters, was to no avail, and he dissolved Parliament on 4 February. He had acted, in part, to block attempts by republicans both inside and outside Parliament to win over elements within the army. The dissolution was followed by another purge of the army, weeding out political opponents and successfully restoring order. During the last months of Cromwell's life, thought was giving to summoning another parliament to stem the regime's spiralling debts and also, some hoped, to revive kingship. However, another failed royalist conspiracy and the resulting treason trials, together with the Protector's declining health, delayed such plans and nothing had been decided by the time of Cromwell's death.

The only major speeches of this period of which full versions survive are his three speeches to Parliament in January and February 1658. In some ways, they confirm this sense of decline and emptiness. They were quite brief, much shorter than many he had delivered to Parliament in 1654–5 and 1656–7, and several times Cromwell referred or alluded to his growing infirmities. In his speech of 25 January, again stressing the great dangers which the nation faced both at home and abroad, he likened himself to a watchman, 'being set on a watch-tower, to see what may be for the good of these nations and what may be for the preventing of evil'. From his vantage point he could see the dangers posed by the Spanish, Catholics and royalists abroad, by closet royalists and other political and religious radicals at home and by unrest in Scotland and Ireland. But far from responding to this rallying cry, the Protector's words went unheeded and divisions worsened. Cromwell's dissolution speech of 4 February was blunt and curt, attacking the Commons in particular for failing to work with him, in accordance with Parliament's own constitution or for the good of the nation. He was particularly scathing about attempts to 'seduce' the army, developments which 'have not been according to God nor according to truth'.

In both speeches Cromwell repeated once again his assertion that he had not sought his office – 'I speak it before God, angels and men, I did not' – and instead pointed out to MPs that they themselves 'drew me to accept of the place I now stand in'. He now held office under Parliament's own Humble Petition and so, he reminded MPs, 'you sought me' to be Lord Protector 'and you brought me to it'. Parliament had requested and persuaded him to accept the office, but he had done so, he suggested, only reluctantly and because Parliament agreed to share the heavy burdens of government. He claimed that he would just as gladly have returned to private life:

> I can say it in the presence of God, in comparison of which all we that are here are like poor creeping ants upon the earth, that I would have been glad, as to my own conscience and spirit, to have been living under a woodside to have kept a flock of sheep, rather than to have undertaken such a place as this was.[48]

The argument was forced and is neither convincing nor entirely honest. On 4 February Cromwell condemned MPs for questioning rather than working within the constitutional system which they had written and persuaded him to accept the previous summer. But he completely ignored the fact that many MPs present during the second session, including all the leading republican critics of the Protectoral regime, had played no part in drafting and amending the new constitution, and had not given any form of consent to it. Well over a hundred MPs had been entirely absent from the first session of the Parliament, most of them formally excluded from the House by the Council. It was the return of these members in the second session – under the new constitution there was no provision for excluding them – as well as the presence of a new second chamber, to which many pro-regime MPs had been elevated, which lies behind the hostility of the Commons.

However, against these signs of decline should be placed

indications of success and continuing optimism. In contrast to the rather empty domestic policy, the foreign policy of the regime was bringing military success, territorial gain and enhanced international respect, albeit at a high financial price. It was in this period that attempts by the Spanish to regain Jamaica were strongly repulsed and the island firmly secured, that, both alone and in alliance with the French, English forces gained several victories over the Spanish on land and sea, and that, arising from this successful alliance, England took control of Dunkirk. The dispatches of London-based diplomats confirm that Cromwell was continuing to take a keen interest in foreign affairs and that, when his health permitted, he was still holding both formal audiences and less formal discussions with diplomatic representatives. Because of these successes abroad, and because of the ability of the regime to maintain peace at home, when he met Parliament on 20 January 1658 at the opening of the second session, Cromwell was able briefly to regain something of the optimism of earlier years, to see clear signs that the favour of God had returned, perhaps to banish from his mind those doubts which had crept upon him in the wake of the repeated failures of 1655. Returning once more to the eighty-fifth psalm, Cromwell noted how God had been 'favourable unto His land', pardoning the 'iniquities' of His people, and so removed His wrath. 'Sometimes', Cromwell claimed, 'God pardoneth nations also. And if the enjoyment of our present peace and other mercies may be witnesses for God, we feel and we see them every day.'[49] Nor was the failure of this Parliament an irredeemably shattering experience. Cromwell acted swiftly and decisively to restore the unity and loyalty of the army, and we possess brief summaries of robust speeches delivered by Cromwell both to the army officers and to the lord mayor, aldermen and councillors of the City during the spring and summer of 1658.

Cromwell had suffered several bouts of ill-health during the Protectorate. A number of contemporary commentators noted signs of a more serious physical decline in 1657–8. The Protector's attendances at Council meetings may reflect this. Cromwell attended only 55 of the 152 meetings recorded from July 1657 until 2 September 1658. But there was a sharp decline within this period, for of the seventy-two meetings held from January to 2 September 1658, Cromwell attended just nineteen. By summer 1658 the Protector's health was causing business to drift along without a clear decision, for the prolonged discussions on proposals that another parliament be summoned forthwith were never brought to a conclusive and constructive end. Cromwell's favourite daughter, Elizabeth, died of cancer at Hampton Court in early August. A month later, on the afternoon of 3 September, his lucky day, the anniversaries of Dunbar and Worcester and, less propitious, the meeting of his first Protectorate Parliament, Cromwell died at Whitehall Palace, apparently from a recurrent fever or 'ague'. An unsuccessful embalming caused Cromwell's mortal remains to be quietly buried in Westminster Abbey sometime during September. The subsequent lying and standing in state at Somerset House during October and early November and the state funeral on 23 November centred on one or more life-size movable effigies, crafted in wood and with a wax face and features and on a – probably empty – coffin. Versions of Cromwell's last words or prayers uttered on 3 September, like most of the colourful accounts of his final days and death-bed scenes in which they are to be found, were written and published with an eye on propaganda, and may owe more to the myth than to the man.

As Lord Protector, Cromwell is not always an edifying sight. As head of state, Cromwell did many things which seem to contradict his earlier calls for justice and liberty and which, at times, come uncomfortably close to some of the policies of Charles I. To draw a modern parallel, it is always easier for an MP in opposition or on the back-benches to be idealistic and to retain pure principles; once in government, cold, harsh necessities often lead to messy compromise and unwelcome entanglements. Even if Cromwell's repeated calls upon God and the Lord's will as justification are accepted as entirely genuine and without a trace of hypocrisy, other elements jar. He did resort to imprisonment without trial, albeit sparingly, he was at least partly responsible for the imposition of the system headed by the Major-Generals, complete with its novel and unparliamentary tax upon former royalists, and he did ride roughshod over some parliamentary rights and privileges, especially in September 1654 when he closed the House, imposed a new test upon MPs and thereby effectively excluded a large number of MPs. Although in his great speeches to Parliament Cromwell could be eloquent, even genuinely moving, he also had an unpleasant knack for twisting events, placing upon them an interpretation so strained and selective as to appear duplicitous and unconvincing. Many of the allegations he made in his speeches were certainly unfair, and some may have been deliberate lies. However much he saw himself doing God's will and working for the greater good of the nation and its people, it is impossible to avoid the conclusion that the Protector and his entire regime were always an imposition, ultimately surviving only through army backing. The Instrument of Government was drafted and imposed by the army, the Humble and Additional Petitions by a Parliament elected on a novel and restricted franchise and then heavily purged. Equally, much of Cromwell's work as Protector either failed during his lifetime or collapsed soon after his death. He had achieved only a limited and enforced form of settlement, and one which perished within a few months of his death. His other goal, reformation, had fared even worse. When Cromwell died, sin was still rife, little progress had been made in law reform and even the much-vaunted liberty of conscience had encouraged religious fragmentation and provoked hostile reaction. The case against Protector Cromwell is a strong one.

There is, however, a far more positive side to the Protectorate and to Cromwell as Protector. Not all of the regime's achievements were wiped away in 1659-60, and several left enduring and perhaps beneficent legacies. The broad liberty of conscience, so dear to Cromwell's heart, had fostered a degree of Protestant plurality so wide and deep that never again could the state church claim an effective monopoly of belief and a generation later toleration for Protestants was legally accepted. The Protectorate's foreign policy, again a field in which Cromwell seems to have played a decisive personal role, brought the nation territorial acquisitions, many of which were retained for decades or centuries and proved extremely valuable, and a degree of international confidence and prestige which may have laid the foundations for later glories. Similarly, the Protector's work to unite Scotland and

Ireland more closely with England in political and administrative terms, as much as his earlier military campaigns there, may have laid the foundations for later, more durable unions. But the Protector's reputation should rest on far more than these legacies. Ultimately, it should rest on the decency of the man and his regime. He never lost a sense of humility, an awareness of the frailty both of himself and others, and a corresponding compassion for his fellow man. He does not come across as a power-hungry, self-seeking, uncaring tyrant. Wherever possible, he tried to compromise and reconcile, to include rather than exclude, to win active support or passive acquiescence rather than to compel or crush. It was in this spirit that he attempted, with partial though not complete success, to heal the divisions of the civil war and to bring peace, unity and settlement. But that spirit alone might also have led to kingship, and to enhanced personal power and wealth. It is to Cromwell's credit that, at least until ill-health overtook him near the end, he never lost a driving zeal to reform society, a desire to extirpate sin, a mission to secure the Promised Land. However futile that vision may have proved during Cromwell's own lifetime and however strange, distant and almost incomprehensible it may appear to modern eyes, it was that visionary element which drove Cromwell on in an attempt to improve society and its people and which meant that, unlike many post-revolutionary leaders before and since, he never became a corrupt, power-drunk, self-interested wreck. If he failed, he did so nobly.

PART III

CONCLUSIONS

7

THE FACES OF CROMWELL

Cromwell's death in September 1658 was followed by attempts to place his life and career in context. His state funeral was badly organized and no funeral sermon was delivered or subsequently published. There were, however, a number of memorial services for the late Protector, and at least two of the sermons preached on those occasions found their way into print, together with memorial verses by Marvell, Dryden and others. No official or state-sponsored biography appeared, but at least three full-length biographical studies were published between Cromwell's death and the Restoration, written by Richard Flecknoe, Samuel Carrington and 'L. S.', the otherwise anonymous author of *The Perfect Politician*.

These three biographies have much in common. They all skate very briefly over Cromwell's life before 1642, tend to focus on the interregnum and, to a greater or lesser degree, become narratives of key events and policies post-1649 rather than tightly focusing on Cromwell's own role and personal contribution. In their approach to the man, however, the three diverge quite sharply. Flecknoe and Carrington are overwhelmingly favourable towards Cromwell, Flecknoe dismissing the 'envy and malice' of others to produce a highly flattering conclusion –

> That a Greater and more Excellent personage had no where been produc't by this latter Age; nor (perhaps) in our Nation by any former ones. And if men anciently have been judged fit for Empire only for the Greatnesse of their bodies; He certainly was most fit for it, for the Greatness of his mind.

– while Carrington makes Cromwell's continuing humility and compassion the dominant feature of his career post-1649: 'Those who shall read the Histories of such like Revolutions as these will finde that they never attained so high a pitch of Grandor, by such meek and merciful means and so void of passion.'[1]

In contrast, *The Perfect Politician* takes a generally more critical line, underscoring even apparently complimentary or neutral passages with barbed comments, as in the account of Cromwell's attempts to readmit the Jews – 'our Protector having a large (I say not conscience, but) heart, and being of tender bowels, his charity extended so far, as to plead for the re-entertainment of these guests' – and alleging that ambition and cunning could be seen even in Cromwell's different speaking styles:

> His Speeches were for the most part ambiguous, especially in publicke meetings; wherein he rather left others to pick out the meanings, then did it himself. But when Offenders came under his own examination, then would he speak plain English, and declare his power unto them in a ranting stile.

The author claims that all the developments in Cromwell's life and career, including his championing of religious liberty and his rejection of the crown, were aimed at personal advancement and the acquisition of power:

> We finde him in the beginning of England's Distractions, a most active Instrument to carry on the Cause for King and Parliament; this pretence holding water, and proving prosperous, he then became the main stickler for Liberty of Conscience without any limitation. This toleration became his Master-piece in Politicks; for it procured him a party that stuck close in all cases of necessity. These Libertines in general, being divided into several particular Fractions . . . did all of them serve as steps to mount our Protector to the highest pitch of Preferment. After he had made use of all that could augment his Interest, then Humility condescended to look thorow his fingers at a crown; but still waving the ayrie title of King, he rather chose to accept the substantial Power of Protector.

However, the author clearly retained much admiration for Cromwell's achievements and *The Perfect Politician* is by no means unremittingly condemnatory. The closing words of the biography, written from the vantage point of 1659–60, with the Protectorate long gone and the army-backed regime which replaced it tottering, capture this ambivalence perfectly:

> To take him in the whole, he was a Man better fitted to make a Prince of, then the People was to receive him: this we see sufficiently in the management of the Government to his Death. But afterwards, the sudden disaster which befel his Posterity was so admirable, that it cannot be imputed to any thing else but Digitus Dei.[2]

If contemporaries such as these were puzzled by many aspects of Cromwell's character and career and produced such starkly differing assessments, it is all the more impossible for historians writing centuries later to produce a comprehensive, all-encompassing or definitive portrait. No interpretation will ever command the total support and approval of historians and biographers and no conclusions are likely to rise above doubt and criticism in their own day and the need for future revision in the light of further work. None the less, it may prove useful to pull together some of the themes of Cromwell's life and career and to summarize of some of the key facets of the man.

Appearance, Health and Character

> His body was wel compact and strong, his stature under 6 foote (I beleeve about two inches) his head so shaped, as you might see it a storehouse and shop both of a vast treasury of natural parts. His temper exceeding fyery, as I have known, but the flame of it kept downe, for the most part, or soon allayed with thos moral endowments he had. He was naturally compassionate towards objects in distresse, even to an effeminate measure; though God had made him

a heart, wherein was left little roume for any fear, but what was due to himselfe, of which there was a large proportion, yet did he exceed in tendernesse towards sufferers. A larger soul, I thinke, hath seldome dwelt in a house of clay than his was. I do believe, if his story were impartialy transmitted, and the unprejudiced world wel possest with it, she would adde him to her nine worthies, and make up that number a decemviri. He lived and dyed in comfortable communion with God, as judicious persons neer him wel observed. He was that Mordecai that sought the welfare of his people, and spake peace to his seed, yet were his temptations such, as it appeared frequently, that he, that hath grace enough for many men, may have too little for himself; the treasure he had being but in an earthen vessel, and that equally defiled with original sin, as any other man's nature is.[3]

This justifiably famous and much quoted pen-portrait of Cromwell was written in 1659 by John Maidstone, formerly steward and cofferer to the late Protector. As a close personal servant and colleague, Maidstone was very well placed to observe both his master's physical appearance and his personality traits, and there is good reason, therefore, to accept the veracity of this account. Around the same time, Flecknoe and Carrington published briefer sketches within their biographies. Flecknoe claimed that Cromwell 'was of stature rather well set then tall; strong and robustious of constitution; of visage Leonin, the true phisiognomy [of] all great and martial men, yet as much Lamb in the Chamber as Lion in the field, courteous, affable and obliging to all', Carrington that 'he somewhat exceeded the usual middle stature, but was well proportioned accordingly, being of a becoming fatness, well shaped, having a masculine face, a sparkling eye, both courteous and harsh at once according as there was occasion'.[4]

Maidstone, Flecknoe and Carrington were writing in 1659, after Cromwell's death, and their sketches were probably based on impressions drawn from the final stages of Cromwell's career, most notably the Protectorate. Other accounts present images of a younger Cromwell, the Cromwell of the early 1640s at the beginning of his political career. However, they were written or published many years later, and they must be approached with some caution, for they may well have been embellished by hindsight and the knowledge of Cromwell's subsequent career. For example, in his *Memoirs*, Sir Philip Warwick claimed to recall how, coming to the House one morning in November 1640, during the opening weeks of the Long Parliament, he

> perceived a gentleman speaking, (whom I knew not,) very ordinarily apparelled, for it was a plain cloth-suit, which seemed to have been made by an ill country tailor; his linen was plain, and not very clean, and I remember a speck or two of blood upon his little band, which was not much larger than his collar; his hat was without a hat-band, his stature was of a good size, his sword stuck close to his side, his countenance swolen and reddish, his voice sharp and untuneable, and his eloquence full of fervour, for the subject matter would not bear much of reason . . . And yet I lived to see this very gentleman, whom out of no ill will to him I thus describe, by multiplied good successes, and by real, but usurped power, (having had a better tailor, and more converse among good company) . . . appear of a great and majestic deportment and comely presence. Of him therefore I will say no more, but that verily I believe he was extraordinarily designed for those extraordinary things, which one while most wickedly and facinorously he acted, and at another as successfully and greatly performed.[5]

Again, in his published *Memoirs*, Sir Richard Bulstrode claimed to have recalled another exchange early in the Long Parliament, when Lord Digby asked John Hampden to identify an MP who had spoken in the House that day. Hampden identified the 'slovenly fellow . . . who hath no ornament in his speech' as Cromwell, supposedly adding a prediction that, if it came to war, Cromwell would become 'one of the greatest men of England'.[6]

As well as pen-portraits of this sort, we also possess a number of illustrative likenesses of Cromwell. Most famous are the portraits. The earliest, probably dating from the late 1640s, was painted by Robert Walker, and shows Cromwell three-quarter length in dark armour. In the early 1650s Samuel Cooper produced a string of miniatures of Cromwell, usually of the head and shoulders alone, sometimes showing Cromwell in shirt and coat, sometimes in armour. The best in this series appears incomplete and may have served as a master study from which replicas could be produced. Slightly later, perhaps in 1653–4 around the beginning of the Protectorate, Cromwell was painted by Sir Peter Lely, who again produced a head and shoulders likeness, usually in armour and within an oval frame. In each case, a number of different versions survive, some by the principal artist, some by other hands. As well as these and other contemporary portraits, there are a number of engravings which were published during Cromwell's lifetime, the busts and profiles of Cromwell which Thomas Simon produced for the coins and medals of the Protectorate, copies of a death mask taken in 1658 and photographs of the semi-mummified head, reputed to be Cromwell's, finally buried in 1960.

Several points emerge from these illustrative images. Firstly, we possess no likeness of the young Cromwell. The earliest image is probably a line engraving produced in the mid-1640s, one of a series showing parliamentary officers first published in 1647. Although some attempt has been made to capture facial characteristics, the series as a whole is crude and roughly executed. Our earliest reliable likeness is probably the Walker portrait, executed in the late 1640s when Cromwell was approaching his fiftieth year. Thus all the surviving and reliable images which we possess date from the final decade of his life. Secondly, even within this fairly short time-span, we can trace clear signs of ageing. The Walker portrait shows a man still in his prime, hardly youthful and with an unmistakably receding hair-line, but none the less not yet ravaged by old age and ill-health. By the 1650s both had visibly taken their toll. Cooper's Cromwell is largely bald on the top of his head, though tufts remain high on the forehead, he is clearly heavier and fatter, with distinct jowls and a barrel chest, and the face is more deeply lined. Thirdly, the surviving portraiture reflects a sense of realism and simplicity. The anecdote that Cromwell instructed Lely to be truthful in his portrait and to include warts and other imperfections, first surfaced third hand in the early eighteenth century and may be apocryphal, but the surviving portraits do not seem to have been designed to disguise imperfections or unduly to flatter. Warts appear on his chin, forehead and by his right eye. In the 1640s and 1650s alike Cromwell chose to be portrayed in fairly simple clothes, in dark armour or in a simple band shirt collar and coat. Even in the most splendidly posed portrait, dating from 1650–1 and showing Cromwell on horseback with the Thames and the City of London in the background, Cromwell's only sops at sartorial show are frilly shirt cuffs and a rather extravagant set of feathers in his broad-brimmed hat. His hair, dark brown, is always shown worn long at the back and the sides. The surviving portraits also show him with a rather thin moustache of lighter-coloured hue and a tuft of hair below his bottom lip, perhaps caused by his inability to shave over or around the largest of his warts. Cooper gives him slaty blue eyes, but Walker and Lely both show dark brown eyes. In none of the surviving likenesses does Cromwell wear jewellery.

In October 1655 the Venetian ambassador was granted an audience with the Protector, a description of whom he swiftly dispatched to Venice:

> He is fifty-six years of age, with a very scanty beard, of sanguine complexion, medium stature, robust, of martial presence. He had a deep and profound expression, wears a large sword at his side, is both soldier and orator and is skilled in both persuasion and action.

The Venetian ambassador observed and reported upon another characteristic: 'I found him somewhat pulled in appearance, with signs that his health is not stable and perfect. I noticed that as he stood uncovered the hand holding his hat trembled.'[7] In autumn 1655 Cromwell was, indeed, recovering from one of the bouts of ill-health which afflicted him with increasing frequency and severity during the Protectorate. Most of the accounts of the illnesses which supposedly afflicted him in early life are to be found in much later sources of questionable veracity, but we do know that when Cromwell consulted Sir Theodore Mayerne in London in September 1628, the doctor noted a range of physical problems, including coughing, the presence of excessive phlegm and digestive disorders. He appears to have been reasonably healthy during the 1640s, active both in Parliament and on campaign, the latter involving quite extensive travelling around England and Wales. We hear only of occasional trouble with boils, which continued to afflict him with greater severity during the 1650s. But by then he had more serious physical problems, apparently stemming from service in Ireland in 1649–50 – we have reports of one fairly brief but severe bout of ill-health in the latter half of 1649 – compounded by an even more intense and much more prolonged attack in Scotland during the first half of 1651. This seems to have been some sort of recurrent fever, perhaps of a malaria type and first acquired in Ireland, which became increasingly debilitating and severe, which may have been responsible both for the trembling hands noted by the Venetian ambassador and for the increasingly shaky handwriting and signature evident in documents, and which was probably the principal cause of his death.

The recurrent fevers which afflicted Cromwell during the last decade of his life seem to have brought with them mental impairment of a type still associated with attacks of malaria and other fever-related illnesses. Such impairment was only temporary, and there is no strong or convincing evidence for long-term mental decline. Although the speeches which Cromwell made during the second session of the second Protectorate Parliament in January and February 1658 were uncharacteristically short, we know that in March he delivered a speech of over two hours' duration to the lord mayor, aldermen and councillors of the City and that during the same period he responded decisively to military discontent by vigorously reasserting his authority through both words and action. On the other hand, there are suggestions that, throughout his adult life, Cromwell's emotions tended to swing wildly from high to low, from elation and euphoria to extended periods of deep depression, and that these fluctuations were so extreme and the periods of depression so bleak that they might be seen as a form of mental illness. Much of the evidence upon which such a case might rest is unreliable, drawn from sources which were clearly biased, written long after Cromwell's death or compiled by authors who had had little or no personal contact with Cromwell. For example, the story that as a young man in Huntingdon Cromwell repeatedly, both by day and by night, called out his doctor because of unfounded fears that he was dying and because he believed that he was having visions and being visited by spirits, first surfaced in the memoirs of the royalist Sir Philip Warwick, published at the beginning of the eighteenth century. Again, the story that, after his great victory at Dunbar, 'Oliver was carried on as with a divine impulse. He did laugh so excessively as if he had been drunk, and his eyes sparkled with spirits', was written after the Restoration by the antiquarian John Aubrey, who claimed to have heard it from an unnamed acquaintance 'who was present'.[8] Similarly, stories that as a senior soldier and politician he continued to indulge in crude, childish humour, flicking colleagues with ink or throwing cushions at them, particularly at times of tension and pressure, generally rest upon a single author and cannot be corroborated.

There is no doubt that Cromwell was an emotional man and that, from time to time during the decades of military and political conflict, those emotions swung from high to low. In 1628 Mayerne had diagnosed acute depression as the underlying cause of many of Cromwell's more physical afflictions, and his letters and speeches of the 1640s and 1650s point to periods of despondency and gloom, at times verging on an utter despair from which he was saved only by his faith in God. Equally, there is no doubting his elation in the wake of military and political success, the euphoria breaking through in the letters which he wrote after the battles of Marston Moor, Dunbar and Worcester and after the vote of no addresses of January 1648, and in the speeches with which he opened both the Nominated Assembly and his first Protectorate Parliament. It would have been strange, indeed, if the letters which he wrote within hours of his major military victories had been anything other than imbued with a sense of great joy and elation. Sometimes, too, high emotion ran away with him. His angry arguments in 1630 over the new Huntingdon charter carried him before the Privy Council and, briefly, into custody, and during the opening years of the Long Parliament his passion, perhaps exacerbated by an inexperience of parliamentary procedures, was often counterproductive and occasionally earned him stiff rebuke. In the first two years of the war, his criticisms of his military and social superiors, culminating in his detailed testimony against the Earl of Manchester, were sometimes ill-judged or unwise. At the army's Reading debates in 1647, Cromwell acknowledged that he was often accused of going 'too fast', of underestimating 'dangers' and of 'alwayes making hast, and more some times perhaps then good speede'.[9] In a letter of October 1651 he wrote of his 'weaknesses' and 'inordinate passions'.[10] But even in the closing years of his life and career, as an experienced politician and head of state, he could still be headstrong. He angrily turned on the senior army officers in February 1657 and put them in their place with a stinging recital of home truths, bolstered – if surviving accounts of the tirade are accurate – with a measure of distortion and invention.

However, there is also evidence that, when faced with a major decision, a complex situation or some other personal or political crisis, Cromwell could withdraw into himself, to become introspective and hesitant. Cromwell explained this as a need to seek the Lord, to spend time searching for a better understanding of where God and divine providence were leading. His critics, both contemporaries and many later historians, interpret this as evidence of uncertainty, over-caution, chronic inaction and an unwillingness to commit himself. Examples might be found in spring 1647, when he was torn between loyalty to Parliament and to the army, the latter half of 1647 and the period 1652–3, when he wrestled with suggestions that the army be used to intervene in central government, the latter half of 1648, when he agonized over military intervention and regicide, and spring 1657, when he gave the impression of being uncertain whether or not to accept the crown. In some cases, the agonizing was ended by the decisive action of others – Joyce's seizure of the King in 1647, the decision of London-based officers to purge Parliament in December 1648, the intervention of moderates within the Nominated Assembly to terminate its power. On other occasions, Cromwell himself eventually reached a clear decision and then acted decisively to implement it and thus change events – his tardy but then very active support for regicide, his ejection of the Rump, his firm rejection of the crown. This pattern, with phases of inaction and introspection, and of high activity and decisive interventions, is sometimes described as symptomatic of a manic depressive, but the comparison seems strained. For long periods during the 1640s and 1650s, Cromwell seems to have been neither manic nor depressive, neither excessively euphoric nor engulfed in a slough of despair. Instead, he appears to have been working steadily and in an emotionally balanced way to tackle his military and political workload. Although there is no denying the periods of depression and inaction, and of euphoric activity, overall Cromwell does not come across as someone who could be described in medical terms as emotionally disturbed or mentally ill.

Family and Personal Life

Cromwell appears to have had a happy, strong and supportive family life. His father died when he was still in his teens, but his mother survived until 1654. For the last thirty years or more of her life, she lived with her only surviving son and his wife. In April 1649 Cromwell wrote that she was 'in such a condition of illness' that he felt he could not leave her, though military service did, of necessity, separate them for much of the 1640s.[11] Although Cromwell makes respectful but loving reference to her in several letters addressed to other members of the family, no correspondence between mother and son is known to survive. In contrast, we do possess three letters which Cromwell wrote to his wife, Elizabeth, in 1650–1, during the closing stages of the Scottish campaign. They express a love and tenderness which sound a little gruff to a modern ear – 'Thou art dearer to me than any creature; let that suffice.' – but which appear deep:

> My Dearest, I could not satisfy myself to omit this post, although I have not much to write; yet indeed I love to write to my dear, who is very much in my heart. It joys me to hear thy soul prospereth; the Lord increase His favours to thee more and more.[12]

Although Cromwell makes reference to receiving regular letters from his wife, just one survives, dating from December 1650. She gently chides him for not writing more often both to herself and to others in London, and she also expresses a longing to see him again, if it be the Lord's will:

> I should rejoys to hear your desire in seing me, but I desire to submit to the provedns of God, howping the Lord, houe hath separated us, and heth oftune brought us together agane, wil in heis good time breng us agane, to the prase of heis name. Truly my lif is but half a lif in your abseinse, deid not the Lord make it up in heimself, which I must ackoleg to the prase of heis grace.[13]

Despite vague allegations of infidelity in early manhood and even airier rumours of a later affection for John Lambert's wife, there is no convincing evidence for any extra-marital liaisons and every reason to believe that Cromwell's marriage was strong. The marriage produced nine children, born between 1621 and 1638. Elizabeth survived her husband and spent her last years at Northborough, Cambridgeshire, with one of her daughters and her husband. She died there in 1665.

Although Cromwell's two brothers died young, seven sisters survived into adulthood, and he clearly remained in regular contact with several. Three of them married prominent parliamentarian soldiers and politicians, most notably Anna, who in 1636 married John Disbrowe, later a Major-General and one of Cromwell's Protectoral Councillors. In a surviving letter of December 1651 to his unmarried sister Elizabeth at Ely, Cromwell thanked her for her many letters, apologized for replying so infrequently and enclosed a gift of £20 'as a small token of my love'.[14]

Of Cromwell's nine children, only one – James, born and died in January 1632 – did not survive infancy. However, two more sons died young, Robert in his teens of unspecified causes while at school at Felsted in 1639, and Oliver junior in his early twenties of smallpox while serving at Newport Pagnell garrison in 1644. No letters to these two sons are extant, and in his surviving correspondence, Cromwell makes no more than passing references to their deaths. Cromwell's four daughters all married during his lifetime. His eldest daughter Bridget married successively Henry Ireton, sometime Cromwell's political confidant, military colleague and commander in Ireland, and Charles Fleetwood, sometime governor of Ireland, a Major-General and a Protectoral Councillor. The youngest two daughters, Mary and Frances, both wedded during the Protectorate, both marrying into established aristocratic families. There survives only a handful of letters from Cromwell to his daughters. The fullest and most interesting, of October 1646 to his newly married daughter Bridget, is warm and loving, though Cromwell encourages her to seek the Lord:

> Who ever tasted that the Lord is gracious, without some sense of self, vanity, and badness? Who ever tasted that graciousness of His, and could go less in desire, and less in pressing after full enjoyment? Dear Heart, press on; let not husband, let not anything cool thy affections after Christ. I hope he will be an occasion to inflame them. That which is best worthy of love in thy husband is that of the image of Christ he bears. Look on that, and love it best, and all the rest for that. I pray for thee and him; do so for me.[15]

There also survives a series of letters which Cromwell wrote to his son Henry in Ireland in the latter half of the 1650s. Most are concerned with official business, relating to Henry's role as governor of Ireland, but a few contain more personal thoughts and messages. Again, religious exhortation dominates. Thus in April 1656 Cromwell wrote to his son, urging Henry 'with singleness of heart [to] make the glory of the Lord' his overriding aim:

> Study still to be innocent, and to answer every occasion, roll yourself upon God, which to do needs much grace. Cry to the Lord to give you a plain single heart. Take heed of being over-jealous, lest your apprehensions of others cause you to offend. Know that uprightness will preserve you; in this be confident against men.[16]

We know far more about Cromwell's relationship with his eldest surviving son, Richard, for we possess a string of letters which he wrote from 1649 until 1651 to Richard himself, to Richard's new wife Dorothy, and to Dorothy's father, Richard

Maijor. Although Maijor had struck a hard bargain and had caused the marriage negotiations to drag on intermittently for over a year, Cromwell clearly took to him and for a time maintained a close and personal correspondence with this Hampshire gentleman. He looked to Maijor to watch over Richard and to correct what he perceived to be faults in his son and heir. The correspondence reveals that Cromwell, though a loving and affectionate father, believed that his son was not above reproach. He saw in Richard not only a lack of devotion to God and to business but also a worrying attachment to good and expensive living. These faults he labelled 'idleness'. Cromwell's letters to Maijor during 1649 repeatedly stress that Richard must 'be serious, the times requiring it' and that his son's education was far from complete:

> I would have him mind and understand business, read a little history, study the mathematics and cosmography: – these are good, with subordination to the things of God. Better than idleness, or mere outward worldly contents. These fit for public services, for which a man is born.

At the same time, Cromwell wrote to his daughter-in-law, Dorothy, urging her to 'make it above all things your business to seek the Lord' and 'to provoke your husband likewise thereunto'. In spring 1650 he wrote direct to Richard, noting in his recent letters some signs of improvement, but exhorting him with renewed zeal to 'labour to know God in Christ'.

> Take heed of an unactive vain Spirit. Recreate yourself with Sir Walter Raughleye's History: it's a body of history, and will add much more to your understanding than fragments of story. Intend to understand the estate I have settled; it's your concernment to know it all, and how it stands.

Although clearly proud of his first grandchild, Cromwell remained concerned about his son – 'I know my son is idle' – telling Maijor in July 1650 that Richard was in need of 'good counsel', for 'he is in the dangerous time of his age, and it's a very vain world'. Cromwell's forebodings were well founded, for by summer 1651 he had heard that 'my Son hath exceeded his allowance, and is in debt'. In June he wrote to Maijor, carefully laying out his own thoughts and asking Maijor to convey them to his son-in-law:

> Truly I cannot commend him therein; wisdom requiring his living within compass . . . I desire to be understood that I grudge him not laudable recreations, nor an honourable carriage of himself in them . . . Truly I can find in my heart to allow him not only a sufficiency but more, for his good. But if pleasure and self-satisfaction be made the business of a man's life, so much cost laid out upon it, so much time spent in it, as rather answers appetite than the will of God, or is comely before His Saints, I scruple to feed this humour; and God forbid that his being my son should be his allowance to live not pleasingly to our Heavenly Father, who hath raised me out of the dust to what I am! I desire you in faithfulness . . . to advise him to approve himself to the Lord in his course of life; and to search His statutes for a rule to conscience, and to seek grace from Christ to enable [him] to walk therein. This hath life in it, and will come to somewhat: what is a poor creature without this? This will not abridge of lawful pleasures; but teach us an use of them as will have the peace of a good conscience going along with it . . . Truly I love him, he is dear to me; so is his Wife; and for their sakes do I thus write. They shall not want comfort nor encouragement from me, so far as I may afford it. But indeed I cannot think I do well to feed a voluptuous humour in my Son, if he should make pleasures the business of his life, in a time when some precious Saints are bleeding, and breathing out their last, for the safety of the rest.[17]

The letter to Maijor sets out very clearly Cromwell's own attitude towards recreations and worldly pleasures. Cromwell was not a kill-joy and certainly did not oppose all recreation and enjoyment. But such activities should be pursued with moderation, should not become too costly in money or time and under no circumstances should cause men to become more distant from God or to neglect God's work. It was on these grounds that he condemned his own son and others for pursuing worldly pleasures immoderately. This outlook formed part of what Cromwell saw as a wide-ranging programme of godly reformation, and he argued that sinful, back-sliding mortals should be encouraged through example and injunction – moral as much as legal – to mend their ways. He practised what he preached. In the 1640s and 1650s Cromwell clearly gave over much of his time to work, military and political, and to religious devotions. But he also sought modest enjoyment and relaxation. He smoked a pipe and took ale, and from time to time he hosted lavish dinners or banquets for fellow officers, City dignitaries, foreign diplomats and others. Although he felt that music should play no part in divine service, he was otherwise fond of music and singing. As Protector, he reportedly had organs installed at Whitehall and Hampton Court, and his household included a Master of the Music, gentlemen of the music and a number of 'lads brought up to music'. Instrumental music, singing and dancing played an important role at many of the principal social occasions of the Protectorate, not least the wedding celebrations of his two youngest daughters. He saved parts of Charles I's great art collection and acquired further pieces to adorn the rooms at Whitehall and Hampton Court. He enjoyed hawking – one of his earliest surviving letters concerns a lost hawk – and clearly appreciated fine horses. He must have ridden since boyhood and rose to fame as a cavalry commander. In 1643 he negotiated to buy for his personal use a couple of the best horses captured in battle, and during the 1650s he acquired a string of fine horses. Foreign heads of state and their diplomatic representatives quickly learnt that one of the surest ways to win the Protector's ear was to present him with horses.

Cromwell was better able to indulge his generally mod-est tastes during the 1640s and 1650s because of his grow-ing personal wealth. It is very hard accurately to quantify this. Neither a will nor any form of inventory or survey of the property which he held at death appears to survive. Equally, during the Protectorate it becomes hard to distin-guish between Cromwell's personal property, which could be sold off or passed on to his heirs, and state property which was merely 'vested' in him through his office of Lord Protector. None the less, it is clear that Cromwell became extremely rich and that this personal wealth increased hugely during the last twenty years of his life. Down to the mid- or late 1630s, Cromwell probably had an income of no more than a few hundred pounds per year. During the 1640s that increased many times over, both because of his growing military salary and through a series of one-off gifts or grants made to him in cash or land by a grateful Parliament. He acquired land and property scattered throughout much of England and Wales, but with particular concentrations in East Anglia, Hampshire, Gloucestershire and South Wales. By the end of the 1640s his total income – military salary and income from property – probably came to well over £10,000 per annum. It seems to have increased again during the 1650s.

It is noticeable that contemporaries very rarely accused Cromwell of material corruption. During the last decade of his life, he was subject to steady flow of printed attacks, and allegations of pride, ambition and self-seeking abound. But these allegations were couched in political terms, accusing Cromwell of seeking power and high office in order to slake his thirst for political control and to establish a personal tyranny and despotism. Several pamphlets did attack the material corruption, greed and profiteering of the interregnum regimes in general and of the Protectorate in particular, but they tended to focus upon other figures, civilian politicians and military men, and only rarely levelled fire at Cromwell himself. As Protector, Cromwell was all too aware that he might be accused of material greed as well as political ambition. In April 1656 he warned his son Henry against 'studying to lay for yourself the foundation of a great estate', for it would prove a 'snare' to him, not only because God 'abhors' such 'evil', but also because it would set a bad example, for observers 'will be confirmed in covetousness'.[18] In May 1654 Richard Maijor tried to persuade the Protector to invest in some sort of property or business venture which he was setting up. Cromwell's reply is revealing. He confessed that the 'business' was attractive and that he had both land in Essex and money in hand which could have 'gone towards it'.

But indeed I am so unwilling to be a seeker after the world, having had so much favour from the Lord in giving me so much without seeking; and so unwilling that men should think me so, which they will though you only appear in it (for they will, by one means or another, know it), – that indeed I dare not meddle nor proceed therein. Thus I have told you my plain thoughts.[19]

Soldier and Politician

'It is obvious to all, he studied Men more than Books', commented the anonymous author of *The Perfect Politician*.[20] Cromwell was far from stupid and had received the solid education of a gentleman's son, including a spell at Cambridge University, though he left well before completing his studies or obtaining a degree. He may have obtained a smattering of legal knowledge by attending one of the London Inns for a time – Carrington commented that 'his parents designed him for the Study of the Civill Law, which is the foundation of the Politicks'[21] – though the evidence is inconclusive. He could read and write English well enough and had adequate Latin. In 1650 he recommended that his son study business, mathematics, cosmography and 'a little' history, particularly Raleigh's *History of the World*. But Cromwell does not come across as a great intellectual or a highly original thinker, and there is little sign that he had an unusually wide or deep academic knowledge. In presenting a set of financial accounts to Parliament in April 1657, he claimed that the business was 'exceedingly past my understanding, for I have as little skill in Arithmetic as I have in the Law'; earlier in the same speech he had pleaded ignorance of legal terms and claimed that, although he had heard talk of 'demurrers', such matters were beyond his understanding.[22] His surviving letters and speeches reveal no more than a passing acquaintance with classical and recent British history, and certainly do not point to a man of wide academic, literary and historical tastes. Instead, Cromwell usually drew on a single book for his intellectual and literary references, and all his speeches and many of his letters were weighed down with repeated references to the Bible, far more often to the Old than to the New Testament.

This apparently somewhat narrow academic and intellectual background was reinforced by a comparative lack of practical experience. During the 1620s and 1630s Cromwell had been a small-scale East Anglian farmer, at or near the bottom of the gentry class. He may well have strayed no further than East Anglia, the east Midlands and London. In 1640 Cromwell probably had no military experience at all, had never been a county JP, had played no more than quite minor roles in town and county administration and had served inconspicuously in a single Parliament. When the political and military conflict of the years after 1640 catapulted Cromwell ever higher, he had only a very limited intellectual and practical grounding upon which to draw. The military and political skills which he displayed in the 1640s and 1650s were built upon slender foundations.

Cromwell has often been described as a natural military genius and compared with several of the outstanding military figures which Britain has produced, most notably Marlborough, Wellington and Montgomery. There is no doubting that during the 1640s Cromwell swiftly acquired and exercised a range of military skills and that he emerged as one of the most successful commanders of the entire civil war, a path which carried him from an inexperienced captain to all-conquering commander-in-chief in less than eight years. Cromwell explained this in terms of God's providence, arguing that he was unworthy and unskilled and that the Lord's intervention alone had enabled him to gain victories and to recover from occasional reverses. Consistent with this is Cromwell's oft-repeated claim that, in raising his own regiment, he recruited 'godly' and 'honest' men, and his oft-repeated advice to others that they should do likewise. Such men would be more likely to win God's favour and to be the instruments of His providences and, more prosaically, they would also tend to be strongly motivated by a belief that they were doing God's work and to accept more readily both self-discipline and the sort of tight discipline which Cromwell and his subordinate officers imposed. It was this discipline which enabled Cromwell – unlike many cavalry commanders

– to keep tight control of his cavalry on the battlefield, to prevent the horse charging off the battlefield in pursuit of their broken enemy and instead then to regroup and to tear into the vulnerable enemy foot. He also learnt very early the value of keeping one or two waves of cavalry in reserve, to be deployed at the vital moment to support the first attack and to relieve units which had met with unexpected pressure or a reverse. These skills were bolstered both by attention to details of pay and supply – seen most clearly in the long, painstaking preparations for the Irish campaign – and by a conviction that the war was necessary and just and that, whatever may then follow in political and constitutional affairs, it was vital to score a complete military victory. In many ways, Cromwell was the most successful military commander of the civil war, and his reputation was built upon solid and often outstanding achievements.

Cromwell never suffered clear defeat in a field engagement, and although he was involved in some unfortunately indecisive battles, notably the second battle of Newbury in 1644, most of the battles in which he fought, both as a subordinate officer and as overall commander, produced decisive victory. However, the record was not entirely unblemished. He was fortunate to escape with his life at Winceby in October 1643, for his horse was shot dead under him and, unmounted and vulnerable, he came close to being dispatched by the royalist Sir Ingram Hopton. None of Cromwell's surviving letters gives an account of this battle, and it is not clear whether the incident could be ascribed to inexperience or overconfidence. It was Sir Thomas Fairfax, not Cromwell, who made the decisive contribution at Winceby and who brought victory. Cromwell was reportedly wounded in the neck at Marston Moor, though not seriously, and was able to return to the field. Indeed, his contribution was probably crucial to the successful outcome. But three months later, at the second battle of Newbury, he appears to have attacked too late, failing to co-ordinate his manoeuvre with those of the other parliamentary commanders, and then to have been less than dynamic on the battlefield. His attitude during and after the battle formed one of the planks of the detailed charges which Manchester subsequently levelled against him, but the matter was dropped without either a full investigation or any form of verdict or conclusion. As second-in-command at Naseby in 1645 and as the overall commander at Worcester in 1651, Cromwell secured decisive victories, though on both occasions the royalists were heavily outnumbered and the parliamentarians therefore had an enormous advantage before a shot had been fired. In contrast, at Preston in 1648 and at Dunbar in 1650, he engaged and defeated armies which outnumbered his own, on both occasions very skilfully avoiding meeting the total enemy strength head on. At Preston he engaged only part of the Scottish army, while the remainder was strung out south of the town, and at Dunbar he began by attacking the right flank of the Scottish army and only then tore into the centre and other wing, relying upon the awkward contour of the ground and the inexperience of the Scots to prevent Scottish realignment. Cromwell's record in field engagements was not entirely faultless, but it was a very strong one, and probably better than that of any other senior officer who fought throughout the civil wars.

It is difficult to avoid the conclusion that Cromwell was not so skilled at siege warfare or at a more protracted, manoeuvre-type campaign. He was involved in a number of sieges in England during the war of 1642–6, generally quite brief operations which ended with a surrender on terms. The main exception was the siege of Basing House in autumn 1645, concluded by bloody storm and slaughter. In Wales in summer 1648, Cromwell was not so convincing, clearly underestimating the difficulties presented by the castle and walled town of Pembroke and the tenacity of his opponents. When the operation proved far more protracted than Cromwell had hoped or expected, he made a premature and unsuccessful attempt to storm. The Irish campaign of 1649–50 saw no field engagements and was instead dominated by a series of sieges and attacks upon towns and castles around the east and south coast of Ireland. Thus both geographically and militarily the campaign was quite limited and specialized in its nature. The results were mixed, with hard-won and terrible victories at Drogheda and Wexford, further success at Kilkenny and Clonmel, though only at a high cost in parliamentarian dead, and failure at Duncannon and Waterford. Although the Scottish campaign of 1650–1 brought Cromwell two of his greatest victories in battle, the campaign as a whole was frustrating and marked by inactivity. It demonstrated the inability of the English to bring to battle an enemy who skilfully used the geographical and logistical potential of their home country, as well as Cromwell's own caution and perhaps uncertainty in the face of such tactics.

The brevity and limited nature of Cromwell's military career must also be emphasized. His soldiering lasted barely nine years, from the young captain's action in Cambridge in August 1642 to the Lord General's crowning victory at Worcester in September 1651. He did not become commander-in-chief until summer 1650, little more than a year before his final action. Although at times during the latter half of the civil war of 1642–6 he led detached units on small campaigns around Oxfordshire or in central southern England, he did not command his own field army until 1648. In only two battles, Dunbar and Worcester, did he command armies numbering more than 10,000 men. Within England, most of Cromwell's campaigns took place in the south, the south-west and the east and southern Midlands. Edgehill excepted, he did not fight in the west Midlands, and Marston Moor and the Preston campaign excepted, he did not fight in northern England. His only experience of campaigning in Wales came in summer 1648, involving the capture of the town – though not the castle – of Chepstow and the operation against the town and castle of Pembroke. The military and geographical limitations of the Irish campaign have already been noted. In Scotland the rather desultory campaign was focused on the central lowlands, principally the east coast south of the Firth of Forth and the area encompassed by the towns of Edinburgh, Glasgow and Stirling. Apart from the campaigns in Ireland and Scotland in 1649–51, Cromwell did not meet any foreign enemies and he did not take part in war by land or by sea against Continental powers. Thus because of the scale, nature and duration of Cromwell's military experience, it is probably unfair and misleading to compare him either with the great Continental commanders of the seventeenth century, who saw action in the Thirty Years War, the wars of Louis XIV or the wars against the Turks, or with later British commanders, all of whom won fame in international warfare. Cromwell was triumphant in the British wars. Therein lies his unique greatness.

Two traits underpinned Cromwell's political approach and outlook from the mid-1640s, when he began to play a significant role in central government and national politics, until his death twelve years later. The first, alluded to above, was his lack of profound or original ideas. Cromwell was not a great political theorist and he tended to be led by, or to react to, initiatives and ideas formulated by others. When the debates held at Reading and Putney during 1647 turned from the role of the army, upon which Cromwell had plenty to say, to deeper political and constitutional matters, his recorded contributions quickly dwindled. Other officers, particularly Ireton, took the lead, displaying a sharpness of mind which was perhaps beyond Cromwell. The constitutional theorizing which produced the Nominated Assembly in 1653 emanated from debates in the Council of Officers reportedly dominated by John Lambert and Thomas Harrison, not from Cromwell either acting alone or imposing his distinctive will. Although he requested and obtained revisions to the Instrument of Government and the Humble Petition and Advice, both Protectoral constitutions were initiated and drafted by others. In 1657–8 he repeatedly claimed that most of the key domestic policy developments from 1653 onwards had been initiated by the army or the Council, though here Cromwell was probably being disingenuous.

The second trait was Cromwell's flexibility, most clearly enunciated at Reading in July 1647, when he asserted that he was not 'wedded and glewed to formes of Governement'.[23] For Cromwell, the importance lay in the ends not the means, and if the government appeared to be doing God's work and bringing closer God's eternal salvation, he was not too concerned about the precise form which that mortal and transitory government took. Thus Cromwell was willing to support different forms, to experiment, and to abandon a government which no longer appeared to have divine support or to be working towards God's chosen ends. According to his interpretation of God's will, he shifted between supporting monarchical and republican forms of government. At times, he laid great stress upon the sovereignty of the people and the sanctity of parliament, yet at other times he could dismiss popular opinion, snarling that the important thing was the people's 'good, not what pleases them',[24] and he was involved in the purging and ejection of elected parliaments and in the establishment of a non-elected assembly. At that point, in spring 1653, he seemed to share many of the millenarian assumptions of the Fifth Monarchists and others, but he clearly shied away from them later in the 1650s, in several speeches bitterly condemning claims by Fifth Monarchists 'to entitle themselves on this principle, that they are the only men to rule kingdoms, govern nations, and give laws to people'.[25] He came to view the Protectoral system of government as an effective means to pursuing God-given ends, though even then he was willing to change the forms, perhaps seriously contemplating taking the crown in spring 1657 and around the same time hinting that the entire Protectorate was a temporary experiment.

In several of his speeches during the Protectorate, Cromwell asserted that the chief ends of government were 'maintaining of the liberty of these nations; our civil liberties, as men; our spiritual liberties, as Christians'. Of the two, he claimed that the religious goal, 'the preservation of the professors thereof, to give them all due and just liberty, and to assert the truths of God', was foremost, but he argued that care for 'civil liberties and interests of the nations' was 'the next best God hath given men in the world . . . to fence the people of God in their interest'.[26] Cromwell wanted everyone to share in the peace and well-being of the commonwealth, to enjoy their liberty and their own property free from illegal interference, protected by the law and the magistrate. He was aware that injustices and imperfections continued, and he sought, both via his own reformist initiatives as Protector and by urging various parliaments to undertake reform, to reduce or remove some of these imperfections. Cromwell concentrated upon the unduly harsh nature of some laws and the inefficiency and unwarrantable expense of the legal system. On several occasions, most notably in the letter which he wrote after the battle of Dunbar in 1650, he also called for a measure of social justice, asserting that 'if there be any one that makes many poor to make a few rich, that suits not a Commonwealth'.[27] On the other hand, he strongly defended the established, hierarchical social order, referred to both liberty and property as 'badges of the kingdom of Christ'[28] and fiercely condemned any institution or group – the Nominated Assembly, the Levellers and other radical sects – which appeared to be threatening the existing social order or to be advocating enforced redistribution of property. Similarly, he supported only modest extensions to the franchise and strongly condemned any proposal to extend the vote to those with little or no property. Cromwell was no social revolutionary.

Cromwell and Religion

From his conversion experience at some point in the 1630s until his death, Cromwell possessed a deep and overriding belief in an active and all-powerful God, who was guiding the nation and its people along His chosen path and who had summoned Cromwell to be one of His servants and instruments in that work. Here, most historians now agree, was the driving force which pushed Cromwell forward and which shaped most of his subsequent thoughts and actions. From the mid-1630s until his death, almost all Cromwell's surviving letters and recorded speeches are loaded with references to the Bible and allusions to God and God's will. Repeatedly during the 1640s and 1650s, he justified the key developments which he initiated or in which he was involved – the civil war itself, Pride's Purge, regicide, the Irish and Scottish campaigns, the ejection of the Rump, the rejection of the crown and so on – in terms of God's will. The Lord had brought them about, and Cromwell was participating merely as God's servant. In our more secular age, this can all too easily be dismissed as cant, as a false veneer to cover his very mortal actions and ambitions and to apply pressure on political opponents. Some contemporaries thought the same, most notably the authors of *The Hunting of Foxes*, who in 1649 famously alleged that 'You shall scarce speak to Cromwell about anything, but he will lay his hand on his breast, elevate his eyes, and call God to record; he will weep, howl and repent, even while he doth smite you under the first rib.'[29] But a belief in God's controlling hand emerges so fervently and so consistently in Cromwell's letters, even those addressed to close personal friends and family, that it is impossible to dismiss such expressions as conscious and deliberate falsehoods.

Cromwell believed sincerely that God was active in the world and that the Lord guided and directed all the key military and political developments of the 1640s and 1650s. At the end of August 1650, as he and his army were trudging back towards Dunbar on an overnight march, an attempt by the Scots to engage the rear of the army was thwarted when 'the Lord by His good Providence put a cloud over the moon';[30] even the movement of a cloud was directed by God. Time and again, Cromwell stressed that he was utterly worthless and unfit; his military and political colleagues were equally unworthy. It was the Lord alone who had employed and empowered such pitiful creatures to secure victory and to advance the godly cause. Thus Cromwell repeatedly begged that all glory and credit for victory should lie with the Lord, not with His mortal servants, though such mortals might draw comfort and strength from the knowledge that they were doing the Lord's work and were pleasing to Him. Conversely, defeats and setbacks were seen as warnings from God, indicating that in some way the Lord was displeased and was testing or admonishing His servants. Several times during the 1640s and 1650s, and over key issues, Cromwell came to believe that divisions among, and defeats suffered by, the parliamentary cause were divine rebukes, signs that somehow he and his colleagues had parted from the chosen path, sinned themselves or condoned sins in others, and so earned God's disfavour. Thus God was delivering a warning, to which the recipients should respond by searching out and extirpating sins and errors. For example, Cromwell came to interpret the divisions of 1647 both among the parliamentary army and between that army and Parliament, culminating in the slide into renewed civil war in 1648, as a sign of God's disfavour, caused by their attempts to negotiate with Charles I. Again, the failure of the first Protectorate Parliament and the defeat in Hispaniola in 1655 apparently triggered in Cromwell another, more personal bout of self-doubt and inquiry, born of a suspicion that the Lord's favour had been lost, perhaps in part because of his own failings. Cromwell's providentialism might strengthen and reassure in times of success, but at the price of intensifying the uncertainties and terrors of failure.

In several speeches delivered during the Protectorate, Cromwell made clear his belief that the Lord had chosen the nation for special treatment and favour. Repeatedly referring to the biblical story of Moses leading his people out of Egypt, he claimed that the nation and its people had come through a period of bondage and trial, were currently in the wilderness purging their sins, but were approaching the Promised Land. Hence his attempts, first seen in letters written during the later 1640s but broadcast with greater assurance through words and action during the 1650s, to institute reforms which would reduce the level of sin and immorality and produce a more godly nation, as well as to encourage other institutions and officials to pass further legislation against mortal sins and to enforce more effectively existing measures. Thus the cause of godly reformation would be advanced. Although the high tide of Cromwell's millenarianism apparently turned in 1653 and thereafter his letters and speeches made fewer explicit references to the second coming, he continued to see a necessity for preparing the nation and its people for the day when 'Jesus Christ will have a time to set up his reign in our hearts', as he put it in 1654.[31] To Cromwell, these divine ends alone mattered; the worldly means by which they might be achieved were immaterial. In autumn 1647 Cromwell approvingly quoted St Paul's reference to mortal government as but 'drosse and dunge in comparison of Christ'.[32]

Just as Cromwell did not care much about worldly forms of government, as long as they facilitated progress towards divine ends, so he was not too concerned about the outward forms of religion and religious organization. Repeatedly during the 1640s and 1650s he stressed that a variety of Protestant churches all contained an element of God's truth and should flourish. What mattered to Cromwell was that people should understand God's fundamental truths and should earn salvation. He disliked dividing people up into distinct churches and labelling them as a particular variety of Protestant. Equally, it is impossible to categorize Cromwell as belonging to a particular denomination or confessional group, independent, presbyterian or whatever. Instead, he wanted broad religious liberty, in the belief that all the Protestant faiths contained some element of God's truth, and in the hope that, in due course, they would all coalesce to reveal a complete and united picture. This desire for ultimate religious unity appears opaquely or clearly in a number of Cromwell's letters and speeches, most notably in a letter to Robert Hammond of late 1648: 'I profess to thee I desire from my heart, I have prayed for it, I have waited for the day to see union and right understanding between the godly people (Scots, English, Jews, Gentiles, Presbyterians, Independents, Anabaptists, and all).'[33]

Religious freedom or 'liberty of conscience' became a cornerstone of Cromwell's religious aspirations and policies. He condemned the pre-war church for denying such liberty, for oppressing and persecuting good Protestants and for forcing thousands of them to emigrate to the New World. Several times, he claimed that the desire to secure liberty of conscience was the main factor which had motivated him and others to take up arms and to continue the bloody and terrible war – 'all the money of this nation would not have tempted men to fight, upon such an account as they have engaged, if they had not had hopes of liberty, better than they had from Episcopacy' – and had become the central principle and objective of the entire parliamentary cause: 'undoubtedly this is the peculiar interest all this while contended for'.[34] This liberty was not total and, both because it operated within certain limits and because its ultimate goal was religious unity not permanent plurality, it is misleading and anachronistic to equate it with the modern concept of religious toleration. It is noticeable that in his letters and speeches Cromwell usually cited just three denominations – presbyterians, independents and baptists – as examples of Protestant groups which contain elements of God's truth, though in practice during the 1650s as a whole and Cromwell's Protectorate in particular, liberty was extended to other individuals and groups. However, Cromwell was adamant that those whose religious practices disrupted the peace or challenged magistracy – itself divinely appointed – or contained elements which went beyond fundamental truths and strayed into blasphemy and heresy, were not to enjoy liberty. The very opposite – the existing laws against blasphemy, heresy and civil disturbance should be swiftly and rigorously imposed by the magistracy. Time and again, he stressed that liberty of conscience would not be used as a cover for heresy or as a shield to protect heretics from the law.

More often, however, Cromwell laid stress on the need to prevent the persecution of those who possessed an element of God's truth and to stop one religious group attacking another. Time and again, he condemned the attitude of men who now enjoyed liberty but who were attempting to prevent others sharing that liberty. Late in 1654 Cromwell reportedly bewailed, 'Where shall wee have men of a Universall Spirit? Every one desires to have liberty, but none will give it.'[35] In a speech to Parliament in January 1658, he condemned the way in which the sects attacked one another as 'an appetite to variety, to be not only making wounds, but as if we should see one making wounds in a man's side and would desire nothing more than to be groping and grovelling with his fingers in those wounds'.[36] But Cromwell's fullest and most eloquent exposition of the point is to be found in his speech of January 1655, dissolving the first Protectorate Parliament:

> I say, you might have had opportunity to have settled peace and quietness amongst all professing Godliness, and might have been instrumental, if not to have healed the breaches, yet to have kept the Godly of all judgments from running one upon another ... Are these things done? Or anything towards them? Is there not yet upon the spirits of men a strange itch? Nothing will satisfy them, unless they can put their finger upon their brethren's consciences, to pinch him there. To do this was no part of the contest we had with the common adversary; for religion was not the thing at the first contested for, but God brought it to that issue at last, and give it to us by way of redundancy, and at last it proved that which was most dear to us. And wherein consisted this, more

than in obtaining that liberty from the tyranny of the bishops to all species of Protestants, to worship God according to their own light and consciences? ... Those that were sound in the faith, how proper was it for them to labour for liberty, for a just liberty, that men should not be trampled upon for their consciences? Had not they laboured but lately under the weight of persecutions, and was it fit for them to sit heavy upon others? Is it ingenuous to ask liberty, and not to give it? What greater hypocrisy than for those who were oppressed by the bishops, to become the greatest oppressors themselves so soon as their yoke was removed? I could wish that they who call for liberty now also, had not too much of that spirit, if the power were in their hands.[37]

In his burning desire to extend and defend liberty, we see Cromwell at his most attractive; in his expectation that the nation would share this vision and link arms with him, we see him at his most futile. Herein rest the triumph and the tragedy of Oliver Cromwell.

SELECT BIBLIOGRAPHY

Biographies of Cromwell abound. Although our knowledge of the man and the period has advanced considerably since their day, the biographies written by the two greatest late Victorian historians of the period – S. R. Gardiner, *Oliver Cromwell* (London, 1901) and C. H. Firth, *Oliver Cromwell and the Rule of the Puritans* (London, 1900) – remain masterpieces; S. R. Gardiner's *Cromwell's Place in History* (London, 1897) and his multi-volumed *History of the Great Civil War* (4 vols, London, 1893) and *History of the Commonwealth and Protectorate* (4 vols, London, 1903) also contain very valuable material on Cromwell, as does C. H. Firth's *The Last Years of the Protectorate* (2 vols, London, 1909), which continued Gardiner's narrative account down to 1658. Of the more recent biographies, J. Buchan, *Oliver Cromwell* (London, 1934) is particularly elegant, R. S. Paul, *The Lord Protector* (London, 1955) is strong on religion and Cromwell's faith, C. Hill, *God's Englishman* (Harmondsworth, 1970) is a brilliant thematic study rather than a straightforward life and forcefully puts the case for Cromwell abandoning his radical past and becoming more conservative in the 1650s, A. Fraser, *Cromwell, Our Chief of Men* (1973) is probably the biography best known outside academic circles, I. Roots (ed.), *Cromwell, A Profile* (London, 1973) is an important collection of essays on the man and his policies, and J. Gillingham, *Cromwell. Portrait of a Soldier* (London, 1976) focuses, as its title suggests, on Cromwell's military career.

During the 1980s A. B. Worden published four stimulating articles, mostly on the theme of Cromwell and religion: 'Toleration and the Cromwellian Protectorate', in W. J. Sheils (ed.), *Persecution and Toleration: Studies in Church History* XXI (Oxford, 1984); 'Providence and Politics in Cromwellian England', in *Past and Present* 109 (1985); an exploration of how Cromwell interpreted the apparent withdrawal of God's support and possibly feared an element of personal responsibility in 'Oliver Cromwell and the Sin of Achan', published in D. Beales and G. Best (eds), *History, Society and the Churches* (Cambridge, 1985); and, on a more literary theme, 'The Politics of Marvell's Horation Ode', in *The Historical Journal* 27 (1984).

Two outstanding studies were published while this book was in preparation. B. Coward, *Oliver Cromwell* (Harlow, 1991) is a clear and well-researched biography, which strongly argues that, far from abandoning his radical past in the 1650s, to the end Cromwell remained true to the cause of reformation. J. S. Morrill (ed.), *Oliver Cromwell and the English Revolution* (Harlow, 1990) is a collection of essays on different themes but of a consistently high standard. Morrill himself has contributed an outstanding re-evaluation of Cromwell's early life, which will serve as the foundation for all subsequent accounts; Morrill also argues that Cromwell acted during the opening years of the Long Parliament as an agent for more powerful and experienced kinsmen and colleagues. J. S. A. Adamson explores Cromwell's role in the Long Parliament, in contrast arguing that in 1640–2 he was acting in isolation. A. Woolrych assesses Cromwell the soldier, D. Hirst Cromwell as Lord Protector, and D. Stevenson Cromwell's attitude to Scotland and Ireland. J. C. Davis and A. Fletcher respectively explore Cromwell's own personal faith and his religious policy, while J. Sommerville places Cromwell's political ideas in the wider context of English political thought. Morrill ends this excellent collection by surveying the views of Cromwell which surfaced in print during his own lifetime. This theme is continued and extended in R. C. Richardson (ed.), *Images of Oliver Cromwell* (Manchester, 1993), a collection of essays in memory of R. Howell and many of them by him, which examines how different ages and countries have thrown up differing interpretations of Cromwell.

The best account of the mythology surrounding Cromwell is A. Smith, 'The Image of Cromwell in Folklore and Tradition', in *Folklore* 79 (1968). See also P. Gaunt, 'To Tyburn and

Beyond: The Mortal Remains of Oliver Cromwell' and I. Roots, 'Cromwell's Head', both in *Cromwelliana* (1986–7). On Cromwell and iconoclasm, see G. F. Nuttall, 'Was Cromwell an Iconoclast?', in *Transactions of the Congregational History Society* 12 (1933–6); also valuable is Nuttall's response to R. S. Paul's biography of Cromwell, 'The Lord Protector: Reflections on Dr Paul's Life of Cromwell', in *Congregational Quarterly* 33 (1955). S. Roberts, 'Work in Progress I. The Wealth of Oliver Cromwell', in *Cromwelliana* (1994), sets out what we know and do not know about Cromwell's property and material wealth. The best account of Cromwell's portraiture is D. Piper, *The Contemporary Portraits of Oliver Cromwell* (Walpole Society, London, 1958). P. Gaunt, *The Cromwellian Gazetteer* (Gloucester, 1987) is a guide to sites associated with Cromwell and the parliamentary cause in general; it includes a list and maps of Cromwell's known itinerary during the last twenty years or so of his life. R. Hutton, *The British Republic 1649–60* (Basingstoke, 1990) is notable both as the most recent fairly detailed synthesis of work on the interregnum and for a portrayal of Cromwell which is harsher than many modern interpretations and which the author himself describes as 'slightly more critical than the norm'. Cromwell continues to divide.

Apart from Morrill's pioneering chapter in his own collection *Oliver Cromwell and the English Revolution* and the relevant sections of the full-length biographies, there is little specifically on Cromwell's early life pre-1640 apart from B. Quintrell's 'Oliver Cromwell and Distraint of Knighthood', in *Bulletin of the Institute of Historical Research* 57 (1984). Cromwell's parliamentary career 1640–6 and beyond is best followed through the relevant sections of the essays by Morrill and Adamson in Morrill's collection. C. Holmes, 'Colonel King and Lincolnshire Politics, 1642–6', in *The Historical Journal* 16 (1973), and C. Holmes, *The Eastern Association in the English Civil War* (Cambridge, 1974) contain much material on Cromwell's military career in 1643–4, including something on the background to his clash with Manchester. The latter is explored in an important and informative article by A. N. B. Cotton, 'Cromwell and the Self-Denying Ordinance', in *History* 62 (1977).

G. E. Aylmer, 'Was Oliver Cromwell a Member of the Army

in 1646–7 or Not?', in *History* 56 (1971) emphasizes uncertainty and ambiguity, while C. Hoover, 'Cromwell's Status and Pay in 1646–7', in *The Historical Journal* 23 (1980) is more confident that he did remain a member of the New Model Army. A. Woolrych, *Soldiers and Statesmen* (Oxford, 1987) is an outstanding and detailed account of the role of the army and army politics in 1647–8, containing much on Cromwell's role, actions and outlook. The account of events at Corkbush Field, Ware, in November 1647 given by Woolrych and others is more convincing than that of M. Kishlansky, 'What Happened at Ware', in *The Historical Journal* 25 (1982). I. Gentles, *The New Model Army in England, Ireland and Scotland, 1645–53* (Oxford, 1992) is a compelling account of the army's military campaigns and political involvement, with frequent reference to Cromwell's role and actions. Unlike the present author, Gentles believes that at Preston Cromwell's army was roughly equal in size to the Scottish army, and he argues that Pontefract remained a serious threat and obstacle in late 1648; hence Cromwell's prolonged operation against the outpost was justified on military grounds and should not be taken as evidence of a reluctance to return to London.

D. Underdown, *Pride's Purge* (Oxford, 1971), A. B. Worden, *The Rump Parliament* (Cambridge, 1974) and A. Woolrych, *Commonwealth to Protectorate* (Oxford, 1982) together provide an outstanding and detailed analytical narrative of the years 1648 to 1653, with much to say about the role and activities of Cromwell. Worden and Woolrych include detailed reassessments – slightly different but not entirely incompatible – of the Rump's constitutional bill and the reasons for Cromwell's actions of April 1653. Although in part superseded by these accounts, C. H. Firth, 'Cromwell and the Expulsion of the Long Parliament', in *English Historical Review* 8 (1893) is still useful.

The best general introduction to Cromwell's campaign in Ireland and Scotland in 1649–51 is to be found in Gentles, *The New Model Army*. See also the more detailed accounts of certain events and aspects in W. S. Douglas, *Cromwell's Scotch Campaigns: 1650–1* (London, 1898), C. H. Firth, 'The Battle of Dunbar', in *Transactions of the Royal Historical Society*, new series 14 (1900), J. G. Simms, 'Cromwell's Siege of Waterford,

1649', in *The Irish Sword* 4 (1959–60), J. G. Simms, 'Cromwell at Drogheda, 1649', in *The Irish Sword* XI (1973–4), and J. Burke, 'The New Model Army and the Problems of Siege Warfare, 1649–51', in *Irish Historical Studies* 27 (1990).

There is surprisingly little political analysis of Cromwell's role as Lord Protector, though D. Hirst's chapter in Morrill's collection contains valuable insights, and the relevant sections of several biographies include a measure of political analysis. On a more ceremonial theme, R. Sherwood, *The Court of Oliver Cromwell* (Cambridge, 1977) is a thorough and perceptive examination of Cromwell's court and household as Lord Protector.

On Cromwell's Protectorate Parliaments, the seminal work was H. R. Trevor-Roper's 1956 article, 'Oliver Cromwell and his Parliaments', subsequently reprinted in several collections, most notably Roots (ed.), *Cromwell, A Profile*. R. Howell questioned several of Trevor-Roper's assumptions and interpretations in 'Cromwell and his Parliaments: The Trevor-Roper Thesis Revisited', reprinted in Richardson (ed.), *Images of Oliver Cromwell*. P. Gaunt, 'Law-Making in the First Protectorate Parliament', in C. Jones, M. Newitt and S. Roberts (eds), *Politics and People in Revolutionary England* (Oxford, 1986) and I. Roots, 'Lawmaking in the Second Protectorate Parliament', in H. Hearder and H. R. Loyn (eds), *British Government and Administration* (Cardiff, 1974) reassess Cromwell's two Protectorate Parliaments and throw new light upon the Protector. See also the more detailed accounts of specific events and developments provided by P. Gaunt, 'Cromwell's Purge? Exclusions and the First Protectorate Parliament', in *Parliamentary History* 6 (1987), T. A. Wilson and F. J. Merli, 'Naylor's Case and the Dilemma of the Protectorate', in *University of Birmingham Historical Journal* 10 (1965–6), and C. H. Firth, 'Cromwell and the Crown', in *English Historical Review* 17 and 18 (1902 and 1903), which remains the most detailed analysis of that episode. P. Gaunt, 'Oliver Cromwell and his Protectorate Parliaments: Co-operation, Conflict and Control', in I. Roots (ed.), *'Founding a Firm State'? Aspects of the Interregnum* (Exeter, forthcoming, due late 1995) attempts a broader review of Cromwell's relationship with his two Protectorate Parliaments.

P. Gaunt, '"The Single Person's Confidants and Dependants"? Oliver Cromwell and his Protectoral Councillors', in *The Historical Journal* 32 (1989) provides some insights into the relative powers of, and the relationship between, Cromwell and his Protectoral Council. However, much of the work on this subject is available only as an unpublished doctoral thesis, P. Gaunt, 'The Councils of the Protectorate, from December 1653 to September 1658' (University of Exeter, 1983), which is heavily based upon the surviving conciliar papers, now in the Public Record Office, London.

The best published study of the role of the army during the Protectorate is A. Woolrych, 'The Cromwellian Protectorate: A Military Dictatorship?', in *History* 75 (1990), which in part draws upon an as yet unpublished doctoral thesis by H. M. Reece; Woolrych answers the question firmly in the negative. For Cromwell's relationship with John Lambert, probably (after Cromwell) the most important military figure for much of the Protectorate, see G. D. Heath, 'Cromwell and Lambert, 1653–7', in Roots (ed.), *Cromwell, A Profile*, and a not entirely satisfactory full-length biography by W. H. Dawson, *Cromwell's Understudy: The Life and Times of General John Lambert* (London, 1938). The Major-Generals, too, deserve fuller study, though some insight into their work and into Cromwell's relationship with them may be gleaned from I. Roots, 'Swordsmen and Decimators', in R. Parry (ed.), *The English Civil War and After* (London, 1970) and from A. Fletcher, 'Oliver Cromwell and the Localities: The Problem of Consent', in Jones, Newitt and Roberts (eds), *Politics and People in Revolutionary England*.

The foreign policy of the Protectorate is another aspect which deserves more research. R. Crabtree, 'The Idea of a Protestant Foreign Policy', in Roots (ed.), *Cromwell, A Profile*, and M. Roberts, 'Cromwell and the Baltic', in his own *Essays in Swedish History* (London, 1967) have much to say about Cromwell's role. Despite its promising title, C. P. Korr, *Cromwell and the New Model Foreign Policy* (Berkeley, Calif., 1975) is merely a review of Anglo-French relations. More helpful are the documents printed within, and the full and perceptive introduction to, M. Roberts (ed.), *Swedish Diplomats at Cromwell's Court 1655–6* (London, 1988). T. Venning, *Cromwellian Foreign Policy* (London, forthcoming, due 1995) is still in press at the time of writing but should go some way towards filling a large gap.

The principal and most reliable sources for a biography of Cromwell are his own writings and utterances. The earliest published collection was T. Carlyle, *The Letters and Speeches of Oliver Cromwell* (2 vols, London, 1845), which went through numerous editions, edited by Carlyle and others and steadily growing in size; several editions were divided into three or four volumes. The best and most reliable was probably that edited by S. C. Lomas and published in three volumes in 1904. W. C. Abbott collected and edited a much larger set, *The Writings and Speeches of Oliver Cromwell* (4 vols, Cambridge, Mass., 1937–47), weighed down with other documents about rather than by Cromwell and with Abbott's own commentary. J. S. Morrill compares and contrasts the Lomas edition of Carlyle with Abbott's work and comes down heavily in favour of the former in 'Textualizing and Contextualizing Cromwell', in *The Historical Journal* 33 (1990). The most reliable and comprehensive collection of Cromwell's state speeches is probably that of C. L. Stainer (ed.), *Speeches of Oliver Cromwell, 1644–58* (Oxford, 1901). I. Roots (ed), *Speeches of Oliver Cromwell* (London, 1989), drawing upon Stainer, reproduces all the major speeches, plus a selection of more private 'conversations'.

J. Bruce and D. Masson (eds), *The Quarrel Between the Earl of Manchester and Oliver Cromwell* (London, 1875) print all the key documents relating to the confrontation of 1644–5. Other vital source material, particularly the accounts of the army's debates at Reading, Putney and elsewhere during 1647–8, is to be found in C. H. Firth (ed.), *The Clarke Papers* volumes I and II (London, 1891 and 1894); they were both reprinted in a single volume and with a new preface by A. Woolrych by the Royal Historical Society, London, 1992. Other sidelights on Cromwell are contained in documents, mostly drawn from the Clarke manuscripts, collected by A. S. P. Woodhouse (ed.), *Puritanism and Liberty* (London, 1938); again, this was reprinted with a new preface by I. Roots by Dent, London, 1992. Two articles by D. Underdown print key parliamentary and military speeches by Cromwell and provide a useful commentary and context: 'The Parliamentary Diary of John Boys, 1647–8', in *Bulletin of the Institute of Historical Research*

39 (1966), and 'Cromwell and the Officers, February 1658', in *English Historical Review* 83 (1968). Most of the broader, state documents of the period can be found in S. R. Gardiner (ed.), *Constitutional Documents of the Puritan Revolution* (Oxford, 1904) and J. P. Kenyon (ed.), *The Stuart Constitution* (2nd edn, Cambridge, 1986). The surviving parliamentary diaries of Cromwell's two Protectorate Parliaments are in J. T. Rutt (ed.), *The Diary of Thomas Burton, Esq.* (4 vols, London, 1828).

NOTES

1 The Man and the Myth

1 W. Bray (ed.), *The Diary of John Evelyn* (2 vols, London, 1901), I, 340–1.
2 John Byng quoted in *Folklore, Myths and Legends of Britain* (London, 1973), p. 268.
3 W. Plover (ed.), *Kilvert's Diary* (3 vols, London, 1938), I, 396.
4 J. Boswell, *The Life of Dr Johnson* (2 vols in 1, London, 1973), II, 479.
5 See, for example, *The English Devil* ([July] 1660), from which the preceding quotation is also drawn.
6 R. Coke, *A Detection of the Court and State of England* (2 vols, London, 1694), II, 31.
7 G. Huehns (ed.), *Selections from Clarendon* (Oxford, 1955), pp. 354–8.
8 T. Carlyle, *Oliver Cromwell's Letters and Speeches* (revised edn, 3 vols, London, 1907), I, 9–10.
9 Ibid., I, 11, 15.
10 Ibid., I, 10.
11 From Carlyle's preface to the third edition of 1849, printed in ibid., I, xxv.
12 Ibid., I, 10.
13 Ibid.
14 Quoted and the source discussed in S. R. Gardiner, *History of the Great Civil War, 1642–9* (reprint edn, 4 vols, London, 1987), III, 316.

2 Early Life, 1599–1642

1 I. Roots (ed.), *Speeches of Oliver Cromwell* [hereafter simply

'Roots'] (London, 1989), p. 42.

2   *The Right Picture of King Oliver from Top to Toe* ([January] 1650), which also alleges that Cromwell had been a brewer, had squandered money given or lent to him, deceived his creditors and caught a dose of 'the French Pox'.
3   Public Record Office, E179/83/398. W. C. Abbott (ed.), *The Writings and Speeches of Oliver Cromwell* [hereafter simply 'Abbott'] (reprint edn, 4 vols, Oxford, 1988), I, 258–9.
4   British Library, Sloane Ms 2069, f. 96v.
5   From Sir Philip Warwick's *Memoirs*, reproduced in Abbott, I, 65.
6   Abbott, I, 96–7.
7   Abbott, I, 80.
8   From Clarendon's *History*, reproduced in Abbott, I, 143.

3   The First Civil War, 1642–1646

1   I. Roots (ed.), *Speeches of Oliver Cromwell* [hereafter simply 'Roots'] (London, 1989), p. 134.
2   W. C. Abbott (ed.), *The Writings and Speeches of Oliver Cromwell* [hereafter simply 'Abbott'] (reprint edn, 4 vols, Oxford, 1988), I, 218, 221, 232.
3   Abbott, I, 236, 251.
4   Abbott, I, 228.
5   D'Ewes *Journal*, reproduced in Abbott, I, 272.
6   Abbott, I, 230.
7   Abbott, I, 240–6.
8   Abbott, I, 248.
9   Roots, p. 134.
10   Roots, p. 134.
11   Abbott, I, 262.
12   Abbott, I, 256.
13   *Special Passages* 9–16 May 1643, reproduced in Abbott, I, 231.
14   Abbott, I, 262.
15   Sir John Hotham's letter quoted in D'Ewes 'Diary', reproduced in Abbott, I, 237.
16   Reproduced in Abbott, I, 216.
17   Abbott, I, 258, 264.
18   Abbott, I, 230, 240–6, 261.
19   *Mercurius Aulicus*, 4–11 November 1643.
20   Abbott, I, 287–8.
21   Abbott, I, 278.

22 Abbott, I, 302.
23 Abbott, I, 292.
24 Abbott, I, 314–16.
25 Abbott, I, 316.
26 Abbott, I, 345.
27 Abbott, I, 340.
28 *Mercurius Civicus*, 23–30 April 1646.
29 Abbott, I, 365.
30 Abbott, I, 377.
31 Abbott, I, 360.
32 Abbott, I, 377–8.
33 Abbott, I, 381–3, 388.
34 Abbott, I, 368–9.
35 Abbott, I, 386–7. *Moderate Intelligencer*, 9–16 October 1645. *Mercurius Civicus*, 9–16 October 1645. *The Scottish Dove*, 10–17 October 1645.
36 *Mercurius Civicus*, 23–30 April 1646.
37 Roots, p. 67.

4 Politics and the Army, 1646–1649

1 W. C. Abbott (ed.), *The Writings and Speeches of Oliver Cromwell* [hereafter simply 'Abbott'] (reprint edn, 4 vols, Oxford, 1988), I, 430.
2 C. H. Firth (ed.), *Memoirs of Edmund Ludlow* (2 vols, Oxford, 1894), I, 144–5. Wogan's narrative is printed in C. H. Firth (ed.), *The Clarke Papers* [hereafter simply 'Clarke'] (4 vols, London, 1891–1901), I, 421–9. Huntingdon's account is printed in F. Maseres (ed.), *Select Tracts Relating to the Civil Wars in England* (2 vols, London, 1815), II, 397–407.
3 Abbott, I, 408.
4 Abbott, I, 410.
5 British Library, Additional Ms 31116, f. 277v, quoted by C. Hoover, 'Cromwell's Status and Pay in 1646–7', *The Historical Journal* 23 (1980), p. 707 n. 18.
6 Abbott, I, 410, 420–1, 430.
7 Clarke, I, xviii. Abbott, I, 428–9.
8 The source, Clement Walker's account, is quoted and discussed in S. R. Gardiner, *History of the Great Civil War, 1642–9* (reprint edn, 4 vols, London, 1987), III, 222. Gardiner is inclined to accept it, believing it to be corroborated by a slightly later account published by Lilburne.

9 Clarke, I, xviii.
10 Clarke, I, 72-3.
11 Clarke, I, 99-100.
12 Abbott, I, 510.
13 Abbott, I, 512.
14 *Two Declarations*, quoted in Gardiner, *History of the Great Civil War*, III, 363.
15 Abbott, I, 506.
16 Quoted and discussed in Gardiner, *History of the Great Civil War*, III, 351.
17 Clarke, I, 177, 178, 179-80, 183-7, 188-9, 190-3, 201-3, 205-7, 209, 211, 212-13.
18 Clarke, I, 209, 226, 229-30, 236-40, 247-51, 255, 257, 258-9, 269-71, 274, 275, 277-8, 279.
19 Clarke, I, 286-7, 288-90, 291-2, 293, 309, 328-9, 331-3, 336, 341, 344-5.
20 Clarke, I, 367, 368-71, 375-6.
21 Clarke, I, 378-83.
22 Clarke, I, 411-12.
23 Clarke, I, 417-18.
24 Abbott, I, 551-2.
25 D. Underdown, 'The Parliament Diary of John Boys, 1647-8', *Bulletin of the Institute of Historical Research* 39 (1966), pp. 152-3.
26 Printed in Abbott, I, 564.
27 Abbott, I, 574-5.
28 Abbott, I, 575-6. Underdown, 'Diary of John Boys', p. 156.
29 Abbott, I, 576.
30 Abbott, I, 577.
31 Firth (ed.), *Ludlow's Memoirs*, I, 184-6.
32 Abbott, I, 585, 588, 590, 591-2, 593.
33 Abbott, I, 598-9.
34 Abbott, I, 606.
35 Abbott, I, 611-23.
36 Abbott, I, 632-3, 634-8.
37 Abbott, I, 619.
38 Abbott, I, 638, 644.
39 Abbott, I, 621.
40 Abbott, I, 690-2.
41 Abbott, I, 676-8, 696-9.
42 Abbott, I, 698.
43 Clarke, II, 146.
44 Clarke, II, xxx. Abbott, I, 719.
45 Abbott, I, 698.

46 I. Roots (ed.), *Speeches of Oliver Cromwell* (London, 1989), pp. 4–5.
47 Abbott, II, 337–8.
48 Abbott, II, 302; A. S. P. Woodhouse, *Puritanism and Liberty* (reprinted edn, London, 1992), pp. 474–8.
49 Abbott, II, 189–90.

5 Enemies and Divisions

1 I. Roots (ed.), *Speeches of Oliver Cromwell* [hereafter simply 'Roots'] (London, 1989), pp. 28–40.
2 Roots, p. 149.
3 W. C. Abbott (ed.), *The Writings and Speeches of Oliver Cromwell* [hereafter simply 'Abbott'] (reprint edn, 4 vols, Oxford, 1988), II, 41–2.
4 Abbott, II, 68.
5 Abbott, II, 74.
6 Abbott, II, 21, 29.
7 Roots, pp. 3–8.
8 Abbott, II, 103–4.
9 Abbott, II, 107.
10 Abbott, II, 110–12.
11 Abbott, II, 118.
12 Abbott, II, 126.
13 Abbott, II, 122, 124, 125–8.
14 Abbott, II, 127.
15 Abbott, II, 135.
16 Abbott, II, 139, 140–3.
17 Abbott, II, 142.
18 Abbott, II, 176.
19 Abbott, II, 160, 171.
20 Abbott, II, 145.
21 Abbott, II, 168.
22 Abbott, II, 146.
23 Abbott, II, 186.
24 Abbott, II, 235.
25 Abbott, II, 173.
26 Abbott, II, 177.
27 Abbott, II, 173–4.
28 Abbott, II, 187.
29 Abbott, II, 285.
30 Abbott, II, 306.

31 Abbott, II, 303.
32 Abbott, II, 324.
33 Abbott, II, 329.
34 Abbott, II, 324–5.
35 Abbott, II, 482.
36 Abbott, II, 335.
37 Abbott, II, 338–9.
38 Abbott, II, 400.
39 Abbott, II, 421.
40 Abbott, II, 433.
41 Abbott, II, 444.
42 Abbott, II, 463.
43 Roots, pp. 42–3.
44 Roots, pp. 30–6.
45 Roots, pp. 11–12.
46 *To the Supreame Authority the Parliament* (12 August 1651).
47 Roots, p. 13.
48 Roots, pp. 205–7.
49 Roots, pp. 207–14.
50 Abbott, II, 575–6.
51 Roots, pp. 13–19.
52 Roots, p. 43.
53 Roots, p. 14.
54 Roots, p. 241.
55 Roots, p. 43.
56 Roots, p. 44.
57 Roots, pp. 14–19.
58 Roots, p. 13.
59 Abbott, III, 5–8.
60 Abbott, III, 13.
61 Roots, p. 20.
62 Roots, p. 45.
63 Roots, p. 8–28.
64 Abbott, III, 89.
65 Roots, p. 45.
66 Roots, p. 34.
67 Roots, p. 111; Abbott, IV, 418.
68 Roots, p. 151.
69 Roots, p. 46.

6 Head of State, 1653–1658

1 W. C. Abbott (ed.), *The Writings and Speeches of Oliver Cromwell* [hereafter simply 'Abbott'] (reprint edn, 4 vols, Oxford, 1988), II, 39.

2 Texts reproduced in S. R. Gardiner, *Constitutional Documents of the Puritan Revolution 1625–1660* (2nd edn, Oxford, 1906), pp. 405–17, 447–64.

3 I. Roots (ed.), *Speeches of Oliver Cromwell* [hereafter simply 'Roots'] (London, 1989), pp. 46–7, 53, 92, 150.

4 C. H. Firth (ed.), *The Clarke Papers* [hereafter simply 'Clarke'] (4 vols, London, 1891–1901), II, xxxvi.

5 Abbott, IV, 449; Roots, p. 156.

6 T. Birch (ed.), *A Collection of the State Papers of John Thurloe, Esquire* (7 vols, London, 1742), V, 424, 426.

7 Ibid., V, 398.

8 S. C. Lomas (ed.), 'The Memoirs of Sir George Courthop', *Camden Miscellany*, XI (London, 1907), p. 141.

9 A. B. Hinds (ed.), *Calendar of State Papers . . . in the Archives and Collections of Venice*, XXX (London, 1930), pp. 230–1.

10 Birch (ed.), *State Papers of Thurloe*, V, 176.

11 Roots, p. 112; Abbott, IV, 418.

12 C. L. Stainer, *Speeches of Oliver Cromwell* (Oxford, 1901), p. 484.

13 Hinds (ed.), *Calendar of State Papers Venice*, XXIX (London, 1929), p. 197.

14 Birch (ed.), *State Papers of Thurloe*, IV, 653.

15 M. Roberts (ed.), *Swedish Diplomats at Cromwell's Court, 1655–1656* (Camden 4th series 36, London, 1988), p. 167.

16 Roots, pp. 28–40, 57.

17 Roots, pp. 30, 41–56.

18 Roots, pp. 57–77.

19 Roots, pp. 59–60.

20 J. T. Rutt (ed.), *Diary of Thomas Burton, Esquire* (4 vols, London, 1828), I, lxxix.

21 Clarke, II, 240.

22 Clarke, II, 240–1.

23 Roots, p. 72.

24 Roots, pp. 78–106.

25 Roots, p. 95.

26 Abbott, III, 671.

27 Abbott, III, 745.

28 Abbott, IV, 548–9.

29 Abbott, III, 857–60.

30 Abbott, III, 859.
31 Abbott, III, 858; IV, 193.
32 Abbott, III, 858.
33 Abbott, III, 756.
34 Abbott, IV, 146.
35 Abbott, IV, 112.
36 Roots, pp. 91-3, 100.
37 Roots, p. 112.
38 Roots, pp. 79-106.
39 Roots, pp. 117, 133.
40 Abbott, IV, 366.
41 Roots, p. 112; Abbott, IV, 418-19.
42 Roots, pp. 113-18.
43 Roots, pp. 118-19, 128-33, 140-1.
44 Roots, pp. 144-5.
45 Roots, pp. 157-62.
46 Roots, p. 111.
47 Roots, pp. 134-7.
48 Roots, pp. 173-93.
49 Roots, pp. 168-73.

7   The Faces of Cromwell

1 R. Flecknoe, *The Idea of His Highness, Oliver* ([April] 1659), preface; S. Carrington, *The History of the Life and Death of His Most Serene Highness Oliver, Late Lord Protector* ([April] 1659), p. 229.
2 *The Perfect Politician* ([February] 1660), pp. 290-1, 346-7, 349-50.
3 T. Birch (ed.), *A Collection of the State Papers of John Thurloe, Esquire* (7 vols, London, 1742), I, 766.
4 Flecknoe, *Idea of His Highness*, pp. 66-7; Carrington, *History of the Life and Death*, p. 243.
5 Sir Philip Warwick, *Memoirs of the Reign of Charles I* (Edinburgh, 1813), pp. 273-5.
6 Sir Richard Bulstrode, *Memoirs and Reflections upon the Reign and Government of King Charles I and Charles II* (London, 1721), pp. 192-3.
7 A. B. Hinds (ed.), *Calendar of State Papers . . . in the Archives and Collections of Venice*, XXX (London, 1930), p. 124.
8 Quoted in W. C. Abbott (ed.), *The Writings and Speeches of Oliver Cromwell* [hereafter simply 'Abbott'] (reprint edn, 4 vols, Oxford, 1988) II, 319.

9 C. H. Firth (ed.), *The Clarke Papers* [hereafter simply 'Clarke'] (4 vols, London, 1891-1901), II, 191.
10 Abbott, II, 483.
11 Abbott, II, 61-2.
12 Abbott, II, 329, 404-5, 412.
13 John Nickolls, *Original Letters and Papers of State Addressed to Oliver Cromwell* (London, 1743), p. 40.
14 Abbott, II, 507-8.
15 Abbott, I, 416.
16 Abbott, IV, 146.
17 Abbott, II, 95, 102-4, 159-60, 235-7, 289, 329-30, 425-6.
18 Abbott, IV, 146.
19 Abbott, III, 280.
20 *The Perfect Politician*, pp. 347-8.
21 Carrington, *History of the Life and Death*, p. 4.
22 I. Roots (ed.), *Speeches of Oliver Cromwell* [hereafter simply 'Roots'] (London, 1989), pp. 157, 162.
23 Clarke, I, 277.
24 Clarke, I, 209.
25 Roots, p. 33.
26 Roots, pp. 116, 169.
27 Abbott, II, 325.
28 Roots, p. 34.
29 Quoted in Abbott, II, 35.
30 Abbott, II, 322.
31 Roots, p. 33.
32 Clarke, I, 370.
33 Abbott, I, 677.
34 Roots, pp. 52, 95.
35 Clarke, II, xxxvi.
36 Roots, p. 180.
37 Roots, pp. 66-7.

INDEX